Suggesting Solutions

Lean is about building and improving stable and predictable systems and processes to deliver to customers high-quality products/services on time by engaging everyone in the organization. Combined with this, organizations need to create an environment of respect for people and continuous learning. It's all about people. People create the product or service, drive innovation, and create systems and processes, and with leadership buy-in and accountability to ensure sustainment with this philosophy, employees will be committed to the organization as they learn and grow personally and professionally.

Lean is a term that describes a way of thinking about and managing companies as an enterprise. Becoming Lean requires the following: the continual pursuit to identify and eliminate waste; the establishment of efficient flow of both information and process; and an unwavering top-level commitment. The concept of continuous improvement applies to any process in any industry.

Based on the contents of ***The Lean Practitioners Field Book***, the purpose of this series is to show, in detail, how any process can be improved utilizing a combination of tasks and people tools and introduces the BASICS Lean® concept. The books are designed for all levels of Lean practitioners and introduces proven tools for analysis and implementation that go beyond the traditional point kaizen event. Each book can be used as a stand-alone volume or used in combination with other titles based on specific needs.

Each book is chock-full of case studies and stories from the authors' own experiences in training organizations that have started or are continuing their Lean journey of continuous improvement. Contents include valuable lessons learned and each chapter concludes with questions pertaining to the focus of the chapter. Numerous photographs enrich and illustrate specific tools used in Lean methodology.

Suggesting Solutions: Brainstorming Creative Ideas to Maximize Productivity explores the process block diagram tool, how to do a Lean layout and Lean master layout and how to create standard work and visual management systems. The goal of this book is to introduce the balance of the tools and how to proceed once the analysis is completed. There are many pieces to a Lean implementation and all of them are interconnected. This book walks through the relationships and how the data presented can be leveraged to prepare for the implementation. It also provides suggest solutions for improvements and making recommendations to management to secure their buy-in and approval.

BASICS Lean® Implementation Series

Baseline: Confronting Reality & Planning the Path for Success
By Charles Protzman, Fred Whiton & Joyce Kerpchar

Assess and Analyze: Discovering the Waste Consuming Your Profits
By Charles Protzman, Fred Whiton & Joyce Kerpchar

Suggesting Solutions: Brainstorming Creative Ideas to Maximize Productivity
By Charles Protzman, Fred Whiton & Joyce Kerpchar

Implementing Lean: Converting Waste to Profit
By Charles Protzman, Fred Whiton & Joyce Kerpchar

Check: Identifying Gaps on the Path to Success
By Charles Protzman, Fred Whiton & Joyce Kerpchar

Sustaining Lean: Creating a Culture of Continuous Improvement
By Charles Protzman, Fred Whiton & Joyce Kerpchar

Suggesting Solutions
Brainstorming Creative Ideas to Maximize Productivity

Charles Protzman, Fred Whiton, and Joyce Kerpchar

Routledge
Taylor & Francis Group

A PRODUCTIVITY PRESS BOOK

First published 2023
by Routledge
605 Third Avenue, New York, NY 10158

and by Routledge
4 Park Square, Milton Park, Abingdon, Oxon, OX14 4RN

Routledge is an imprint of the Taylor & Francis Group, an informa business

ISBN: 978-1-032-02916-0 (hbk)
ISBN: 978-1-032-02915-3 (pbk)
ISBN: 978-1-003-18579-6 (ebk)

DOI: 10.4324/9781003185796

Typeset in Garamond
by KnowledgeWorks Global Ltd.

This book series is dedicated to all the Lean practitioners in the world and to two of the earliest, my friend Kenneth Hopper and my grandfather Charles W. Protzman Sr. Kenneth was a close friend of Charles Sr. and is coauthor with his brother William of a book that describes Charles Sr. and his work for General MacArthur in the Occupation of Japan in some detail: *The Puritan Gift: Reclaiming the American Dream amidst Global Financial Chaos.*

Charles W. Protzman Sr.

Kenneth Hopper

Contents

Acknowledgments

There are many individuals who have contributed to this book, both directly and indirectly, and many others over the years, too many to list here, who have shared their knowledge and experiences with us. We would like to thank all of those who have worked with us on Lean teams in the past and the senior leadership whose support made them successful. This book would not have been possible without your hard work, perseverance, and courage during our Lean journey together. We hope you see this book as the culmination of our respect and appreciation. We apologize if we have overlooked anyone in the following acknowledgments. We would like to thank the following for their contributions to coauthor or contribute to the chapters in this book:

- Special thanks to our Productivity Press editor, Kris Mednansky, who has been terrific at guiding us through our writing project. Kris has been a great source of encouragement and kept us on track as we worked through what became an ever-expanding six-year project.
- Special thanks to all our clients. Without you, this book would not have been possible.
- Russ Scaffede for his insight into the Toyota system and for his valuable contributions through numerous e-mail correspondence and edits with various parts of the book.
- Joel Barker for his permission in referencing the paradigm material so important and integral to Lean implementations and change management.
- Many thanks to the "Hats" team (you know who you are).
- I would like to acknowledge Mark Jamrog of SMC Group. Mark was my first Sensei and introduced me to this Kaikaku-style Lean System Implementation approach based on the Ohno and Shingo teachings.
- Various chapter contributions by Joe and Ed Markiewicz of Ancon Gear.

For the complete list of acknowledgments, testimonials, dedication, etc. please see The Lean Practitioner's Field Book. The purpose of this series was to break down and enhance the original Lean Practitioner's Field Book into six books that are aligned with the BASICS® model.

Authors' Note: Every attempt was made to source materials back to the original authors. In the event we missed someone, please feel free to let us know so we may correct it in any future edition. Many of the spreadsheets depicted were originally hand drawn by Mark Jamrog, SMC Group, put into Excel by Dave O'Koren and Charlie Protzman, and since modified significantly. Most of the base formatting for these spreadsheets can be found in the Shingo, Ohno, Monden, or other industrial engineering handbooks.

About the Authors

Charles Protzman, MBA, CPM, formed Business Improvement Group (B.I.G.), LLC, in November 1997. B.I.G. is in Sarasota Florida. Charlie and his son, Dan along with Mike Meyers, specialize in implementing and training Lean thinking principles and the BASICS® Lean business delivery system (LBDS) in small to fortune 50 companies involved in Manufacturing, Healthcare, Government, and Service Industries.

Charles has written 12 books to date and is the coauthor of Leveraging Lean in Healthcare: Transforming Your Enterprise into a High-Quality Patient Care Delivery System series and is a two-time recipient of the Shingo Research and Professional Publication Award. He has since published *The BASICS® Lean Implementation Model* and *Lean Leadership BASICS®*. Charles has over 38 years of experience in materials and operations management. He spent almost 14 years with AlliedSignal, now Honeywell, where he was an Aerospace Strategic Operations Manager and the first AlliedSignal Lean master. He has received numerous special-recognition and cost-reduction awards. Charles was an external consultant for the Department of Business and Economic Development's (DBED's) Maryland Consortium during and after his tenure with AlliedSignal. With the help of Joyce LaPadula and others, he had input into the resulting DBED world-class criteria document and assisted in the first three initial DBED world-class company assessments. B.I.G. was a Strategic Partner of ValuMetrix Services, a division of Ortho-Clinical Diagnostics, Inc., a Johnson & Johnson company. He is an international Lean consultant and has taught beginner to advanced students' courses in Lean principles and total quality all over the world.

Charlie Protzman states, "My grandfather started me down this path and has influenced my life to this day. My grandfather made four trips to Japan from 1948 to the 1960s. He loved the Japanese people and culture and was passionate and determined to see Japanese manufacturing recover from World War II."

Charles spent the last 24 years with Business Improvement Group, LLC, implementing successful Lean product line conversions, kaizen events, and administrative business system improvements (transactional Lean) worldwide. He is following in the footsteps of his grandfather, who was part of the Civil Communications Section (CCS) of the American Occupation. Prior to recommending Dr. Deming's 1950 visit to Japan, C.W. Protzman Sr. surveyed over 70 Japanese companies in 1948. Starting in late 1948, Homer Sarasohn and C.W. Protzman Sr. taught top executives of prominent Japanese communications companies an eight-week course in American participative management and quality techniques in Osaka and Tokyo. Over 5,100 top Japanese executives had taken the course by 1956. The course continued until 1993. Many of the lessons we taught the Japanese in 1948 are now being taught to Americans as "Lean principles." The Lean principles had their roots in the United States and date back to the early 1700s and later to Taylor, Gilbreth, and Henry Ford. The principles were refined by Taiichi Ohno and expanded by Dr. Shigeo Shingo. Modern-day champions were Norman Bodek (the Grandfather of Lean), Jim Womack, and Dan Jones.

Charles participated in numerous benchmarking and site visits, including a two-week trip to Japan in June 1996 and 2017. He is a master facilitator and trainer in TQM, total quality speed, facilitation, career development, change management, benchmarking, leadership, systems thinking, high-performance work teams, team building, Myers-Briggs® Styles, Lean thinking, and supply chain management. He also participated in Baldrige Examiner and Six Sigma management courses. He was an assistant program manager during "Desert Storm" for the Patriot missile-to-missile fuse development and production program. Charles is a past member of SME, AME, IIE, IEEE, APT, and the International Performance Alliance Group (IPAG), an international team of expert Lean Practitioners (http://www.ipag-consulting.com).

Fred Whiton, MBA, PMP, PE, has 30 years of experience in the aerospace and defense industry, which includes engineering, operations, program and portfolio management, and strategy development. He is employed as a Chief Engineer within Raytheon Intelligence & Space at the time of this book's publication.

Fred has both domestic and international expertise within homeland security, communications command and control intelligence surveillance and reconnaissance sensors and services, military and commercial aerospace systems, and defense systems supporting the US Navy, US Air Force, US Army, US Department of Homeland Security, and the US Intelligence Community across a full range of functions from marketing, concept development, engineering, and production into life cycle sustainment and logistics. Fred began his career as a design engineer at General Dynamics, was promoted to a group engineer at Lockheed Martin, and was a director at Northrop Grumman within the Homeland Defense Government Systems team. As vice president of engineering and operations at Smiths Aerospace, he was the Lean champion for a Lean enterprise journey, working closely with Protzman as the Lean consultant, for a very successful Lean implementation within a union plant, including a new plant designed using Lean principles. Prior to joining Raytheon, Fred was a senior vice president within C4ISR business unit at CACI International and prior to joining CACI was the vice president and general manager of the Tactical Communications and Network Solutions Line of Business within DRS Technologies.

Fred has a BS in mechanical engineering from the University of Maryland, an MS in mechanical engineering from Rensselaer Polytechnic Institute, a master's in engineering administration from The George Washington University, and an MBA from The University of Chicago. He is a professional engineer (PE) in Maryland, a certified project management professional (PMP), served as a commissioner on the Maryland Commission for Manufacturing Competitiveness under Governor Ehrlich, as a commissioner on the Maryland Commission on Autism under Governor O'Malley, and as a member of the boards of directors for the Regional Manufacturing Institute headquartered in Maryland and the First Maryland Disability Trust.

Joyce Kerpchar has over 35 years of experience in the healthcare industry that includes key leadership roles in healthcare operations, IT, health plan management, and innovative program development and strategy. As a Lean champion, mentor, and Six Sigma black belt, she is experienced in organizational lean strategy and leading large-scale healthcare lean initiatives, change management, and IT implementations. Joyce is a coauthor of Leveraging Lean in Healthcare: Transforming Your Enterprise into a High-Quality Patient Care Delivery System, Recipient of the Shingo Research and Professional Publication Award.

She began her career as a board-certified physician's assistant in cardiovascular and thoracic surgery and primary care medicine and received her master's degree in Management. Joyce is passionate about leveraging Lean in healthcare processes to eliminate waste and reduce errors, improve overall quality, and reduce the cost of providing healthcare.

Introduction

This book is part of the BASICS Lean® Implementation Series and was adapted from The Lean Practitioner's Field Book: Proven, Practical, Profitable and Powerful Techniques for Making Lean Really Work. In Book 3, we start with discussing the Suggest Solutions step of the BASICS Lean® Implementation Model. These steps include how to create standard work and the differences between standard work and work instructions, implementing Lean and Strategic Materials solutions, the importance of using Creativity before Capital, and the role Engineering Plays in Lean Solutions.

The books in this BASICS Lean® Implementation Series take the reader on a journey beginning with an overview of Lean principles, culminating with employees developing professionally through the BASICS Lean® Leadership Development Path. Each book has something for everyone from the novice to the seasoned Lean practitioner. A refresher for some at times, it provides soul-searching and thought-provoking questions with examples that will stimulate learning opportunities. Many of us take advantage of these learning opportunities daily. We, the authors, as Lean practitioners, are students still thirsting for knowledge and experiences to assist organizations in their transformations.

This series is designed to be a guide and resource to help you with the ongoing struggle to improve manufacturing, government, and service industries throughout the world. This series embodies true stories, results, and lessons, which we and others have learned during our Lean journeys. The concept of continuous improvement applies to any process in any industry. The purpose of this series is to show, in detail, how any process can be improved utilizing a combination of tasks and people tools. We will introduce proven tools for analysis and implementation that go far beyond the traditional point kaizen event training. Several CEOs have shared with us; had they not implemented Lean, they would not have survived the Recession in 2008 and subsequent downturns.

Many companies prefer not to use their names in this book as they consider Lean a strategic competitive advantage in their industry, and some of these companies have now moved into a leadership position in their respective markets; thus, we may refer to them as Company X throughout the series. We explain to companies that Lean is a 5-year commitment that never ends. About 80–90% of the companies with which we have worked have sustained their Lean journeys based on implementing our BASICS® Lean approach that we will share with you in this book.

The BASICS Lean® Implementation Series discusses the principles and tools in detail as well as the components of the House of Lean. It is a "how to" book that presents an integrated, structured approach identified by the acronym BASICS®, which when combined with an effective business strategy can help ensure the successful transformation of an organization. The Lean concepts described in each book are supported by a plethora of examples drawn from the personal experiences of its many well-known and respected contributors, which range from very small machine shops to Fortune 50 companies.

The BASICS Lean® Implementation Series has both practical applications and applications in academia. It can be used for motivating students to learn many of the Lean concepts and at the end of each chapter there are thought-provoking questions for the reader to help digest the material. The investment in people in terms of training, engagement, empowerment, and personal and professional growth is the key to sustaining Lean and an organization's success. For more on this topic, please see our book Lean Leadership BASICS®. Lean practitioners follow a natural flow, building continually on previous information and experiences. There is a bit of the Lean practitioner in all of us. Hopefully, as you read these books to pursue additional knowledge, as a refresher or for reference, or for academia, it can help expand your knowledge, skills, and abilities on your never-ending Lean journey.

Chapter 1

The BASICS® Model: Suggest Solutions

Quality means doing it right when no one is looking.

Henry Ford

The first S in our BASICS® model stands for Suggest Solutions (see Figure 1.1), and the goal of this chapter is to discuss how to proceed once the analysis is completed. There are many pieces to a Lean implementation, and they are all interconnected. The material in this chapter walks through the relationships and how the data presented to this point can be leveraged to prepare you for your implementation. It will discuss suggested solutions for improvements and making recommendations to management to secure their buy-in and approval. The information obtained from the staff during the value stream map (VSM), process flow analysis (PFA), workflow (operator) analysis (WFA), and changeover analysis will help us develop the key data elements: cycle time, takt time (TT), demand, available time, and total labor time (TLT). We use the analysis to develop standard work, calculate standard work in process (SWIP), design the new layout, and create the new workstation/area design. Materials and inventory management support the new flow of delivering the service or product to the customer. We call it "Feeding the Beast" once the Lean line is up and running. As we reduce the cycle times in each process, our overall throughput time is reduced which is one of our main goals with Lean (see Figure 1.2).

It is important to note that ours is a ready–aim–fire versus a traditional point kaizen or kaizen blitz approach of ready–fire–aim, but it is not analysis paralysis. With enough practice, the Lean tools outlined in this book can be applied as quickly if not quicker than traditional point kaizen events sometimes in the span of hours. However, it can take days, weeks, or months, depending on your process scope to implement a Lean System Implementation using point kaizens for transition of an entire product line.

DOI: 10.4324/9781003185796-1

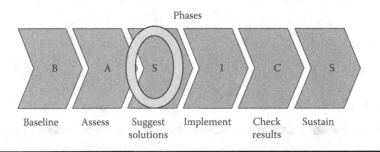

Figure 1.1   BASICS Model—Suggest Solutions.

Solving the Lean Puzzle

We start by developing the target condition. Our target condition when converting from batch to flow will always encompass the following guidelines:

- Alignment of goals from shop floor to CEO.
- One-piece flow production.
- Optimizing the product flow and laying parts and processes out in the proper order of production even if it means repeating equipment, tooling, fixturing, or parts. *The product should never go backward during production.*
- Include sub assembly operations in the main process flow wherever possible.
- Incorporate standing and walking operations.
- Incorporate baton zone line balancing (recently referred to in the literature as self-balancing[1]). Since the late 1990s, we have always called it bumping.
- Work to match cycle time to TT.
- Reduce setup and changeover time to less than 3 minutes for machining with a goal of 0 second for mixed model assembly.
- Implement a flexible Lean layout with materials supplied from the outside and operators on the inside.

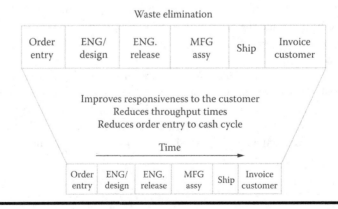

Figure 1.2   Waste elimination funnel—as you reduce waste, you increase velocity or throughput time.

(a)   (b)

Figure 1.3   **(a) Linside storage right and VMI supermarket to the left of the aisle and (b) Tristate Labeling supplied for VMI materials.**

- Implement line side point of use (POU) materials and material warehouses next to or near the line.
- Move toward Kanban or set parts/pallet systems (SPS) systems with vendor-managed inventory (VMI) replenishment systems (see Figure 1.3).
- Flatten bills of materials. Eliminate all kitting and stocking of subassemblies from the stockroom.
- Eliminate traditional stockrooms over time.
- Create and develop adherence to standard work.
- Implement visual controls.
- Implement accountability and discipline throughout the organization.
- Create a learning organization by developing your people.
- Remove silo-based management and move to a cross-functional organization.
- Create accountability-based systems at all organizational levels to ensure success.

Once the initial analysis is completed, we construct a block diagram. The block diagram takes the output from the (to be) PFA and (to be) WFA and combines them into one flow. We develop this tool with the operator and supervisors present. The block diagram sets the stage for the workstation design and layout.

The Process Block Diagram

To construct the process block diagram (see Figure 1.4), we start with our PFA and diagram it on a whiteboard (or piece of paper) in the order of how the part is to be produced whether it is assembled, machined, or both. At this point, don't worry about the current tooling, fixturing, layout constraints, and the size of each part or model or if you have enough space, equipment, operators, etc. We just want to line up each step in the proper order it should be in the process. This is a very difficult process because we tend to let our current state or "as-is" condition influence our process flow decisions. There are usually many ways to build a product. For instance, it can be built up from bottom to top or side to side. Discuss all the

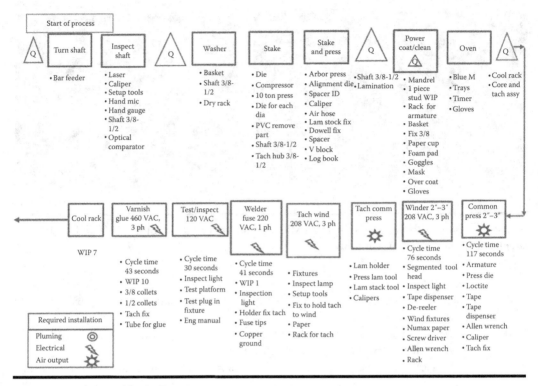

Figure 1.4   Process block diagram.

different alternatives for building the product. Once all the steps are on the board, start to ask the following questions:

■ Do we have all the models in the flow? Can we change the flow to streamline it even more?
■ Does it really flow?
■ Do note where there are subassemblies (or pre-assembly operations). Are the subassemblies in the right order? Can they be incorporated into the line?
■ Is this really the right order for each step from the part or product's viewpoint?
■ Do we have to carry a subassembly with us? Is there a way to build it into the product directly? Can we deliver it without carrying it (i.e., gravity conveyor)?
■ Is there a way we could rearrange and/or combine steps that make more sense or make it easier to assemble? Could we build it from the ground up starting with a subassembly or do we have subassemblies that have to be built in parallel? (This will mean that one of the subassemblies may have to be carried along while the other subassembly is produced.)
■ Would changing the order of steps help in mistake proofing any steps?
■ Would simplifying (removing complexity) help in mistake proofing?

For a mixed model line, we need to review each model and add any unique steps (in a different color) where they fit in the block diagram for each model as necessary. Many times, it is surprising that very few, if any, steps must be added (see Figure 1.5). As one looks at mixed model lines, check routings to see where any variance initially occurs. You may be surprised how far along the value stream this occurs.

Figure 1.5   Mixed model line process block diagram in process—this was for a motor line.

Once we have all the block diagrams, we need to review the list we put together during the WFA to determine what parts, equipment, jigs, tools, fixtures, tooling, etc. are required and list them out under each PFA step on the board. Note where and what type of electric is required, air (high or low pressure), other gases, safety checks, quality checks, etc., is needed. Next, we need to identify where the SWIP will be required and how much.

Constraints

Constraints are not always negative. Sometimes constraints can be enablers.[1] Now let's consider what constraints we have. The first thing you may find is that you need more equipment than you have now. For instance, today you may have a process that looks like Figure 1.6. In the current environment, these may all use the same arbor press or air press. On our new line, we are going to want each step to have its own arbor or air press. If each operation uses the same tooling or tools, we are going to want to duplicate them at each station as well. Part of the target condition is to make sure the product never goes backward in the flow. It can go from one side of the line to the other (i.e., parallel lines), but it should never go backward. So, equipment, tools, tooling, etc. may be a constraint in our future state environment.

We need to identify, at this point, what additional tooling and equipment is desired and whether we have the funds and customer demand to justify its purchase. Eighty percent of the time, we don't require additional funds or may require small expense dollars for tools or equipment but not large capital appropriations; however, there are exceptions. If a large dollar purchase

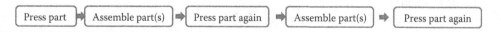

Figure 1.6   Process steps where each press currently uses the same arbor press.

Figure 1.7   Workstation design comes from the video and resulting process block diagram.

is required, we may have to implement the line in phases—that is, pre- and post-purchase of additional equipment.

Once the block diagram is completed, go back and review the PFA and WFA. Use the new block diagram to reorder the steps, eliminate the omitted steps, and create the new *to-be* PFA document. The PFA spreadsheet will predict the improvement to be gained. Do the same for the WFA. Once the steps have been rearranged in the WFA, determine how much labor time will be required for each of the steps in the block diagram and note them on the diagram. The WFA spreadsheet will predict the number of operators required based on the demand which will become the basis for the standard work document and capacity analysis we will create later.

We will use this process block diagram to help us determine the layout and workstation design (see Figure 1.7) for the line. On very simple lines, we can start implementing on the floor from just this block diagram. On more complicated lines, we may draw up a layout with paper dolls or in computer-aided design (CAD)/Visio with rough workstation design, and on very complicated lines, we will design each workstation down to the part and tool locations and may use a simulation program. We normally go to the area and use tape to outline the workstations and simulate building a part. You can also use cardboard cutouts to simulate equipment, parts, and station layouts and to check the flow as you layout the workstation.

Points to Consider

- Make sure you create and walk through the new point-to-point diagram with each product at the block diagram stage.
- Make sure you have work content experts (operators and engineers) in the room during the block diagram phase.
- Experiment with all flow options to see what works best and creates the best results.

- Question the order of every step and keep an open mind during the discussion.
- Work hard to keep all subassemblies on the line versus creating off-line operations. Keep in mind that it is much easier to move things around on the block diagram whiteboard at this phase than once it is implemented on the floor!
- Look for opportunities to remove complexity from the operation both from an equipment (PFA) and an operator perspective (WFA).

Layout Recommendations, Reviews, and Approvals

When implementing Lean lines, we want to implement flexible layouts as customers have changing needs and demands. Remember that layouts are a root cause for much of the waste we see in factories, government, healthcare, and offices. The following items are absolutely required and are nonnegotiable:

- Maximum flexibility
- Operators on the inside
- One-piece flow (or small lot) production
- Parts and tools in the order of the sequence of operations—right tool at right time to perform the task
- Materials fed from outside the line
- Machines in the order of the processes
- Separate human from machine work
- Implementation of standard work methods
- Ability to balance work across operators
- Multi-process cross-trained operators
- Standing/walking, moving operations
- SWIP identified with a quantity and always in place
- Visual controls

The following items are negotiable:

- Process sequence (determined during block diagram)
- Visual control design
- Quantity of finished goods (FG) (goal is to eliminate where possible)
- Quantity of raw materials (RMs) line side and warehouse/supermarket
- Operators walk patterns
- Tool size and types

Cell Layout Design

The shape of a cell is determined by the requirements of the process. There are many cell layouts possible. The advantage to the system kaizen approach over point kaizens is you don't have to change the layout 10 or 15 times over a year. At this stage, we find we can normally get the layout 80%–95% correct the first time; but over time, the layout will continue to evolve and change. Don't get hung up on trying to make the layout so perfect that it never gets implemented. Layouts can be in a U shape, L shape, S shape, C shape, or straight line. Make sure you involve health, safety, and environment (HS&E) to help create or review the layouts. Some guidelines:

- ■ Try to keep the working aisle width to 4.5 ft (1.37 m) and when not possible an absolute minimum width of 3 ft (0.914 m).
- ■ Put machines as close together as humanly possible (don't worry about access panels—cut them in somewhere else, move control boxes, etc.).
- ■ Get rid of excess space, work benches, toolboxes.
- ■ Don't leave room for WIP. We are working on one piece at a time.
- ■ Be sure to get anti fatigue mats or shoe inserts for the people working the new line. It is very likely that people working the new line aren't used to standing and walking.
- ■ Whenever possible, incorporate the building of subassemblies into the line to avoid interference with feeding the subassemblies into the line and line stoppages from subassembly shortages.
- ■ Try to avoid having the working aisle of the line be parallel and immediately next to a main plant aisle to minimize distractions from other employees walking by.
- ■ Consider the ability to, without disrupting the line, regularly remove empty boxes or bins that get returned to suppliers for refill in the layout.

Beware of Isolated Islands[2]

In the layout pictured in Figure 1.8, what do you observe? This person works only at this station all day long. He is basically stuck there by himself. If his cycle time is longer than the TT,

Figure 1.8   Isolated islands create fractional labor.

he will create a bottleneck because the station's layout will not work with two people. If his cycle time is quicker than the TT, he will be idle part of the time or if he keeps working, his parts will back up at the next station. This is an example of an isolated island. At Company X, they created isolated islands so people would not talk! Does this really fix the root cause of the problem in their system?

Fractional Labor

The most important thing to avoid in any layout is isolated islands. Isolated islands are created when operators are positioned in such a way they are boxed in or are so far away from each other they cannot flex and help each other out. This leads to the creation of fractional labor. Fractional labor occurs where we have a stranded operator whose cycle time is less than the TT. We lose the time difference between the TT and the isolated operator's labor or cycle time. When operators can't flex, they become bottlenecks or idle depending on their work content. These layouts are easy to unintentionally create and be stuck with over time especially in office, healthcare, and automated manufacturing environments.

The other root cause of fractional labor is skill set or job classification limitations. When, for instance, an operator can only weld but does not clean their welds or can do the previous or following steps, they become bottlenecks or are saddled with idle time as well. We often see this in batch factories. The other issue is there is now no incentive for the welder to do a clean weld since he/she doesn't have to clean it.

If the operators have knowledge of previous and following processes, they can detect abnormalities in the incoming product. In this case, we would incorporate cleaning the weld as well as part of the welders' standard work. This will ensure quality is built in at the process (clean welds are now an expectation from the welder). We define this as process ownership. Review the block diagram to see if this can be accomplished. Work elements may require realignment to make this happen.

Lesson Learned: When you make welders clean their own welds, less work is required to clean the welds.

The batch or functional layout creates isolated *work center* islands which are caused by both layout and skill set constraints and design. Therefore, there is such an inherent imbalance in WIP inventory in batch factories. Operators may not be able to be assigned any more duties because they either are not capable, may not want to do another job, or cannot flex to help someone else out because they are too far away (distance) or are sitting down. They may have a barrier that precludes them from flexing; an example of this is the nutritional tray line. Notice the operators are boxed in by equipment and carts of dishes or food, and the layout prevents them from performing other tasks.

Bad Layouts

Shapes such as A, B, D, E, F, G, H, K, M, N, O, P, Q, R, or T layouts, for example, could contain isolated islands. We see this in many factories and offices. Some leading Lean universities[3] and some Lean approaches teach that a T-shaped layout is good (see Figure 1.9), primarily when building two different products with the same subassembly or parts. However, when you have people on both sides of a table or conveyor line, the ability to replenish materials without interrupting the operator is lost and the operators cannot flex. Some lines have the operators on the outside of

"T" layout creates
remote islands

Figure 1.9   T-shaped layout creates isolated islands. Isolated islands are bad.

the line surrounded by equipment or materials. Again, materials must be replenished on the operator's side. Operators should be on the inside of the line and materials replenished from the outside.

Traditional electronics assembly (see Figure 1.10), off-line sub assembly operations, and office layout normally contain isolated islands. In assembly operations, there are normally benches set up in advance by the supervisor or on the fly by the operators for the operation listed in the router (traveler or work order process steps) they are working on. The operators take in-process WIP from a cabinet or stockroom, log in to the labor computer, and set up the workstation which is a time-consuming and very inefficient method of assembly.

The next layout is called the bird cage layout (see Figure 1.11). We see this often in machining environments where the operator is trapped inside the equipment layout like a bird in a cage. The operator moves from machine to machine and generally has a bunch of idle time. Each machine is producing different batches of parts that may or may not be in router sequence. We also see

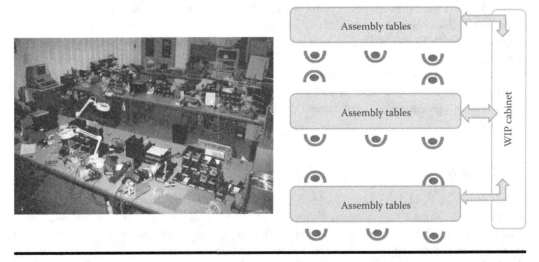

Figure 1.10   Traditional electronics assembly type layout using isolated islands. Isolated islands are bad.

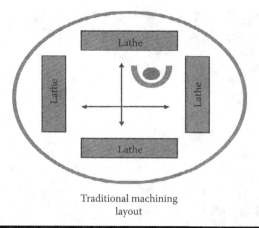

Traditional machining
layout

Figure 1.11   Bird Cage Island is an isolated island. Isolated islands are bad.

this with monument-type machines (see Figure 1.12). Monument machines (Figure 1.13) are very large, very difficult to move, normally requiring concrete foundations or pits. These can be wave solder machines, large presses, etc.

Another problem with existing layouts is the lack of flow; however, ironically, we are told often by managers in the area how well they think the product flows. There seems to be a basic misunderstanding of what the word "flow" means. Flow means once the part starts moving it doesn't stop until it is completed and boxed. If there is any batching in the process, that is, lot delays, the part is not flowing. Products, many times, travel all over the factory or the office before it is finally

Figure 1.12   Monuments include machines with pits concreted into the ground or requiring thick foundations.

Figure 1.13   Monument—wave solder machine.

assembled or completed. We also see this on both small- and large-scale centers of excellence or centralized processes like plating.

Lesson Learned: Isolated islands are bad!

Fishbone Layout

The layout pictured in Figure 1.14 shows a traditional Fishbone layout. This layout was taught as a Demand Flow Technology Lean layout and has been very successful at many companies. It is mainly used when there are a lot of subassemblies to a product. The subassemblies are built on feeders to the main line which looks like a fish bone. The subassembly is then added to the main unit which progresses down the center of the line. This type of line still yields a great improvement over traditional batch lines because it gets the product piece of Lean right but not the entire

Traditional fishbone layout

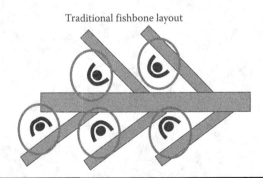

Figure 1.14   Demand flow technology (DFT) fishbone layout used in the past at Dell and many other factories—one piece flow but each branch is an isolated island. Isolated islands are bad. DFT came from the book called Quantum Leap by John Costanza April 1990, Costanza Institute of Technology, Incorporated.

operator piece. This is since each feeder is an isolated island the operators can't flex, and it can never realize its true possible productivity unless it is perfectly station balanced.

Lean Layout Expectations

Lean layouts should promote flexible workspace design. Layout redesigns should result in a decrease in overall space and travel distance needed to perform a task and eliminate/minimize fractional labor. If the redesign does not save space, we need to understand the variables that caused the space to increase. In most cases, space increase would be due to changing technologies for new equipment or dramatic increases in projected volume.

Creating the Lean Layout

Cell Design

Lean layouts allow operators to flex and help each other. The first step required is cross-training. This section will show Lean layout designs with advantages and disadvantages of each. We started with the block diagram which shows how the product flows. The next analysis drills down one more level to workstation design. It is critical to review the layout and workstation design as part of the process improvement. Most batch layouts (see Figure 1.15) are full of the waste of transportation, which leads to the waste of overproduction, waste of inventory, and waste of idle time (waiting). If the layout is not fixed or the workstation design corrected, it may be virtually impossible to achieve the Lean targeted condition and results outlined during the WFA. When the processes are in cells or workspaces in sequence and adjacent to each other, the team members understand their part in the total process. We normally find in batch layouts that the most utilized areas are located

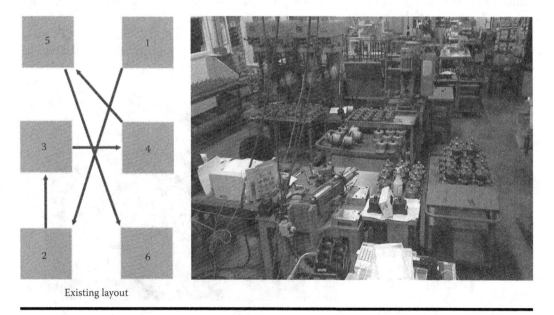

Existing layout

Figure 1.15 Batch layouts include significant WIP storage on racks, carts, pallets etc.

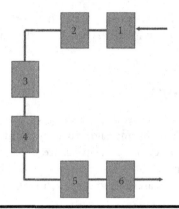

Figure 1.16 U-shape layout.

farthest from the beginning of the process. Some products are so big that operators can work on both sides of the line (i.e., car line) but they should still be on the inside of the line with materials presented from outside or with parts kits (SPS) which travel with the unit.

U-Shaped Layout

The U-shaped layout has some advantages over other shapes (see Figure 1.16). The main benefit is the ability to share resources. The staff is better able to help each other should the need arise. Communication among the staff is easier, especially between the beginning and end of the process or part of the process you are trying to improve. Walking distances are shorter between the beginning and end, and the person can work while they are standing and moving. The staff will be more productive yet potentially feel less fatigued. This layout maximizes the ability to flex the staff across operations. It can be run with one person or multiple persons (see Figure 1.17). If, for example, it is run with three people, one person could do stations 1, 5, and 6 or 1, 2, and 3. If one person runs 1, 5, and 6, that person controls the input and output of the area, so we can never start more than we finish (a pull system). Materials and supplies are replenished from the outside so there is no interruption to those working inside the area.

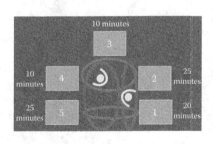 

Figure 1.17 U-shape Layout offers options for workload balancing.

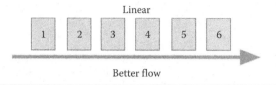

Figure 1.18   Straight line layout.

When building new layouts or work areas, effort should be made to have most of the operations take place in the same area with one team. This facilitates communication, as errors are found and communicated among team members. This motivates team members to problem solve thus avoiding mistakes. U-shaped layouts do not have to run counterclockwise. The advantage to counterclockwise is for those of us who are right-handed it is supposed to make us 0.3% more productive. It is important to note that accommodations need to be made for left-handed people, especially in workstation design.

Disadvantages of U-shaped cells are that the corners of the Us can be difficult to flex and the outside corners of the workstations may not be reachable by the operators. U shapes may be impractical or the workstation that makes the U may be the handoff point for the next cell for long lines with many subassemblies. One sees this in chaku-chaku cells, which we will explain later; however, this tends to make the cell more of a parallel line versus a U shape. Cell layouts should be based on what makes sense for the product and for the master layout as well.

Straight Line Layouts

Straight lines (see Figure 1.18) or linear layouts allow resources to move down the line sequentially for the process. Staff can still flex in a straight line, but the flexing is limited to the operator immediately before or after. The drawback to this layout is that, with one team member, the travel distance is longer from operation one to operation six (see Figure 1.19); however, the process generally dictates the layout, and often, straight lines work best for the master layout. Most car assembly lines are straight line layouts.

Parallel Layouts

Parallel layouts are designed with the staff on the inside to facilitate resource sharing as staff can move across to the other parallel line or down the same line (Figure 1.20). Materials and supplies are replenished from outside the work area or cell to minimize interruptions. This layout works well in a high-mix, low-volume environment. Operators can still flex as if they were in a U-shaped layout that works well for lines that have multiple subassemblies.

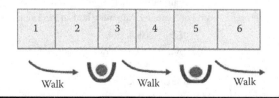

Figure 1.19   Straight line layout allows operators to move work and sets up the line for bumping. However with one operator, the travel distance is longer from start to finish vs. a U-shape layout. The product flow helps determine the layout.

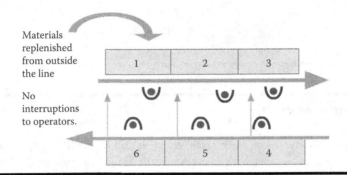

Materials replenished from outside the line

No interruptions to operators.

Figure 1.20 Parallel line layout shows sub-assemblies feeding into a final assembly line. This shortens the throughput time for the first piece. Materials should always be fed from the outside of the cell so as not to interrupt the operators.

Cell Design Types

There are four basic cell designs (see Figure 1.21):

1. Manual assembly
2. Machining cell
3. Hybrid assembly/machining
4. Automated cells

Manual (assembly or manual machines)
If the cell is flexible:
The operators can flex across stations to increase output
If the cell is not flexible:
The operators are tied to stations. Need multiple tools in place
Machine Cells—semiautomated (chaku-chaku)
If the cell is flexible:
The number of operators dictates output
If the cell is not flexible:
The machine bottlenecks dictate output
Totally automated cells
Totally under control of computer. Minimum human involvement
If the cell is flexible:
It is easily changed over to make several different types of products
If the cell is not flexible:
It is only designed to make one type of product. Output is fixed

Figure 1.21 Four basic cell designs.

Each type can be considered flexible or inflexible:

1. A flexible cell for manual assembly is where operators can flex across workstations (baton zone/bumping) and the number of operators control the output with little or no idle time in the cell. The most flexible assembly layout is where the operator can start and finish an entire part at each workstation and each operator is cross-trained across every operation. An inflexible cell is a station-balanced layout where the operators are tied to their stations, and adding operators creates idle time and does not necessarily increase output.

2. A flexible machining or hybrid cell design is one where the operator can flex across machines. This means they are multiprocess and multi-machine capable. In this cell design, the number of operators controls the output. The most flexible cell is a chaku-chaku line. In an inflexible machining layout, the bottleneck machine time is longer than the TLT creating idle time in the cell. No matter how many operators are added, the output remains the same.

3. A flexible automated cell is one that can be easily changed over from one product to the next employing a single-minute exchange of dies (SMED), one-touch exchange of dies (OTED), or zero setup time. An inflexible cell is one where the cell is designed to make only one type of product and the output is fixed.

Other Layout Considerations

Layout and workstation considerations should include baton zones or flex spaces in between work process zones. These areas are located before or after standard work zones (see Figure 1.22) in which operators can flex to absorb minor variations in time.

Chaku-Chaku and Hanedashi

A chaku-chaku cell is a "load–load" cell. It means the equipment has been designed to load and unload itself. It uses a tool called hanedashi. A hanedashi device (see Figure 1.23) is used for automatic unloading to make it perfectly positioned for removal of a workpiece from one operation or process and is critical for a chaku-chaku line. The chaku-chaku line is about the furthest one can go with semi-automation prior to completely automating a cell. The operator picks up and loads the finished part from one machine to the next as they proceed through the

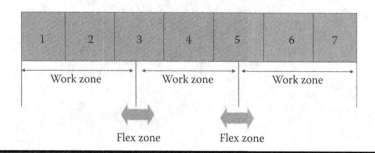

Figure 1.22   Layout showing flex zones for operators. This sets up the line for bumping.

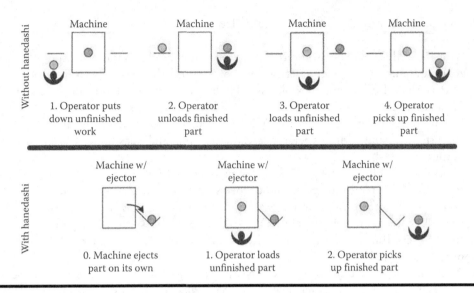

Figure 1.23 Shows cell with and without hanedashi device.

entire cycle. In addition, simple rotating wheels are used for SWIP where necessary for cooling or drying (i.e., epoxy).

Takt Time Board and Line Counters

It helps when day-by-hour charts are in use to install line counters (see Figures 1.24 and 1.25). With standards in place and line counters, it is easy to determine if you are ahead or behind schedule.

Figure 1.24 Electronic schedule board.

Figure 1.25   Electronic end of line counter.

Overarching Guidelines to Layout Redesign

Guideline 1: No Isolated Islands

The golden rule is not to build isolated islands into your layout.

Guideline 2: No or Limited Use of Doors, Drawers, Walls, and Partitions

Walls are bad and drawers hide clutter and provide a space for just in case supplies, which hide problems/waste, which increase inventory and impact the organization financially by having hidden excess cash in unneeded inventory. If cabinets need to be installed, remove the doors. If lockers, doors, or drawers must be installed, make them see through, so when looking for items, they are clearly visible. This will also assist with 5S to de-clutter and keep the area clean. There will be much resistance to this guideline. Staff and especially supervisors and managers will interject many reasons for why we need walls, doors, and drawers. They have become accustomed to what they have today and are challenged to make the paradigm shift to an open shared environment. The company will have to define what a customer area is and what it needs. We have designed many customer areas without doors and drawers, and we tape out items, areas, aisles, doorway paths, etc. (see Figure 1.26).

We have found there is seldom a true need for walls, doors, and drawers. There are some limited cases to allow a wall, such as a mandated (by the customer) wall for security areas, clean rooms, etc. This requirement can occur in firms that are working on defense or national security products. However, depending on the part per million (PPM) requirements, some clean rooms can be made with flexible materials like plastic. In some applications, we have eliminated walls and protected the individual workstations, which at POU is much cheaper than building an entire clean room (see Figure 1.27).

Figure 1.26 Elimination of hard walls and 6 feet partitions in offices allows for line of sight and greater communication.

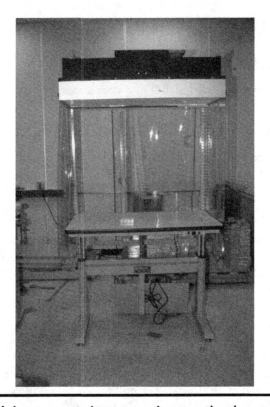

Figure 1.27 Picture of clean room station vs. creating an entire clean room which was a much cheaper implementation. We only protected the operation which needed to meet the high level cleanliness specification.

Figure 1.28 Flexible utilities.

Lesson Learned: Have the courage to challenge conventional guidelines and regulations, as many are antiquated and can be overturned. Some are misinterpretations of regulatory requirements and Occupational Safety and Health Administration (OSHA) guidelines. There are times when we have had to go to government agencies, ISO guidelines, or auditors to get clarifications, additions, or changes to existing guidelines to facilitate Lean designs.

Guideline 3: Flexibility

What you are building today may change tomorrow. Build grid systems or manifolds for air, exhaust, water, and electric facilitates flexibility and extended use (see Figure 1.28). Providing utilities in a grid enables future flexibility. Grid-type layouts allow for plug and play air, water, and utility connections. In addition, should you need to move a piece of equipment to another location to improve the flow, or take on a new line of business, it makes sense to change the sequence. Flexible utilities, even though a bit more costly up front, can make future changes very cost effective. Maintenance should move each piece of equipment with the paradigm that "it can be moved twice as fast the next time." There will be resistance in general to grid utility construction, which can result in more labor up front but will pay off in the long run. We are seeing that more organizations adapt to the use of modular furniture and use clear glass for offices to encourage open door policies.

Guideline 4: Review Layout and Workstation Design for Travel Distance and "Ergonomics," Limit Reaching, and Implement Standing/Walking Operations

Travel and excess motion are non-value-added activities identified as wastes. They also cause fatigue and impact your workforce, so whenever possible, they need to be eliminated or minimized. Sitting may cause staff to reach unnecessarily and the up and down activity may be more detrimental ergonomically than standing. There will be resistance to stand and move rather than sit. Utilize ergonomic floor mats and floor oil removal mats wherever possible (see Figure 1.29). A good tool to use is the ergonomics root cause analysis (see Table 1.1).

Figure 1.29 Floor mats which keep the operator from slipping in oily environments.

Table 1.1 Root Cause for Ergonomics Checklist with Contributing Factors

Root Cause Analysis					
Select the Contributing Factors					
Unsafe Conditions		Unsafe Actions		Behavioral Factors	
Selection	Comments	Selection	Comments	Selection	Comments
Breathing problem		Breathing problem		Anger/ frustration	
Chemical exposure		Exposure		Breathing problem	
Close clearance (congestion)		Failure to clear debris		Complacency	
Defective tools/ equipment		Failure to follow rules/procedures		Did not ask for help	
Excessive reach		Failure to lockout		Did not report unsafe condition	
Exposed electrical		Failure to warn/ signal		Fatigue	
Lack of training		Horseplay		Forgot proper method	
Machine guarding		Improper lifting		Influence of alcohol/drugs	

(Continued)

Table 1.1 *(Continued)* **Root Cause for Ergonomics Checklist with Contributing Factors**

Root Cause Analysis					
Select the Contributing Factors					
Unsafe Conditions		Unsafe Actions		Behavioral Factors	
Selection	Comments	Selection	Comments	Selection	Comments
Noise		Improper use of hands		Influence of illness	
Poor work position		Inattention		Insufficient concern for hazards	
PPE not readily available		Operating at unsafe speed		Insufficient preparation for hazards	
Repetitive motion		Operating without a safety device		Low job skills	
Fire hazard		Operating without authority		Prone easily to tension	
Hazardous arrangement		PPE related		Working overtime	
Hazardous storage		Reaching into moving equipment		Working too fast	
Heavy lifting requirement		Removed safety device		Other	
Hot work surfaces		Tensed environment			
Inadequate lighting		Took unsafe position/posture			
Sharp object		Used unsafe equipment			
Slip/trip hazard		Used wrong tool/ equipment			
Unsecured from movement		Other			
Weather conditions (snow etc.)					
Other					

Source: Submitted by Jennifer Lucachic.

Guideline 5: Oba Gauge (Line of Sight)

The rule is that racks and partitions should be no higher than 4 ft. This is called the Oba gauge. The story is that a 4 ft tall Japanese Lean sensei named Mr. Oba was notorious for insisting nothing in the factory be taller than his eye level. This resulted in the Oba gauge for a visual workplace (see Figure 1.30). The idea is to avoid creating view blockers in your workplace whenever possible. It is also called the 4 ft rule or 1.3 m rule. Six-foot-high cubicle walls and doors create isolated islands or silos in office and work environments. Cubicle walls should be no more than 3 or 4 ft high for offices to encourage line-of-sight management. Provided with the appropriate mechanism, such as padded mats and high counters along with health safety and environmental reviews, we can overcome most, if not all, objections. Many times, in the United States, we adjust the Oba gauge to 5 ft (1.525 m) high.

Guideline 6: Staff Should Be Located on the Inside of the Work Cell and Replenishment Should Be from the Outside

Locating staff on the inside facilitates movement of staff as they can flex across process steps, promotes resource sharing, and provides shorter travel distances. Replenishing supplies from outside the work cell or area limits interruptions of cell activity when supplies are needed.

Before   After

Figure 1.30   OBA gauge example before vs. after line of sight.

Guideline 7: The Layout Should Be Designed with Flow and Visual Controls in Mind

Point-to-point diagrams must be constructed for all proposed layouts. These diagrams should include both the flow of all products and inbound and outbound materials. Cell layouts should remain constant regardless of the number of operators (within reason).

Guideline 8: Co-Locate Executives and Office Staff on or Near the Floor or Areas with Their Products

How can an executive manage a company from a separate building or floor? We need to be co-located on or near the Gemba (see Figure 1.31). This aids in assisting any interruption of flow on the line and ensures a quick response to any problems.

Guideline 9: Don't Plan Rework Inside a Cell

If you absolutely must have a rework area, make sure it is painfully visible and someone is assigned as the owner and held accountable. Statistics on WIP and cash flow and cost of poor quality (COPQ) for the area should be posted and visible. This is a pain point and should be remedied as quickly as possible.

Guideline 10: Develop a Master Layout Early in the Project

The master layout can be constructed in less than a day but sometimes can take a week or more to get it right. It does not have to be perfect but will serve as a guide to the Lean practitioner (LP)

Lean FF 2 (value stream) organization

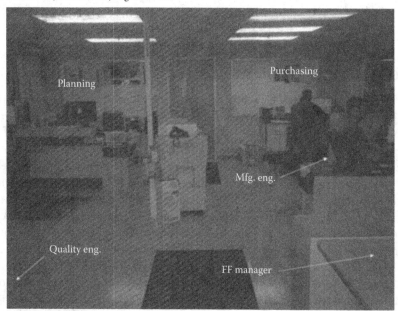

Figure 1.31   Focused factory office.

team and a vision to the rest of the organization on how things may look in the future. We typically get it 80%–90% correct the first time.

Guideline 11: Layout Approval

We recommend that every site develop a layout approval process. Too often, we see lines designed as Lean lines that aren't Lean. If you have no process to approve the layouts or no one knows what a Lean layout looks like and what questions to ask, you end up with what you think is Lean only to find you must redo the line later. We can't emphasize enough how important this gate review can be.

Establish a Lean review board (LRB). There should be a Lean layout expert developed at your site with the power to say no. This person should be thoroughly trained in the Lean principles and be able to offer an explanation and suggestions for layouts that are not acceptable. The layouts should be explained in a meeting to the staff, facilities or engineering department, supervisors, and process owners prior to submission for approval. Reasonable suggestions, which do not violate the principles, should be incorporated. Be careful with new installations not to add additional workspace if data does not support it. Every time we have added additional workspace that people just had to have, it has resulted in the additional workspace collecting junk. An analogy for this would be the exercise bike that becomes a clothes hanger.

Guideline 12: Housekeeping

A place for everything and everything in its place! Each place should be labeled with the equipment name, supply or part name, and location with min and max identifiers. Consider appointing someone or a team to implement 5S kaizens frequently and sponsor office-based shredder days or housekeeping days several times a year. Take before and after pictures of each project area. Video a baseline of your entire plant prior to starting Lean improvements. Someone must be accountable to ensure these 5S activities happen at the prescribed frequency.

How Do We Know When the Layout Is Right?

This is a difficult question to answer, but we find it to be both qualitative and quantitative. Many times, you just know when you get it right. The true test is when point-to-point diagrams work for each model and the overall report card metrics of space, travel distance, number of operators, inventory, percentage of fractional labor, etc. support it.

When the product flows, operator travel is minimized, changeover can be performed quickly, and there is room for expansion; we know the layout is close to being correct. Keep in mind that, as we continue to implement improvements or expand capacity, the layout may need to change. Therefore, walls are (see Figure 1.32) never in the right place and it is important to have workstations and equipment on wheels with quick disconnects to facilitate easy and ongoing layout changes.

As improvements are implemented, we find most layouts will continue to shrink over time. In developing the layout, it is important to separate human work from machine work. Once the layout is in place, we need to immediately implement and audit standard work methods, visual controls, and balance work across all operators and train and cross-train operators as soon as possible to minimize the number of staff required to support the operation. The layout should provide for standing/walking and moving operations and have room for SWIP.

After walls went up

Campaign to remove walls

Walls coming down

Walls down—offices on floor with
partitions—no more hard walls

Figure 1.32   Walls are never in the right place. They always become constraints to flexible layouts.

Struggling to Get the Layout Right?

There are instances where several days or even weeks are spent trying to get the layout right (see Figure 1.33). Sometimes, we have found that one must step away from it for a while and come back to it. Something else that normally works is when we suggest rotating all or part of the layout 90° to see if flow improves. It is important to make sure, where applicable, that machines with the highest volume are located nearest the work entry point(s), i.e., hospital laboratory. Keep in mind that many people design the layout in the right order, within a work cell, in sequence to create flow; however, this is only part of the equation. Yes, it is true that you will get improvement by having the activities in the right sequence and moving activities closer together; however, if you have not looked at smoothing or load balancing the incoming work, in essence, you have only completed part of the task and have not level loaded the work to facilitate flow and, thereby, not eliminated potential bottlenecks.

Put Tools and Materials in Designed Places

If tools and materials don't have designated places, hand motions will be different each cycle. Work will become unstable and confused. Work speed may fall off. Conducting kaizen to overcome

Figure 1.33 Layout review with key stakeholders including operators.

these problems will help to increase work efficiency. It is important to place tools in designated positions. Hang them with balancers or place them in guides so they fall into proper positions by themselves even when put down quickly or roughly. Tools and materials should be laid out close to the employees and positioned so they can be easily picked up. Determine locations and keep the tools and materials in their designated locations to maintain the cycle time. Having tools and materials conveniently located minimizes the amount of employee motion. This reduces time spent on searching for tools. As much as possible, place the tools within the range of normal motion.

Avoid Moving Parts Vertically; Move Parts Horizontally

Moving parts vertically (up and down) which requires extra effort and in time becomes a potential ergonomic issue. To avoid waste of energy, align the heights of the machines so parts can be moved horizontally.

Utilize Gravity to Help Move Parts

Many examples of this principle are visible in factories. Chutes are used to roll products down; sloping part shelves along the assembly lines help to slide boxes into positions. The advantage is low cost or no cost; gravity is your friend (see Figure 1.34).

Place Materials and Tools in the Most Convenient Position

This principle is followed to obtain an optimum motion sequence. Recall the results and avoid changing the direction of motion abruptly. The most convenient position is that which enables the employee to follow a short, smooth path of motion. Table and workstation design is very important to material and tool location optimization to support Lean product flow. Adjust table heights to better fit the work, including material and tool location, and the worker, normally between

Figure 1.34   Gravity is your friend.

37 and 41 in. (0.93–1.04 m) (see Figure 1.35). Generally, the optimum height for a worktable is determined by hanging the upper arm down and bending the elbow at a right angle.

Use Suitable Lighting

Important factors to consider when choosing lighting include lumens, contrast, glare, and color. In all cases, lighting should be arranged so that it shines on the work, not in the worker's eyes—especially

- The assembly zone is the general area in which the equipment and materials are located at a workstation.
- Three zones are defined by their distance from the worker in a seated position (or standing position if the work station is a standing one).
  - The primary zone is closest to the worker. Equipment and materials which are used most frequently or for the longest period of time are placed in the primary zone.
  - The secondary zone is for items that need to be reached or seen on a daily basis, but for shorter periods of time.
  - The reference zone is the area reserved for items which are used occasionally. Use of the reference zone usually requires the worker to move from his/her normal position to access them.

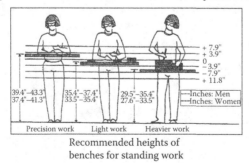

Recommended heights of
benches for standing work

Figure 1.35   Ergonomic heights for standing and walking operations.

important for paint and inspection. Many times, in almost every country, government assistance can be obtained for improving and installing more energy efficient lighting in the workplace.

Ten-Step Master Layout Process

Major planning phases include (see Figure 1.36):

1. Future requirements analysis
2. Issues and problem statement
3. Point-to-point diagram of current or proposed future layout—and findings
4. Group tech matrix (if needed)
5. Ideal layout—one-piece flow from start to finish with capital wish list
6. Assumptions and options
7. Block diagram future state master layout
8. Detail layout
9. Review with HS&E and facilities
10. Implementation planning

Layout Review

We have visited many plants (and hospitals in the past) who asked us to look at their master layout. Normally, they already had drawn up the plans with an architect or in some cases started moving the equipment! So really, what can you say? What answer are they really looking for? "Oh yes, it is a great layout!" At this point, any changes suggested could cost

Current layout product process flow (PPF)

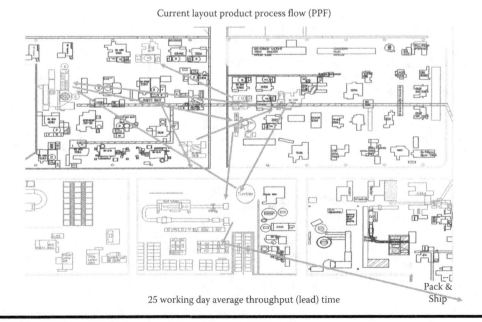

25 working day average throughput (lead) time

Pack & Ship

Figure 1.36   Master layout point-to-point diagram.

thousands or tens of thousands of dollars. If you tell them right away it is a bad layout, they tend to get a bit defensive. Normally, they have a lot of time put into it, sometimes years which is why they sometimes get upset. We suggest we not discuss their layout yet. We can already tell you there are things we will like and things we will want to change. With any layout, no matter how good it is, there are always things we will find at some point to make it better. We suggest instead that we start with a future requirements analysis.

Lesson Learned: If you want a Lean layout, pull in the LPs before you start the layout process and bring in the architect.

Future Requirements Analysis

The first question we ask is, does this support your future requirements over the next five to ten years? (Table 1.2). Normally, the answer is yes. The next question we ask is, what problems are you trying to solve? Normally, we get a blank stare and then we get "We need more space for capacity." We ask what metrics have you evaluated in terms of the layout? What is the minimum and maximum number of people it will handle? How much space have you reduced? Does it reduce cost per square foot in operations? Does it reduce travel distance? Have you eliminated isolated islands? Will it support one-piece flow? Does the product ever travel backward?

Another part of the requirement's analysis is to determine adjacencies. What areas should be next to other areas or feed other lines. There are a variety of tools available to accomplish this from relationship (see Figure 1.37) bubble diagrams to flow charts. At this stage, we may also do a group tech matrix (see Figure 1.38) to determine if we have families to create cells or to make sure the existing cells contain the right parts or even to ensure the families are still correct.

Point-to-Point Diagram

We have them do a point-to-point diagram (see Figure 1.39) of their current state or planned future state master layout (see Figure 1.40). The point-to-point diagram follows the major products through the master layout. Most times, it is very telling and virtually every time, it's a mess. There will always be the 20% or so (Pareto rule) that will not fit the flow. We call these parts misfits.

Lesson Learned: It is amazing how many times we have done this very simple exercise and the problems it immediately reveals in layouts. It only requires a small investment of time to trace each part or model through the factory flow; yet most companies don't take the time to do this. Layouts should be all about the product. The product should dictate the layout, not the other way around.

Table 1.2 Future Requirements Analysis

Available Time		370 minutes									
Year	Line A	TT	Line B	TT	Line C	TT	Total Line A and B	TT	Total Overall	TT
2013	37,144	2.39	64,489	1.38	16,640	5.34	81,129	1.09	118,273	0.75
2014	38,952	2.28	67,254	1.32	30,240	2.94	97,494	0.91	136,446	0.65
2015	40,773	2.18	74,899	1.19	42,720	2.08	117,619	0.75	158,392	0.56

Source: BIG Archives.

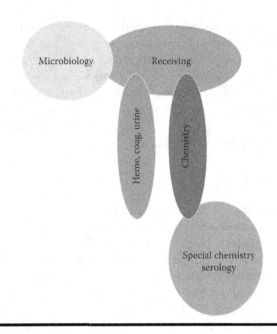

Figure 1.37 Determine adjacencies—what area should be next to what area based on the product process flow?

(32)	Drill Press	Leak Check Bell Jar VARIAN	Sq. Leak Ck Tank PURGE & FILL	Hot Burn In	Cold Burn In	Vibration Burn In	Cal Pos Auto Panel	Test Pos Auto Panel	Auto Breakdown	Pin Insertion Tool	Crimper X2	Solder +GRD LUGS	Vise	Endplay Block 1/2"x8" X2	Arbor Press	130 F Oven	180 F Oven	200 F Oven	400 F Oven	Vacuum Oven HEAT TREAT	Tank Seal Station	490-1018 Tank	32-1024-01 LCA-8	32-1028 Hi Temp	9007095 Black Max	32-1033 White Rubber LCA-4	9007053 Grey SILVER COND.	490-1014-01 Locktite	490-1014-02 Locktite
018-1738-10	X	X					X	X		X	X	X		X	X	X	XXX				X	X	X						
018-1738-9	X	X					X	X	X			X	X	X	X		X												
9000411-2	X	X					X	X		X	X	X				XX	XX	X			X	X	X		X				
9000413-3	X	X					X	X		X	X	X		X	X	XX	XX				X	X	X		X			X	
9000421-1		X					X	X		X	X	X			X	X	X				X	X			X			X	
356745735B5												X																	
45655B51												X																	
018-1958-16	X	X							X			X		X	X	X	XXX				X	X						X	
018-1958-17	X	X					X	X	X			X		X	X	X	XXX				X	X						X	
018-1958-20	X	X					X	X	X			X		X	X	X	XXX				X	X						X	
018-1968-31	X	X				X	X	X	X			X		X			XX				X***							X	
018-1969-12	X	X					X	X	X			X			X						X								
018-1969-13	X	X					X	X	X	X	X	X		X	X	X	XX				X	X						X	
018-1969-14	X	X					X	X	X	X	X	X		X	X						X	X						X	
018-1969-15		X					X	X	X	X	X	X		X	X	X	XXX	X		X	X	X				X		X	
018-1969-16		X					X	X	X	X	X	X		X	X	X	XXX	X		X	X	X				X		X	
018-1969-17		X					X	X	X	X	X	X		X	X	XX	XXXX	X		X	X	X				X		X	
018-1969-18		X					X	X	X	X	X	X		X	X	XX	XXXX	X		X	X	X				X		X	
018-1937 & P30	X			X	X	X		X	X			X**	X	X	X				XXX					X		X			
3567328-0001												X**																	
9000405-1						X*						X**					X									X			
9000407-19	X	X					X	X	X			X									X	X							
9000407-20	X	X					X	X	X			X									X	X							
9000408-21	X	X					X	X	X			X									X	X	X		X			X	X
9000408-22	X	X					X	X	X			X									X	X	X		X			X	X
9000412-1	X	X		X	X		X	X				X		X	X					X	X	X	X		X			X	
9000414-1	X	X					X	X				X		X	X						X	X	X		X			X	
9000910-1		X								X	X	X			X				X		X	X	X						
9000910-2		X								X	X	X			X				X		X	X	X						
018-3001-3		X		X	X	X						X										X					X		
9000003-1 -2			X X X							X	X	X								X						X X	X X		
9000003-3			X X									X								X							XX		

Figure 1.38 Example of group technology matrix.

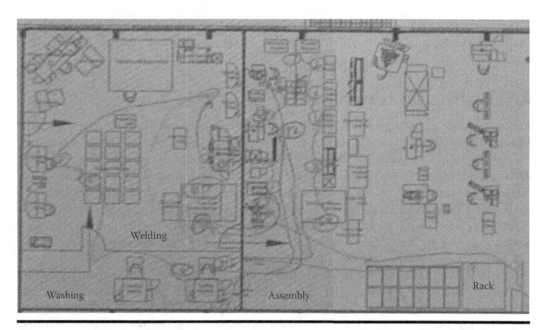

Figure 1.39   Point to point diagram.

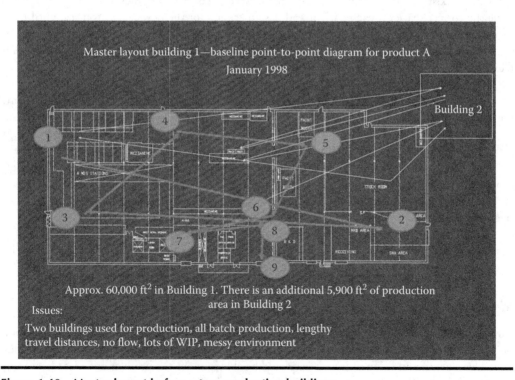

Figure 1.40   Master layout before—two production buildings.

It's not about seeing where things will fit or trying to squeeze machines in here or there, which is a common approach with architects. You must stand your ground with the architects.

Architects versus Lean Hospitals[4]

At hospital X, we submitted several (to scale) conceptual layouts to an architectural firm. The firm refused to draw them up and said they were Mickey Mouse layouts. We asked what he meant by that, and he stated they looked like they were set up with queues like the lines at Disneyworld. We explained our analysis to him and how patients must wait 30–60 minutes on average for results to come back from their tests, so we had created a new area called "observe care" with LazyBoy® chairs and TVs to provide a comfortable area for patients to wait. The architect asked me how many emergency department (ED) layouts I had designed. I said this was my first one. He said I was completely wrong and clueless and that he had done over 100 emergency rooms and that no ED's were designed this way. My next remark was not so kind, but I said to him, "Well I guess that's why all the ED layouts today are so screwed up and patients wait for hours to be seen by the doctor." We explained to the architect how we had conducted the point-to-point diagram and proved the extra costs his layout was driving. It is not surprising he still refused to draw up our layout and the hospital followed his recommendations, not ours. Later, however, I was questioned on all the problems the ED was having with the new layout and asked why we had not provided any layout recommendations. Obviously, someone had buried all our layout suggestions and conversations regarding this. We told this director we did in fact provide 15 different layout options all of which were rejected and sent them copies. We never heard back. Since this type of ED design space never existed before, we had to reach out to several governing bodies and agencies to determine the correct space for each patient and design criteria for the new space. You see, until now, there were treatment rooms but there had never been a results waiting room or dedicated physician exam room. They didn't exist. Since that time, several hospitals now have installed this new Lean Flexcare Track™ concept and patients love it.

Lesson Learned: With Lean, if you get to a point where your layout is not the norm or have to get approvals to make changes, it is normally a sign you are doing something right, not wrong!

Lesson Learned: Layouts drive costs and waste. You don't get many opportunities to design green fields (brand new layouts). However, once you design it, you are stuck with it for the next 30 years. We tried repeatedly with this argument but could not at the time get anyone high enough up to listen. Even though the current ED Director won out with her layout, she ended up being let go due to all problems with her new layout. So, the hospital was still stuck with her layout for another 20+ years.

Lesson Learned: If you have already committed to your layouts, don't ask someone what they think because at that point, it really doesn't matter unless you are truly prepared to spend the money to make the changes they may recommend.

Ideal Layout

Now we need to put an ideal layout together. The ideal layout means we have the new technology we need and all the money in the world, and if it was your business, how would you lay this out to make money? In addition, it means we would be able to move the product one-piece flow from beginning to end. This entails creative thinking and brainstorming.

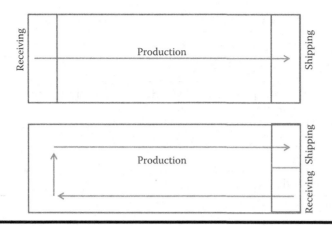

Figure 1.41   U-shape vs. straight line flow. With U-shape, personnel can be shared between shipping and receiving.

We need to look at where we are today and the equipment, we have available. In our ideal layout, we may have a one-piece flow washer, but in our current state, it is a big old batch washer; thus, if we need new equipment to make one-piece flow happen, we need to put a capital request together or design our own system in-house. The ideal layout would have no Kanbans! Remember, inventory is evil and Kanbans are inventory needed to link processes together. This linkage is driving batch processing. Even one-piece flow processing in another building requires the creation of a Kanban so the subassembly or product can be transported to another building. So, in essence, the product is still being batched (segmented batch). Once we find out what we can and cannot acquire in terms of equipment, then we need to look at putting together options for the master layout. The final master layout should flow just like any other layout from RM in to FG shipped out. Some factories are laid out in a straight line and some in a U shape. The U shape allows for easier sharing of resources between receiving and shipping but either method works (see Figure 1.41).

Assumptions and Options and Barriers

The ideal layout will in most cases not be practical right away; therefore, we need to list out what our assumptions will be for our new layout as well as any barriers (see Table 1.3). Generally, we come to develop 10–15 different layout options before we select the right one. Paper dolls (see Figure 1.42) or CAD layout options are good tools for this, and we project the CAD drawing to a whiteboard and use the whiteboard (see Figure 1.43) to review different options.

Other influences are specific goals from the organization. For instance, there may be a goal to save 50% of the overall floor space. Assumptions would include the information in the requirements analysis, the use of current technology, the use of one-piece flow wherever possible, the implementation of a Kanban or SPS system, the use of existing power available in the main panel, and some areas that may still be batched. Different options examine the big picture. If we are building a new building, it may be an option to put either production capability or offices in the new space and the assumptions and options transition into a high-level block layout.

Table 1.3   Issues and Barriers

Why do we use ovens for temperature soak?
Is cycle test at high temperature necessary?
What are customer change requirements? What do they control and what types of changes do we need to communicate?
Tolerance stack-ups
DIRFT-Repeatable processes
Silicone temperature bath
Traceability
Source inspection
Acceptance of tolerances requiring high-tolerance capability
Flexible washer raw material, sorting and tweaking
Perceived lack of engineering resources
Engineering—Why fix it if it works?

Source: BIG Archives.

Figure 1.42   Paper dolls.

Figure 1.43   CAD layout on whiteboard where we can notate changes on the whiteboard while viewing.

Block Layout Draft

The next step is to construct five or ten different options at a high level and avoid agreeing on the first layout attempts. The block layout (see Figure 1.44) is designed to house the entire product line or parts of product lines, machine shops, materials locations, offices, etc. The layout should have an "in" location for receiving and an "out" location for FG. It is best if these are separated but adjacent where staff can be shared. This is not always possible. The overall material (and information) should flow throughout the plant and never go backward. Remember, the layout comes from the product piece of Lean. Once these layouts are completed, use a point-to-point diagram to ensure a streamlined flow of the products and ensure there is room to move all stockroom materials to the material warehouse next to or near the line or in a centralized supermarket. The disadvantage to a centralized supermarket is that the materials must be gathered and moved to each cell via the water spider. A warehouse next to the cell with minimum and maximum inventory levels puts the materials much closer and makes it easier for the supervisor to immediately determine if any shortages exist. Either system will work. In the layout, there must be room for the materials to be replenished outside the lines. Many times, we see product lines where the workstations are up against the wall. If this is the case, we cannot get behind the line to replenish the materials, which means we will interrupt the operators to feed the cell. We need to keep in mind the space and location we will need for future state purchases of equipment or changes in technology. The space should be designated as such on the drawing. It is also good to note where there is space left over

Figure 1.44   Block layout paper dolls.

for growth and label it as such. This layout should be reviewed by management and employees for additional input and considerations.

Detail Layout

The next step is to create the detailed layout for each block. This means we lay in all the work-stations and material racks required to support the line. Again, do a point-to-point diagram for each line to ensure a smooth flow. At this point, it is probable that there is no layout for much of the line; in which case, we will need to leave these areas in the block form until such time as we are able to implement Lean on those lines. We have covered the detail layout earlier in the book.

Layout Lessons Learned:

- Have an "are you ready for the change?" meeting the day before re-layout and another the day after re-layout.
- You can't over-communicate or be over-communicated to.
- You need to spend as much time as possible with the operators on the floor at least a week or two after the change.
- Flexible utilities are generally worth the trouble and expense.
- Turn off gas lines before unhooking equipment.
- The more detailed your layout, the better it will come out.
- Pay attention to the necessities. Don't unplug the water cooler during re-layout.
- Try to have known new pieces of equipment up and running before re-layout.

1. Demo/clear out area A—includes moving cell X
2. Put in office in area A
3. Setup first flexible cell Y lines in area A—Dec 2010
   a. With plan to run line starting Jan 2011
   b. Setup up capsule assy area and Kanban rack
   c. Setup Second flexible cell Y lines in area A—Jan 2010
   d. With plan to run line starting Feb 2011
4. Overlay cell X on existing cell Y Lean line 1
   a. Overlay cell X on existing cell Y Lean line 2
   b. Demo wall and inside door only
   c. Move Lean lines cell X #1 and 2 to new location
   d. Move capsules and electricals to new location
5. Demo weld area and spring room
   Move cell Z and electricals to demo'd area
   Move spring room to machining area across hall
6. Move the cell Y Lean lines to the area vacated by cell Z and electricals demo wire storage room
   Setup capsule and electricals area
7. Setup cell X line 3
8. Setup cell Z lines 1, 2, and 3 and electrical and capsules in area A
   Move cell Z lines to old spring room weld area
9. Setup cell Y Lines 4 and 5

Master layout phases—Phase I
Cell 50

1. Demo/clear out area A—includes moving cell X to south of existing Lean lines

Phase II

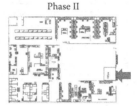

2. Put in office in area A

Figure 1.45   Phased in implementation plan.

Lesson Learned: Avoid getting emotionally tied to just one layout. It happens all the time! Remember, the layout will change over time. The layout should never be larger (i.e., square feet or meters) than the first time it is implemented, and ongoing improvements will constantly shrink the layout. The only exception is if the demand grows, we add another line or more equipment to provide the additional product.

Phased Implementation Plan

We should construct a phased-in implementation plan (see Figure 1.45) with projected costs after the detail layout is complete. This plan should be reviewed by engineering, maintenance, and HS&E who should be involved during the entire layout process. For master layouts, we develop a phased-in plan for the overall layout (see Table 1.4).

ROI Analysis

In some cases, especially if capital is involved, there will probably be a requirement for a return on investment (ROI) analysis (Table 1.5). The analysis should include all the investment costs in terms of expense and capital. We generally don't include internal maintenance labor as an expense as we pay for it as part of doing business; however, external labor and subcontractors should be included in the analysis and budget. The ROI should contain a savings section with payback analysis. Generally, a payback of one or two years is required at most companies; however, we should do the change as it is the right thing to do, but we do need to have the budget, if necessary, to pay for it.

Typical Approach to a Master Layout

Typically, we recommend that companies begin our implementation approach with a pilot area. Once the BASICS® tools are implemented, the companies should have an idea of the time and

Table 1.4   Chronological Phasing by Line

Month	Tasks
Oct-10	Complete valve area move Solicit bids for valve area trench Budget and approve switch layout Solicit bids for switch area move
Nov-10	Order supplies for switch area move and start demo area A Build out Sue's new office
Dec-10	Setup cell X Line 1 in area A
Jan-11	Cell X Line 1 up and running Setup cell X line 2
Feb-11	Cell X Line 2 up and running Setup cell X line 3
Mar-11	Cell X Line 3 up and running
Apr-11	Overlay cell Z on existing cell X lines (optional) Take down wall and one door near source area Move cell Z lines to new location Demo weld area Demo cell Y area Move cell Y over to new cell 30 area Build cell X Line 3
May-11	Run cell X Line 3
	Move cell R to demo'd area
Jun-11	Move cell X lines from area A to area vacated by cell 40 Setup cell R Line 1
Jul-11	Run cell R Line 1 Setup cell R Line 2
Aug-11	Run cell R Line 2 Setup cell R Line 3
Sep-11	Run cell R Line 3
Oct-11	Move cell R Lines to old spring/weld area Setup cell X Line 4 in area a
Nov-11	Run cell X Line 4 Setup cell X Line 5
Dec-11	Run cell X Line 5 Setup cell Z Line 1
Jan-12	Run cell S Line 1 Setup cell S Line 2
Feb-12	Run cell S Line 2 Setup cell S Line 3
Mar-12	Run cell S Line 3

Source: BIG Archives.

Table 1.5 ROI Analysis

Capital				
Qty	Equipment	Price per Unit ($)	Total ($)	
7	Welders	48,000	336,000	
3	Leak check	20,000	60,000	
10	Link gages	8,100	81,000	
2	Laser markers	100,000	200,000	
5	Test equipment	40,000	200,000	
1	Revamp cell X flow bench estimate	15,000	15,000	
Subtotal Capital			**892,000**	
Demo and Construction				
Qty	Area	Price ($)	Total ($)	
1	Switch assy offices	23,000	23,000	
1	Final inspection offices	10,000	10,000	
1	Welding/spring room	33,000	33,000	
Subtotal Demo and Construction			**66,000**	
Grand Total Capital			**958,000**	
Expense-Lean Line Setup				
No. per Lean Line	Total for 14 Lines	Equipment	Price per Unit ($)	Per Cell ($)	Total All Cells ($)
8	84	Workbenches	435	3,480	36,540
5	55	Ovens	420	2,100	23,100
5	60	Regulators	400	2,000	24,000
5	60	Swagelok fittings	900	4,500	54,000
1	14	Grainger/home depot/etc. MISC	1,500	1,500	21,000
1	14	Misc. electrical drops	2,500	2,500	35,000
Subtotal Expense				16,080	193,640
Grand Totals Capital and Expense					**1,151,640**
				Savings per year	**404,982.75**
				Payback	**2.84**

Source: BIG Archives.

Note: The payback of 2.84 years was calculated before the true productivity of the cells was realized. Once we realized 50% increases in productivity, the payback was reduced to 1.2 years.

dedication required to pursue this implementation strategy. When the first project is completed, we suggest they develop an overall implementation plan together. Part of that plan should be to develop a master layout early in the process. The advantage of creating this master layout is that, as we implement ongoing improvement, we can work to move or place the new lines, machines, or workstations where they fit in the overall new Lean master layout.

We have seen companies save a tremendous amount of time and expense getting their layout right the first time as opposed to moving entire areas multiple times per year. At Honeywell, we utilized this strategy when we purchased companies and moved their manufacturing to our plants. We would use the BASICS® tools to figure out how to move and transition their batch processes into Lean processes. This forced us to run the new area Lean. Many companies will move the batch processes "as is" and try to Lean them out later; however, this requires more space initially and loss of productivity until the area is converted over to Lean.

Master layouts should flow from receiving and RMs to the shipping dock just like individual layouts (see Figure 1.46). We utilize the same principles. We also look for adjacencies or areas that make sense to be configured next or near to each other. In the example earlier, we combined production from both buildings into one and increased annual inventory turns close to 60.

In companies, moving some areas is very expensive and difficult because of the need for containment and or operator safety. The biggest opportunity for Lean master layout development is during a redesign of an area or a totally new manufacturing, government building, hospital, or clinic construction, which are called green fields.

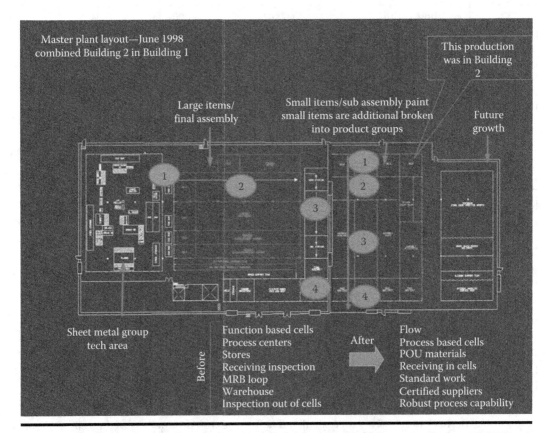

Figure 1.46 Master layout after eliminating need for second building. It's all about FLOW!

Lean and Architects

Layouts are one of the biggest sources of the eight wastes. It is amazing to see how much waste can be built into a layout. How does this happen? Most architects do not consider the process flow and tend to put things where the customer wants them and then work to make everything else fit, which doesn't always mean it flows. We have never seen an architect do a point-to-point diagram. This does not necessarily mean it's never done; we have never witnessed it.

When isolated islands are designed in, the company ends up paying for the fractional labor of that person(s) who becomes idle. There is not a cost for this in the architect's proposal. A significant amount of thought is provided from the implementing department; however, often, there is not much thought given to how the new design may impact other departments. Layouts should be designed to support the overall flow of the products and materials. Overall flow is just as important as the flow within a department. Companies are systems with many departments and information flows interacting simultaneously and continuously.

There is a real need for architects to learn Lean because just about every facility design today is not Lean especially in the healthcare world. Many companies ask us to review a new design for a manufacturing or office building that is so far along in design stage 4 or 6, that any changes would be impossible owing to the high cost of the changes. In new buildings or construction, there may have been thought given to layout adjacencies and equipment placement. We have found that, in many instances working with architectural firms over the years, the architects believe they have considered equipment placement and process when designing workspace; however, often the architects increase space based on what people want versus what they need, or they base it on volume projections and apply square foot multipliers to determine the amount of space needed to support the project.

Recently, there has been an increase in the number of architectural firms now utilizing Lean principles to help guide their design process; however, they may be reluctant to push back when managers and staff ask for non-Lean designs. The layout from the architect should be analyzed using point-to-point diagrams for every product in the process. The overarching goal is to provide a flexible work area and workstation designs that can adapt to future needs and provide an environment conducive to continuous improvement (CI).

Hospital Results—Laboratory

At hospital X in Florida, we were working on Leaning a laboratory, both core and non-core. The architects were told the laboratory expected to double its output over the next three years. So, what did the architects do? They doubled the floor space for both laboratories. Once they doubled the floor space, there was no longer room for both laboratories on the same floor. As a result, the decision was made to move the non-core laboratory off site to a soon to be built two-story building. By the end of our Lean laboratory project, we were able to reduce the architect's footprint for the core laboratory by close to 30% and the non-core laboratory by the same margin. In addition, both laboratories could have remained on the same floor. But since the new building was so far along in the design process, they continued down that path. By moving the non-core laboratory to another building, a whole new set of additional waste was created.

Master Layout Results

Hospital X in Florida had a foodservice master plan which showed the department was below the average for existing volumes. Hospital X was going to experience a 30% increase in volumes and the master plan for food service reflected a 50% space increase, necessitating expansion of the existing facility to a new excavation site since the current area could not accommodate that size of expansion. This created a level of cost that could not initially be approved. We worked with the Lean team to analyze exactly how much more space would be required if we moved to a one-piece flow model. Six months into this major Lean project, it was determined that the new space excavation was not needed, and, in addition, the expansion was reduced from 50% to 20% to meet the new volume projections. Instead of a major expansion involving new construction, a renovation in existing space was planned. This was a multi-million-dollar savings for the hospital!

Workstation Design

We discussed the importance of engaging frontline staff, frontline supervisors, and managers in the process of layout. Everyone should also be involved in workstation design (see Figure 1.47). Often, we find that workstations are changed on the fly at every shift change based on how the next employee or next shift performs their work. It is critical that the frontline staff is fully engaged in the redesigning of their workstations, as it reinforces their acceptance.

We recommend that team members consisting of frontline staff and supervisor plan out the workstation and locate all supplies and needs on the drawing. Workstations should be designed to the product flow (not the operator time). The team needs to decide on quantity and location for inventory and buffer or backup supplies and discuss the replenishment or restocking of supplies to determine the impact to workstation design. It is recommended that, if multi-shifts and staff are sharing work areas, each person on each shift can review the workstation redesign and process and there are standards and audits put in place to ensure compliance.

Workstations should be constructed at stand-up height generally 38–40 in. (approx. 1 m) for jobs done with the hands. Even though we are all at different heights, our arms are generally within 1–3 in. (3–8 cm) of each other (see Figure 1.48). However, for workstations that have microscopes or are height, i.e., *eye* dependent, the workstation or object on the workstation will have to be set up so the height is adjustable. There are all different types of workstations. One can buy erector set-style workstations (see Figure 1.49), which can be expensive, or fabricate his or her

Figure 1.47 Workstation design. How much space does Larry really need?

Figure 1.48 Heights of arms are only a couple of inches different, whereas eye heights vary significantly.

Figure 1.49 Erector type workstations are easy to build and customize.

Creativity-based tool holder at POU and standard WIP location label

Mixed model cell—Parts, tools and epoxy lined up in order of use. Second bin (behind first bin) is for next model build. The parts setup for the next model is performed on external time by the water spider.

Figure 1.50 Workstation design—lining up tools and materials in order of use at point of use.

own rather cheaply. Each workstation should be on wheels where possible with air and other utilities designed to be as flexible as possible.

A good operator will show you how their workstation should be set up as shown upon review of the videos. It is important to notice where they move their eyes, where they place their hands, parts, and tools during their operations. We will normally run a pilot or mockup with the operator or office person when setting up the new workstation. We literally go step by step, following the block diagram as we go, lining up their materials (see Figure 1.50) and supplies in the proper sequence as they are building or processing the parts to minimize reaching and excess motions. We draw an outline around it (or use tape) and label it. This is a very time-consuming process that requires much patience by the person we are working with and the Lean team or supervisor.

Once we get everything in place, we have the operator run the workstation and adjust (see Figure 1.51), since operators will normally forget something, or something will not be in the right place. When we are comfortable that everything is set up correctly and they have practiced it, we will video them and review the video. After reviewing the video, we will make other improvements or adjustments as necessary. Once we are satisfied, the lines and flow are running well, we will perform a formal redesign of all the workstations. Simple stand-up workstations on wheels with lights are very flexible and allow for easy improvements or adjustments (see Figure 1.52).

There may be cases where we duplicate equipment or supplies on the workstations ensuring the product keeps moving forward and allows the opportunity for other operators to bump. If we were to set everything up on one workstation with the supplies not in the exact order, that is, we put a fixture in the middle of the workstation, this would force the operator to stay in one place, probably sitting, and would not allow anyone else to flex in and help. This also almost always leads to more quality issues.

Lesson Learned: Standing and walking is up to 30% more efficient than sit-down operations. We also need to develop solutions that work well for our physically challenged individuals.

Figure 1.51 Workstation design—all tools and materials labeled.

Materials Should Be Fed from the Back of the Workstation

Many catalogs have non-Lean choices in terms of workstations and bin shelving (see Figure 1.53). Flow racks should be used wherever possible and fed from behind.

Batching Fixtures and Workstations Must Be Modified or Removed

Batching fixtures need to be modified to support one-piece flow (see Figure 1.54), which is an example of mistake proofing. Once the fixture is modified to support one-piece flow, the operator can only do one piece at a time on the fixture.[7]

Figure 1.52 Creating workbenches which can be daisy chained and are totally flexible. We moved an entire factory over a weekend.

Before   After

Figure 1.53   Bad workstation design—can't feed materials from behind.

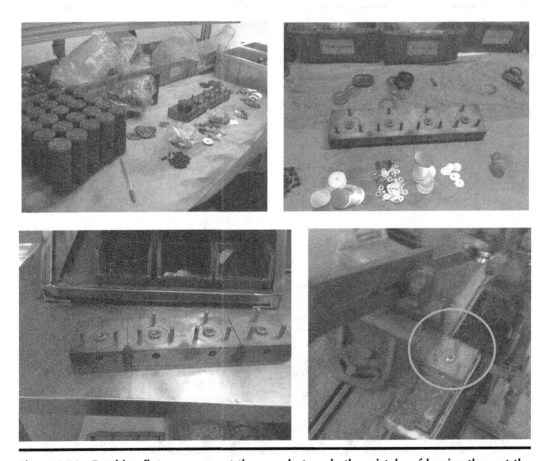

Figure 1.54   Batching fixtures—we cut these up but made the mistake of leaving them at the workstation so they welded them back together. We cut them apart again and trashed the other three fixtures.

Figure 1.55   Bad workstation design. Can't feed from behind. Tool board keeps tools from not being at point of use.

Plan for Every Tool

Tool boards (often known as shadow boards) (see Figure 1.55) are a very popular place to start with 5S. Initially, this is a big improvement over how the tools were managed; however, tool boards are still very inefficient. Because the tools are now centralized, they force the operator to go back and forth to the tool board. When used on large lines, the tools will disappear off the boards during the day, populate in and around the units being built by the operators, and return to the tool boards at night.

The Lean goal is to place the exact tool where it is needed, when it is needed, even if it means duplicating tools. As one gets further down the Lean path, one finds they are spending a lot of money on new shadow boards because the shadows keep changing due to the introduction of new tools or most likely the elimination of many tools as engineering works to standardize parts and tooling. One-sided bin racks, on which most tools hang, are also inefficient. The problem with one-sided bin racks is that the bins cannot be fed from behind and then there is no incentive to put in a two-bin system.

The plan for every tool is like the plan for every part (PFEP). The plan describes the tools used and important information to consider about the tool. Each tool should be identified (where possible) as to its location so if it is found anywhere in the factory, one knows exactly where it belongs (see Table 1.6). For instance, the location C1–2–Op1 would tell you cell 1, station 2, operation 1.

Tooling Placement

Each tool required should be at the workstation (see Figures 1.56 and 1.57). We generally don't label the tools or solidify their location until the line has been running for a week or so. Tools in this case include machines, i.e., marking machines, arbor presses, air presses, required to do the job. Like the parts, this may require duplication of equipment to keep the products flowing. If you combine two press operations at a station with one machine, it may inhibit your ability to properly flex the team members when the line is running!

Table 1.6   Plan for Every Tool

Tool required
Customized or standard catalog?
If customized, does it have a drawing number?
Cell or product line and station location
Station location
Supplier
Number required
Requires special training?
Specifications (i.e., torque settings, etc.)
Calibration required? If yes, note frequency
Maintenance required?
Does it require consumables? If yes, what consumables?

Figure 1.56   Tools at point of use and labeled to denote the assembly cell and station.

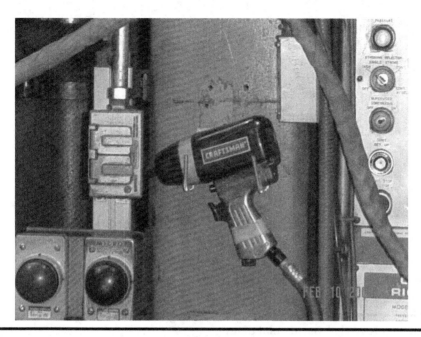

Figure 1.57   Tool used for setup right at point of use.

Once we have time to see what tools are necessary and where, we look for ways to present the tools to the team members, which will minimize their motions and thought processes when using the tool. It should be automatic to just reach down (without looking) and grab the tool (see Figure 1.58). We also use tool balancers and other types of overhead tool presentation devices to reduce fatigue and motions. In many cases, if two bits are required, we will supply two power screwdrivers. But there are some nonnegotiable points here:

- The tools must be laid out in order of assembly.
- The tools must be arranged to minimize operator motions such as reaching.
- The tools must be color coded, scribed or somehow identified by line and station.

Tooling Notes

1. Evaluate tooling needs early—there should be enough to accommodate peak production of any part.
2. Tooling should be for one-piece flow only in general—no multi-cavity trays except for SWIP, that is, curing or similar operations.
3. Assess for convenient storage and access to workstation.
4. Tooling design must be ergonomic.
5. Should be low maintenance with little/no calibration required.
6. Presentation of tools should be designed for standing and walking operations.

Lesson Learned: Use the highest skilled person to run the line during initial layout to eliminate the bugs and achieve single piece flow. This process should be used even if the line is designed for many operators and will highlight missing tools and/or materials, table heights,

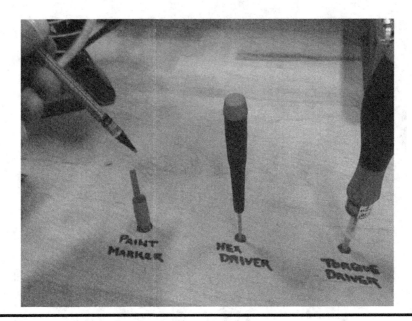

Figure 1.58   Tools labeled and at point of use.

order of materials and tools, etc. Next, bring additional people into the line one at a time and let each person run the line by themselves first, which will make it immediately obvious where cross-training is required.

Personal Tools versus Company-Owned Tools

Many companies, especially in machine shops, require their employees to bring in their own tools or, in some cases, will provide a tool allowance so they can purchase their own tools. What are the problems with personal tools? (Figure 1.59)

- ■ Each person must have a toolbox—ties up space.
- ■ No one will lend tools—can you blame them?
- ■ If you need a tool, it is locked up.

The biggest problem however is when a team member comes up with a great idea and designs and modifies a tool to do the job. There is a saying: "Want to know who has the right tool to do the job? Look for the operator who does the job the fastest. Invariably they have or made the right tool to get the job done."[5] Since they own the tool, it is now in their locked toolbox. If they are out for a day, it could shut the operation down.

Toolboxes

Toolboxes are bad. Why do we say this? As an example, try searching for a 0.5 in. wrench or #3 screwdriver. Most toolboxes are unorganized and a mess; even organized toolboxes are wasteful as operators are always searching for a tool. The boxes require valuable floor space and have locks on them so if you need a tool and you don't have the key or combination, there is no way to get it. We

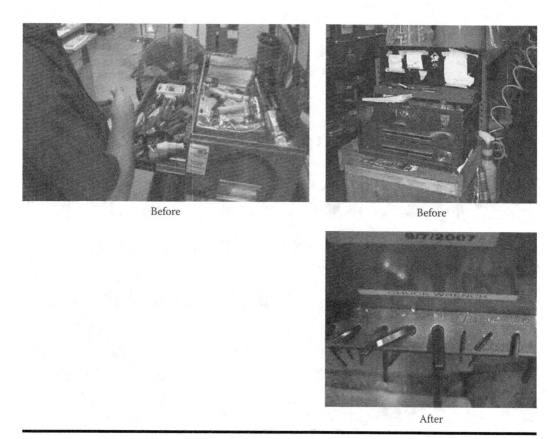

Before   Before

After

Figure 1.59   Move to company tools and organize with just what is needed.

have seen (see Figure 1.60) assemblies wait to be assembled from second shift until the first shift because the second shift didn't have the right tool or worse, they tried to use the wrong tool that was available and damaged and subsequently scrapped the assembly. How many times have you tried to do something around the house and didn't have the right tool? Operators want to work and will use any available tool. This usually violates standard work and increases the probability of a quality issue.

Lesson Learned: If operators don't have the correct tool, they will make the best with the tools they have available.

Homework: Watch any assembler or maintenance person for a day and record what waste you observe.

Exercise: Locate and take a toolbox off the floor and place it on a table. Next, get several additional screwdrivers and wrenches and lay them on the table as well. Label each one. Then ask for two volunteers. One volunteer stands in front of the toolbox and the other in front of the labeled tools. Next, start a stopwatch and ask each person to find a 0.5 in. open-end wrench. The toolbox person (it can even be the person who owns the toolbox) immediately starts pulling out drawers and the person next to them immediately picks up their wrench. Continue to work at the pace of the person with the labeled tools, which is a very eye-opening exercise. Compare the times it took for each one. The person with the toolbox will get very frustrated as you continue to read off the tools before he can even find the first one. Follow up by asking each one what they learned.

Figure 1.60 Problems with tool boxes.

Tools for Machine Setups

In this Ancon Gear example, the setup tooling is attached right to the machine. In the past, it was inside a cabinet, drawer, or toolbox with many other tools that resulted in wasted time searching. By building these tool holders and 5S'ing the tools, it reduced their setup times across the shop tremendously and increased their production capacity: freed up waste = additional capacity (see Figure 1.61).

Problem with Shadowed Tools

The problem with shadow tools and boxes is that the tools are centralized and not in order of use. This means the operator must constantly move to get their tools or they take the tools with them and leave them on the work bench until the end of the day when they put them back (see Figure 1.62).

Sitting versus Standing and Walking Operations

Any good ergonomics and safety person will confirm that moving and walking is better for you than sitting all day. Sitting creates many problems and standing in one place is also bad for you. Standing/moving operations also promote operator and/or office staff flexibility and health

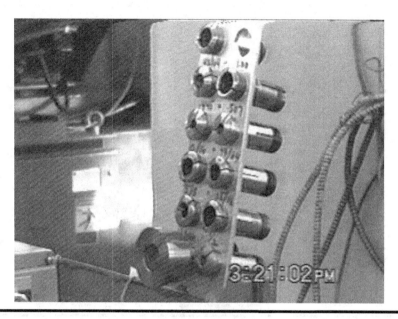

Figure 1.61 Setup tooling at point of use.

(see Figure 1.63). Sitting can lead to back problems and obesity, which can eventually lead to the possibility of early mortality.[6] You may need to transition from sitting to standing by adjusting bench or desk heights that will allow the option to stand and perform activities. These will make the transition easier, as staff will find the task or activity they are performing easier to do if they stand.

A person who sits is more likely to either build inventory or to wait (adding seconds or minutes to a process), as it takes more effort to get up from a chair rather than rotate around when

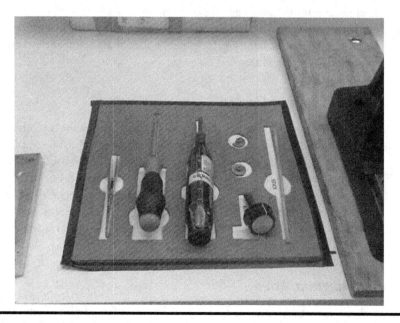

Figure 1.62 Shadowed tools in Lean foam—it's a good first step but not long term solution.

Figure 1.63 Ergonomic stand up desk.

standing. You will find that team members who are used to sitting for tasks may resist the suggestion of standing and walking, and vice versa. Standing and walking are up to 30% more efficient. If sitting is necessary, we put in standing height sit-down chairs. A general guideline for allowing stand-up chairs on the line is for operations or tasks where a person would have to stand in one place with no movement for 10–15 minutes at a time. We want workstations to be as flexible as possible. This means workstations with wheels and no hard piping, conduit, or tubing unless one is designing for very high-pressure air or gas applications. Workstations need to be safe and ergonomically designed with standing mats. Lean, ergonomics, and safety all work very well together and are part of our respect for humanity principle. We should always make provisions in our workstations for workers with disabilities.

Implementing Workstation Design

You must stay with the line for several days if not weeks to make sure it runs correctly. This means to continuously watch what is going on and coaching the operators all the time until they start to figure it out. We start by laying out all the parts in order and continue working with the operators on iterations of improvement all geared around making their job easier (see Figure 1.64). This means making sure they are following standard work and maintaining proper SWIP levels. It also means fixing any problems immediately or as quickly as possible. To enable this, we create a quick response team of quality, materials, engineers, and maintenance folks to be ready at the drop of a hat to help the new cell's team members.

Point-to-Point Diagram After

The best way to check any workstation, cell, or master layout design is with a point-to-point diagram to make sure the parts and products flow (see Figure 1.65). When you install a rack and have

Figure 1.64   Workstation design is ongoing.

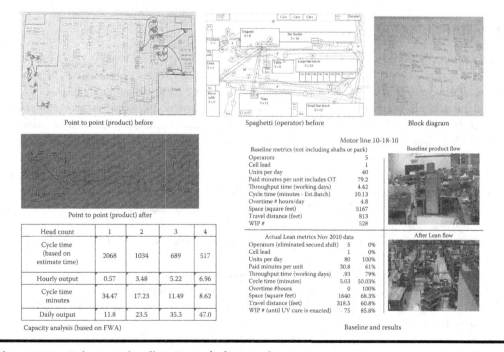

Figure 1.65   Point to point diagram and after results.

| If the parts are lined up in this direction the operator and product may have to travel backwards. Best case they are stuck at the workstation and bumping becomes difficult. With this design bins are not duplicated but the chances of truly standardizing this work are near impossible. | If the parts are lined up in this direction the operator and product continue to move forward and it is much easier to hand off the part, however, it means we must duplicate parts where necessary. This setup is very easy to standardize work. |

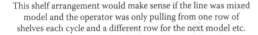

This shelf arrangement would make sense if the line was mixed model and the operator was only pulling from one row of shelves each cycle and a different row for the next model etc.

Figure 1.66   Workstation design—how parts should flow.

parts at three to four levels high, it is important to have the parts run vertically up or down the rack versus horizontally. If they run horizontally, the operator will have to continuously move left to right, and it will tie them up at that station. See the Lean storyboard pictured in Figure 1.66.

Station Balancing and Load Balancing

A deeply misunderstood concept is that workstations must be designed to meet the TT or a balanced cycle time. This is not necessary if the operators can flex across the stations. The problem with designing stations to TT is that the TT or number of operators may change or there may be a lot of variation in the process. To station balance the line, we are faced with having to change the workstation every time the TT changes to give the operators the same amount of work. So, we potentially lose the product flow to balance the line. Questions to ask during the workstation design process are as follows:

- Do we have the right amount of inventory? We need a minimum amount of SWIP to meet the TT and do it safely. The SWIP at the line or in the area is based on TT and the throughput time.
- Are workstations designed based on what logically makes sense to build the product or paperwork process?
- Work zones and standard work need to be designed for plus or minus two operators based on the number of operators required to meet the current cycle time or TT.
- Workstations should be designed to support peak demand with maximum model type options.
- The layout should not change based on changing the number of operators.
- The layout may change based on ongoing improvements.

- Supplies and tools should be in the exact order of use and should be within reach, even if duplicate supplies are required.
- Do you have doors and drawers built in as hiding places? Some drawer applications are ok, that is, for computer keyboards or station changeover tooling.
- Is the furniture bolted or is it readily movable?
- What is the state of the infrastructure? If a new piece of equipment had to be added, how difficult or costly would it be to partially redesign the work area?
- Have you calculated the distances the product and staff need to travel between processes and to get the supplies they need to do their jobs?
- Where are the staff members located in relation to the flow of the work that needs to be performed?
- Are there collisions that may occur between staff members or opportunities for products to get mixed up?
- Are there walls or doors impeding flow?
- Can you visually identify bottlenecks within the process?
- Are tasks or processes that occur sequentially located near each other to enable flexing of resources?
- All supplies are available and in the right order as needed. We need to verify the placement, order, and sequence of the supplies for each work area or station and that each is labeled by area and location.
- What size and amount of supplies are needed? Do you really need a drawer full of office supplies?
- How many workstations are really needed? Many times, people argue for more space but don't really need it. If you give it to them, they will *junk* it up!

Proper Sizing of the Quantity of Supplies Needed

During one company 5S kaizen, they found enough office supplies in just the accounting area to last well over two years and this is the office responsible for budgeting and lowering costs!

Fit Up

We use the term fit up to designate what actions need to be taken to supply utilities to the line, install new equipment, increase power to an area, etc., to support the installation of the line. We have normally noted these ahead of time in the block diagram. The next step is to meet with the physical plant/maintenance manager and physically go to the floor or office area and check to see what will be required to get the line up and running. We are looking at electrical connections, type of voltage required, and where we can get power, air line connections, high-pressure gas lines, water lines, sensors, etc. We work with maintenance and HS&E to make sure all regulatory requirements are met, and the line is prepped to move safely. This is also a great time to perform a failure modes effects analysis (FMEA) and create a risk mitigation plan. It is amazing how often we think we are going to go to bring up a line only to find we have some major installation issues. Had we tried to bring the lineup, we would have ended up being down for several days to fix the problems. We also experienced this issue in point kaizen events where the ready–fire–aim approach caused major problems.

Monument centralized solder machine   One piece flow solder machine

Figure 1.67 Example of right sized machines—converted from batch monument to one piece flow solder machine.

The optimum situation is when we have the room to set up the new line in parallel with the old line still running. This allows us to work out the *kinks* prior to tearing down the old line. We do push back on HS&E when they mandate the use of non-flexible utilities other than (high-pressure gas lines) where local regulations allow flexible cord drops and quick disconnects. We also suggest that maintenance label all their lines with voltages, breaker information, flow directions on the pipes, etc. It is surprising how often this is not standard operating procedure (SOP) for maintenance.

Lesson Learned: Labeling lines should be part of any visual management activity. In the case of piping with valving on the lines, it's critical to understand flow when transferring materials or what valves need to be closed in the case of an abnormality.

Make sure all equipment is right sized (see Figure 1.67) and available and utilities are considered prior to the implementation. Facilities and HS&E should be involved in the layout process. One must take into consideration mechanical and electrical fit up requirements like high-voltage electrical connections, water lines, air flow lines, gas lines, or venting/ducting requirements. Some equipment when initially considered doesn't consider other pieces of equipment that may be necessary to support it like manifolds, cooling add-ons, or hydraulic modules. Sinks and wash stations can be made to support one-piece flow. Monuments many times can be right sized to support one-piece flow. Make sure everything necessary is near each office workstation, that is, fax, phones, and copiers. (Again, the larger layout will drive adjacencies, but remember what may be needed related to support these in the adjacent work areas.)

Centralized versus Decentralized

The great debate is as follows: do we buy one big, centralized printer/copier/fax/scanner or do we put one on each person's desk? Information systems will always vote to centralize. They will argue economies of scale. However, what it really means is less work for them, that is, one drop and one router location and one machine for maintenance. The drawback is when that one machine goes down or someone ties it up with a larger printing job, everyone else is stuck dead in the water. In addition, everyone must walk to the printer. That generally necessitates conversations with everyone on the way and sometimes lines form at the printer. We have found it much more productive to have the right type of office equipment at the desk of the person doing the job.

Bringing Up the Line

If you have not involved the operators up to this point, you will experience their wrath! It is important to realize that when you first install the line, the hidden factory or problems will surface immediately. This is where one begins to first see some of the hidden waste. The waste that is hidden by WIP everywhere will rear its ugly head! We generally call the first week of implementation affectionately as hell week. No matter how much you have planned and tried to negotiate the change management course, it will all catch up with you here.

Stall Tactic

Beware of the stall tactic. This is where the organization or person you are dealing with puts up excuse after excuse as to why the line cannot be implemented yet. At first, it may be difficult to recognize as the excuses seem plausible; eventually it becomes obvious the stall tactic is in full gear. You must address and remove all the excuses before the line will flow.

Free Beer Tomorrow

How often we ask for something to be done; it can be anything, and the response is that it is too complicated, or it is too difficult to do right now; we will do it later (see Figure 1.68). That is, free beer tomorrow; but the promised free beer never comes. Many times, we want to get it just perfect the first time. The focus must stay on production, eliminating waste, and making the operator's job as easy as possible. If the operator is struggling, we need to fix their problem right away, even

Figure 1.68   Free beer tomorrow—fix it now!

if it is only temporary—that is ok. It is not fair to the operator to make them wait until something is ordered or approved or studied to death.

Waiting to Solve Every Possible Situation

Many times, we find people (sometimes cultures) whose every idea is repeatedly shut down because they are trying to make the suggested solution fit every possible situation or worst-case scenario. When we run into this, we suggest that companies try it in phases: phase I (pilot the idea on just one piece to see if it works), phase II (go after the 80% of cases where it might work), and phase III (go after the difficult remaining 20%).

Lesson Learned: You must take away everyone's excuses (valid or not) for why Lean won't work, or one-piece flow won't work before the line will really run well. Like peeling an onion, you must remove each layer (excuse) one at a time to reach the center.

Training

Prior to implementing the line, we must run all the operators through at a minimum of 2–3 hours Lean course. This includes a batch versus flow exercise where we teach them baton zone/bumping handoffs. This training is very important to gain buy-in and to prepare them for what is coming. We cover a simple overview of what Lean is and do a before and after Lean exercise. We all know that learning by doing is an effective learning methodology. We will discuss more about bumping later in the book.

When we run our first-round batch versus Lean exercise, we let them see the power of one-piece flow. We try to simulate any existing issues on the line during both the before, batch, and after, one-piece flow. This can be with Legos® or with real parts. Once the exercise is completed, we show them how to bump. The secret here is to always start with the team leader (TL) (or group leader/supervisor) and have the TL build the part by himself/herself first. This gives the TL some credibility with their team. We select the next person to run the line and have them run the entire line. Sometimes this means we must do some additional training. This highlights immediately the need for cross-training on the line. Once both are proficient, we have them work together. We start with the TL and when they get about halfway through the building process, we tell the second person to start. Once the TL has completed their first unit, we have them *bump* back to the second person. They take the work from the second person and continue from there and the first person goes back to start. What normally happens is that the second person doesn't want to stop or let go of their piece until their operation is completed. This is normal. However, the facilitator, typically the LP, must intervene and tell the second person he/she must hand off the part. The first objection is that we are going to have quality problems. It is true, but not if we have standard work in place! Now is the time to emphasize the importance of standard work. We also need to make sure the operators communicate during the handoff if something needs to be completed. There are occasionally times where the second operator must complete a process (i.e., soldering a wire), but we have found this to be less than 1% of the time. This assumes that the line has been properly set up to support bumping.

Production is Most Important

When bringing up a line, making the numbers, that is, meeting the daily production plan, should be a primary focus. Too often, we see where implementations disrupt production, or the focus is on making a workstation perfect versus making sure the line continues to run. We still have made commitments to our customers whether we're starting up a new Lean line or implementing another Lean initiative that we must make sure we meet.

Parallel Implementation

Production is near and dear to all our hearts. We work diligently to keep this in mind whenever we implement a new line. As stated earlier, the best implementation is where one can execute pilots and still have the main line running. Many times, this option is available. A pilot has little or no impact on the main production line. As problems surface, they can be dealt with immediately without affecting the main line. Sometimes, there are duplicate sets of equipment, or we may be purchasing new equipment and have some free space to bring up the new line in parallel. If the line only requires worktables and cheap equipment, this can easily be an option. In some cases, there may be space available to get the utilities and hard piping (if absolutely required) in place prior to moving the line. The second shift is also an option for trying out new concepts without interfering with production.

Start with the Team Leader or Group Leader/Supervisor

When implementing the line, we should follow the same process as the training. Start with the TL and have them run the entire line by themselves. This assumes the TL can run the entire line. Sometimes, we find this is not the case! A TL must not only understand the line but must also be able to perform all the processes (functions) on the line for which they are responsible.

As the name implies, they are leaders and a leader leads by example. If there are absences, they must be able to fill in for the process that has the absent operator. The ability for the TL to do all processes on the line helps develop respect as well. This aspect will be discussed in greater detail a bit later. By having the TL run the line first, we will expose any immediate problems or issues that the team did not contemplate or, if they did, be able to see the severity of how it impacts the line. After, the TL has each other operator run the line by themselves. If they cannot run the entire line, note what stations they can perform on a cross-training matrix. The next step is to go back to the TL running it by himself/herself. When the TL is about halfway, add the next person to the start of the line. When the TL completes a unit, have them *bump* the first person back to the start of the line and the TL continues to assemble their part. Continue to add each person in over 15 minutes to 0.5 hour intervals so each person has time to adjust to the new process.

Quick Response Team

Prior to implementing the line, we need to designate a quick response team. This team should be composed of maintenance, process engineering (with design on call), quality materials, HS&E, and the Lean team members. This team should be on hand initially for the first few hours the line is running to be able to immediately react to problems. After, the team should be on call so in the event of a problem, the TL can call them. There should be a Lean team member on hand for the first two to three weeks or maybe more if the line is complex to monitor the line and coach the TL and team members. The team members will naturally start to come up with ideas on how to improve the process. Unfortunately, they are not always Lean solutions. Many times, they involve batching or changing the standard work to work around a problem instead of fixing it. Recall that Lean is all about identifying and eliminating problems and not Band-Aiding® or creating workarounds for the problem. If a temporary solution is identified, there should be an action plan for countermeasures with target dates and responsibility assigned for the solution.

Lean Roles and Responsibilities

The Importance of the Lean Practitioner Staying with the Line during Start Up

At a company in China, the final operator in the line (who was a temporary contract employee) decided he wanted to change the standard work because he felt the parts, he was carrying, were too heavy. The parts were within the ergonomic guidelines for the job. So instead of following the process that was to (1) unload and load the closing machine, (2) to unload and load the testing machine, (3) to unload and load the filling machine, and (4) to unload and load a final test machine, he decided to change things up. First, he took the part from the 1st operator and set it on the floor. Then he moved to the end of the line and unloaded the final test machine, then traveled back to the filling machine. He grabbed the part from the filling machine and put it in the final test machine. He then went to the test machine and moved the part from the test machine to the filling machine. Next, he moved to the closing machine and grabbed the part sitting there (and of course now there was now more than one part sitting there) and finally he loaded the test machine.

If no one was there to watch the line, they would not have been able to figure out why the operator changed up the standard work. He basically decided to do the standard work backwards. We immediately instructed the operator to follow the standard work. The operator said the parts would be too heavy and he would have to set them down in between each machine to do the standard work properly. We told him that was ok if he didn't slam them down and that we would add brackets to hold the SWIP but until we did, he needed to follow the new process. He proceeded to bang each part on the floor as he set it down. Somehow sensing he was upset, we stopped the line and had a private chat with him. We explained we understood the problem and would work on the solution right away, but his current behavior would not be tolerated. He settled down and we installed the brackets and once again life was good.

Lesson Learned: It takes a lot of courage to instruct the operators and stick to your guns, but if you don't reinforce the proper standard work procedures, the team members will get into bad habits. This is called discipline and is not a bad thing. We must set guidelines and stick to them. In this case, the operator highlighted a problem, and it was corrected. This is the nature of the beast!

Lesson Learned: Sometimes, it is uncomfortable to correct an operator especially in the beginning or when multiple corrections are necessary. But without discipline or continued reinforcement of the standard work, the line will not run properly, and productivity will suffer.

Role of the General Manager or VP of Operations

- Responsible for standardizing operations and ensuring all documentation is updated. Should be tied into company SOP or policy and procedures. Follow their leader's standard work.
- Conduct Gemba walks.
- Set targets for direct reports to reduce throughput and cycle time for production processes.
- Provide a growth opportunity for production personnel.
- Make sure one-piece flow or small lot production is in place.
- Lines are stopped when problems are found and containment and/or countermeasures are implemented (A3 and plan–do–check–act [PDCA]).

- Materials are supplied from outside the cell.
- Layouts are designed for one-piece flow and reviewed with a point-to-point diagram.
- Schedules are level loaded and managed.
- Group leaders are held accountable to make the numbers.
- Everyone must understand the importance of standardized work.
- Group leaders/managers on the floor and in the office must be held accountable for standardized work compliance.
- Responsible for making this a way of life on the factory floor.
- The engineering department should be held responsible for the exact accuracy of the information within the standard work and Lean line packages.
- The mindset should be we pay better than market wages and we expect high levels of performance in return.
- Create value stream managers versus functional managers.
- Each line should have their top ten action list of problems with an A3 in process for each one.
- Office personnel who impact the day-to-day operation of the cell should have their desk or workstation located close to the cell.
- Group leaders/managers should be held accountable for the 5S audit results. The cell/office area should be prepared as if the president or major customer was coming through at any time. Some call this a tour ready facility.
- Senior management visits should be unannounced.
- Set simple, measurable, achievable, reasonable, and trackable (SMART) goals and use the day-to-day approach to metrics.
- Use process focus metrics—discourage the day-to-day mentality.

Role of the Manufacturing Manager (If the Position Exists)

- Encourage employee suggestions.
- Conduct Gemba walks and follow their leader's standard work.
- Encourage adherence to standard work.
- Encourage cross-training and job rotation—make sure they are posted and visible.
- Encourage development of process focused metrics.
- Make sure the line leader (TL) is always 100% on the floor. Any meetings they need to attend should be scheduled before or after the shift. Fifty percent of their time should be spent on soliciting ideas and implementing improvements.
- Ensure a quick response to problems.
- Develop your people.
- Create focus factory teams and daily huddles to discuss business and CI ideas.

Activities of the Engineering Manager

- Design products with Lean, including total productive maintenance (TPM) and serviceability issues in mind. Follow their leader's standard work.
- Set targets for direct reports to reduce throughput and cycle time for engineering processes.
- Engineers should own their design throughout the life of the product.
- Engineers should be responsible to transition their product to production and build what they design themselves. Most Lean improvement can and should be designed into the products.

- Video your design processes and send designs to manufacture with the PFA, full-work analysis, and setup time studies and standard work outlined.
- Work with production operators during development of assembly products.
- Implement design for assembly analysis on all programs.
- Monitor to ensure engineering change requests is handled promptly—requires SOP procedure in place.
- Engineers should start out their careers as assemblers for the first six months to a year on the Lean line.
- Do Gemba walks.

Role of the Group Leader[7]

The group leader (supervisor/manager) must own the line and have the responsibility to make it successful. Otherwise, the pressure will be on the LP to make it successful. This almost never works as the group leader will take a hands-off approach so they can blame the LP in the event something goes wrong or, worst case, sabotage the LPs. The LP needs to work with the group leader to get them on board and, if they can't, must escalate this to the next level for resolution. It is essential to have the group leader on board because they will be responsible for driving Lean in their area once the LP leaves:

1. Follow their leader's standard work. Verify attendance at shift start
2. Check safety features
3. Perform quality checks
4. Monitor 5S compliance
5. Perform/assist with preventive maintenance activities
6. Train and oversee training with a job instruction method
7. Facilitate problem-solving
8. Crossover with previous/next shift's facilitator
9. Spend 95% of work time on the production floor
10. Assist with and participate in model rollout
11. React to performance indicators such as schedule attainment
12. Focus on the process
13. Understand company policies and practice them in your work area
14. Encourage good teamwork in your group
15. Understand and implement your company's Lean production system
16. Develop close working relationships with every group and team member
17. Use visual controls to improve time and understanding of the group's goals
18. Resolve daily problems with appropriate countermeasures
19. Drive to achieve and maintain standardized operations on the shop floor
20. Monitor metrics for each cell. Coach TLs
21. Capture all ideas that surface
22. Keep a logbook for the shifts for communication of any major changes
23. Review SWIP and FG inventory—within min/max levels
24. Review attendance/vacation plan for known absences
25. Look for any abnormal conditions that might delay the start of production
26. Identify any special production needs for the day
27. Review attendance—complete job rotations for the day based on absences, restrictions, etc.

28. Help the TLs solve any startup problems
29. Report manpower needs to an assistant manager (request for support)
30. Record absenteeism or tardiness on team attendance calendar
31. Prepare for any needed disciplinary feedback
32. Walk through area daily to confirm the following:
    a. Safety compliance
    b. Hazardous waste compliance
    c. RM levels
    d. General area 5S
33. Interact with every team member daily—develop trust and respect
34. Pre-shift meeting with manager and other group leaders
35. Team wellness checks
36. Check and update evacuation lists
37. Daily safety walk
38. Daily PPE audits
39. Update all visual management boards
40. Process diagnostic checks
41. Daily stand-up meetings
42. Operator process certifications—standard work compliance
43. Previous shift/day quality investigations and follow-ups
44. Recertify team when changes have been made to standard work
45. Follow-up on issues from previous shift that:
    a. Review status of team member suggestions. Support or facilitate as needed
    b. Develop plan for team member cross-training; coordinate with TL to do training
    c. Review initial control charts and check sheets are being completed properly and are in control

Role of the Working Team Leader

When bringing up the line, the TL's as well as the group leader's role is to work to make the line successful. In the beginning, the TL will be involved in running the line with their team members joining in one by one. The next step is to get the TL to back off and stand and watch the line. The LP needs to tread carefully here. We want to coach the TL but not give them all the answers. We need to ask questions designed to get them to think and come up with the necessary answers. The TL should:

■ Follow their leader's standard work. Make the numbers and meet the schedule.
■ Understand how the line runs and run it properly. Know each job thoroughly and be able to train others in standard work and hitting the times.
■ Manage SWIP in the cell.
■ Ensure that the day-by-hour chart and the month-by-the-day chart are filled out.
■ Ensure enough materials are available for production.
■ Deploy people properly, make sure people stay in the areas, and flex as required and make sure vacation plans are considered.
■ Handle people issues (disciplinary issues).
■ Clearly display the standardized work in the area.
■ Cross-train everyone in the cell and rotate jobs at desired frequency.
■ Create a top ten problem action list for the team and for upper management.
■ Manage breaks, lunch, and start times.

- Take swift and effective action on ideas generated by the team.
- Update the standard work.
- Make sure people have tools and materials to do their jobs.
- Float into the line as needed or ensure someone is available to float.
- Responsible for immediately responding to problems on the line with appropriate action and document on the day-by-hour chart.
- Be a leader and lead the cell.
- Create an atmosphere that encourages standard work practices.
- Run the daily team meeting.
- Make timely and effective decisions.
- Be able to prioritize and delegate.
- Be the role model for the cell (i.e., attitude, breaks).
- Role model the behavior you expect from the cell. Know each job thoroughly and be able to train others in standard work and hitting the times.
- 5S the area daily. Responsible for 5S in the area and constantly improving 5S scores.
- Solicit CI ideas from the team and implement them swiftly.
- Review production orders or schedules to ascertain product data such as types, quantities, and specifications of products and scheduled delivery dates to plan department operations.
- Create TPM checklists as applicable and follow up to ensure TPM checklists are completed in a timely manner. Clean and inspect machines and equipment to ensure specific operational performance and optimum utilization. Document unplanned downtime on machines and use root cause corrective action and problem-solving models to fix problems.
- Utilize ongoing video of operations and review with operators as required to implement and document CIs.
- Resolve worker grievances or submit unsettled grievances to the production superintendent for action.
- Determine manpower requirements and adjust based on customer demand and material input. Flex people in and out of the cell as required. Zero idle time is the goal.
- Coordinate with other product teams to obtain and expedite required materials and assure compliance with processes, procedures, specifications, and quality standards.
- Address needs online as they arise.
- Look for improvement opportunities.
- Investigate/troubleshoot quality, equipment, parts, and other issues as they arise.
- Escalate items to group leaders that cannot be dealt with at their level.
- Complete shift communication log.
- One-on-one communication with team members on their team.
- Identify line downtime.
- Complete hourly production summary with issues and solutions upon investigation.
- Respond to line calls.
- Confirm team is following standard work.

Role of the Operators

- Always work safely and advise the TL (supervisor) of any safety or ergonomic issues
- Wear proper PPE equipment
- Follow company procedures
- Do not rush when working

- Follow the standard work
- Always be 100% proud of their actions
- Provide 100% effort
- Be critical in the evaluation of their work
- Follow 5S instructions
- Follow TPM instructions
- Provide ideas on how to perform work better
- Help implement ideas
- Learn new jobs (cross-training)
- Be open to new ideas
- Help new team members in the cell
- Present ideas to the TL
- Highlight problems or abnormalities

Rules and Assumptions for Running the Line

- Work is not done in a station unless the unit is in that station.
- TT and/or cycle time are defined for the line each day.
- Define max number of people that can work effectively at each station at a time.
- No steps are performed on a unit out of standard work sequence (included in flexing).
- If there is nowhere for a person to flex, the line leader decides what tasks that person is to work on or what area that person is to go to.
- When there are more than two people working on a unit, the line leader needs to make sure the work is being performed properly until there is enough discipline in place to eliminate the need for direct supervision.
- Operators should never be idle.
- A unit should never be started if it is short parts. In the event it is, and management makes the decision to run with shortages, it should require:
  - The unit being red tagged with the shortage or problem identified and who owns the resolution of the problem along with the completion date/time for the unit and special handling instructions (i.e., where the unit is going once off the line). Communicated red tag status in daily meetings. Red tag unit flows as normal, built to shortage(s) and taken off the line and reworked off-line in the rework area.

The Family Test for Operator Jobs

- Is the job safe enough that you would let your family member do the job?
- Would you be pleased if the end customer was a family member for the unit you are working on?
- Would your family be proud of the way you are working and conducting yourself?

Flip Chart to Capture Problems and Ideas

When first bringing up the line, have a flip chart and markers ready on the floor (or office) to capture any problems or ideas that are found. The LP should work with the TL to assign actions and due dates to work on the problems or implement the ideas.

Discipline

Many times, the TL does not have the authority to discipline the workers. If this is the case, the group leader (manager) must be present and available to the TL to correct any problems that arise throughout the first week. Since there is normally no andon or communication signal in place, we suggest the TL have a cell phone or walkie talkie to get in touch with those needed so they can work through the issues.

The Team Leader Must Stay on the Line!

This is one of the most difficult issues much of the time to resolve. Normally, the TL is called to many meetings or has other tasks or sometimes other lines to run. In this system, the TL needs to be available 100% of the time for cross-training, filling in on the line when a team member must use the facilities or experiences some type of problem. The TL must get the quick response team to track down the resolutions, so they don't have to leave the line.

Don't Interrupt the Line Team Members

One of the first things we see when bringing up a new Lean line is how often the team members are interrupted by all types of personnel from engineers to material handlers asking them questions. This doesn't work in our new line. When you interrupt the operator, they get out of their standard work rhythm, lose their place, and often make mistakes, which adds another level of frustration to an already frustrating first week. Very nicely suggest to the person interrupting, they contact the TL or group leader from now on and not the operators, and it is also important to resist the urge to change things too much right away.

Create Lean Line Package

The Lean line package is made up of several starting documents required to bring up the line. These include the following:

- Role of the operator
- Guidelines for running the line
- TL duties (first level of supervision, working line leader, supervisor, etc.)
- Group leader duties (manager)—this is the beginning of leader standard work
- Guidelines for water spider
- Water spider duties
- Quality's duties
- Guidelines for TPM
- Guidelines for 5S
- Role of day-by-hour chart
- Standard job sheet
- SWIP locations and amount

These documents are dynamic and become a WIP. You can discuss it with the team ahead of time, but it won't make sense until everyone is confronted with the new line setup and is trying to figure out how to react to it. The first problem we encounter is that we normally don't have all the parts. The organization must determine who is going to do what jobs to make the line work. So, the Lean line packages are generally created on day one or two and pretty much completed by the end of the first week.

Rules for Stations

- Need a minimum number of stations to support the SWIP required to meet the TT and do it safely.
- The SWIP on the line is based on TT and number of operators and the work content of the units.
- Stations are initially designed based on what logically makes sense to build the product.
- Work zones need to be designed for the operators based on the number of operators required to meet the TT plus/minus two operators.
- Stations should be designed to support peak demand with max mixed model options.
- The layout should not change based on changing the number of operators.
- The layout may change based on ongoing improvements.
- One may need to add a temporary buffer station to accommodate a quality problem on the line. The quality problem should have an owner and a planned date of resolution. The buffer should not be removed until the quality problem is resolved.

Guidelines for Running the Line

During this time, we recommend assembling a Lean line package. Part of that package is guidelines for running the line. These change on each line as each line is unique. Here is an example:

- Have quality, delivery, inventory, and productivity (+QDIP) huddle meetings once a day.
- Record day-by-hour chart and month-by-day and month-by-month chart.
- Do not run orders if they are short of any parts. Check for Kanban parts as well.
- Continue to work on your part until you are bumped. Person closest to shipping will bump the prior person and take part from them. Let your part go right away.
- Must follow standard work in the cell.
- May rotate positions any time.
- Run one-piece flow.
- Place failures in the red bin at test and bump.
- Cell Lead must support the line first before working or reworking or repairing units.
- SWIP should be always in place (where marked) and lines should be left wet (which means with all standard WIP in place) at the end of the day.

Prework Order Checklist

These are examples of items that may appear on the preorder checklist.

- Verify all parts are available for order.
- Try to set up orders to minimize changeovers during the day.
- Make sure all parts are washed/ready for assembly.
- Check for any special requirements for the order. Any special requirements that cannot be done on the line must be done ahead of time.

- Stage all parts on the line.
- Replace empty bins as needed.
- Print out inspection sheet.
- Move orders in the computer system to consume component parts, if required.
- Move previous order to FG.
- Highlight special parts and instructions on work orders. Make sure packing list instructions show on the back of the packet with special instructions highlighted.

Sample of Water Spider Job Duties

Once the water spider position is created, it will be important to clarify the roles and responsibilities. Many times, these jobs were previously shared by the TL, group leader, material/stock handler, or warehouse person. Water spiders can be positioned as simple material handlers or what we call *smart* water spiders that can substitute in for any job on the line as necessary. Examples of guidelines for the water spider are:

- Verify all parts are available for order.
- Try to set up orders to minimize changeovers during the day.
- Review parts for cosmetic defects and make sure all operations were carried out (this should go away in the future).
- Make sure O-rings are pre-greased.
- Do not run two small lots in a row unless necessary.
- Check part number for any customer options.
- Stage all parts online.
- Replace empty bins as needed.
- Take the machine Kanbans to the appropriate machining cell.
- Print out all labels and separate (for now) into ten-piece increments (Pitch).
- Highlight special parts and instructions on work orders. Make sure packing list instructions show on the back of the packet with special instructions highlighted.
- Substitute into line as necessary for restroom breaks or high labor content units.
- Replenish all bins, grease, and consumables.
- Make sure the preorder checklist is completed and with work order prior to the start of the job.
- Stay an hour ahead of the line. Make sure the line keeps running efficiently.
- Check all orders for today and lookout next two days for parts shortages.
- Lead the cleanup at the end of the shift. Make sure the area is 5S'd prior to leaving.
- Make sure all WIP is in place prior to leaving (line should be wet).
- Make sure the line runs one-piece flow and SWIP is in place.
- Scrap parts in the system as necessary.
- Move parts in the system as necessary.
- Encourage CI ideas from the line and advise assembly managers.
- Replenish stock/Kanban locations according to the production schedule or heijunka system.
- Maintain Kanbans and move bins to lines as called out in work order parts lists.
- Provide tools and materials to the production workers.
- Verify lot numbers are accurate.
- Verify that cure/shelf-life expiration dates are up to date on consumable materials.
- Report shortages, scrap, and empty Kanbans to the supervisor.

- Contact suppliers per PFEP to advise when Kanbans need replenishing.
- Advise movement of carousel items that should be on the floor (eventually this will go away).
- Other duties as assigned to supervisor.
- May have to enter a day-by-hour plan and update day-by-hour and month-by-day charts.
- May have to assist with video, analyzing, and updating standard work.
- May need to train new workers and reinforce standard work.

Sample Checklist for Operators TPM

Daily

- Check the oil level on the test stand each day
- Check the oil bottle and level on the machine each day on the oiler
- Check oil level on each press
- Clean all machines in the cell
- Replace Allen bolt Kanban
- Check paint supply

Weekly

- Check oil drill presses

Sample Operator Guidelines for 5S

- Sweep the line each day
- Make sure all bins are full and in the proper locations
- Make sure all tools are properly stored
- Make sure all equipment is turned off in home positions
- Make sure the day-by-hour sheet is completed

Every Team Leader Should Have a Stopwatch and Camera at Their Fingertips

Each TL should know the cycle times for each operation on the line as part of the leader standard work. They should have a stopwatch, which is part of most cell phones today, available to check on the cycle times for both people and machines to make sure the standard operations are being followed. A camera can be very helpful to capture problems on the line or ideas for improvements. These photos can be a great trigger for action and to provide before versus after examples of improvements. Many times, we keep a chrono-file of line analysis and improvements, which is a great reference tool for the TL.

Role of the Day-by-Hour Chart at First Introduction

The first day that we create the day-by-hour chart, we use it for ideas. The next day, we used it to record actual production only. The next day(s), once we have had a chance to train the group leader and TL in its use, we implement the plan portion. There may be some initial resistance to putting in the plan. The TL will say we will never meet that plan and we will demotivate the team! We explain the plan is necessary to provide a target condition for the team members. Half of us in the world have styles that require a goal to achieve. Everyone should understand that hitting the goal the first week is probably not realistic but eventually will be achievable as we fix the problems. The purpose of the day-by-hour chart is not to make the team feel good. This hourly goal is a goal that initially will be a stretch and won't necessarily be reached in the first week but in time using Lean principles to identify and eliminate waste or problems will be rewarded through consistently meeting this hourly target until we challenge this target due to perhaps an increased demand.

The purpose of the chart is like an audit sheet, which is to drive improvement and make sure we are following the standard work. We must explain to the team that the purpose of the plan is to visually highlight what is possible based on the analysis and the times predicted during the omit session. Anytime we don't hit the plan, it means there was some problem that got in our way. So, when we have an hour where we don't meet the plan, we need to write down the issue or problem. By this time, however, some countermeasure should have been taken, if possible, by the quick response team. When it is not possible, this action is turned over to the management because obviously it must be some type of a barrier, which the quick response team is not prepared or doesn't have the authority to deal with.

First Week Implementation Points

Working off the WIP

One of the first implementation steps in any new Lean line is working off the excess WIP inventory. We generally put the inventory roughly where it would be had it been assembled on the line. We start working it off from the process closest to the customer and work our way back. If SWIP will be required, consider this so that not all the WIP is consumed before starting the line.

Resist the Urge to Make the Day by Hour Small or Put in the Computer

We have some very bright people that are now black belts, Lean experts, or Lean masters. However, sometimes an asset can be a liability. We find that it is normally the most intelligent of us that figures out they can put the day by hour in the computer. Isn't that a great solution they reason? Now we don't have to do double work of entering it on the flip chart and into the computer to capture it. However, imagine replacing the scoreboard at a major sports event and shrinking it to an A4 size (letter) piece of paper or putting it into someone's personal computer! What would be the crowd response? It is no different on the shop floor except they initially don't know any better. No one has shared the information with them before, so what's the difference now? The day by hour is one of our most highly prized visual controls. Remember, anyone who walks through the area should know if they are on plan, most importantly the team members. Even putting day-by-hour boards on large flat screens defeats the main purpose of a day-by-hour board, which is to capture problems. Any worker on the line should be able to go to the board and write down a problem. A computer station makes this more difficult and will probably result in the worker not capturing the problem.

Lesson Learned: As Yoda said, sometimes we "must unlearn what we have learned."[8]

What to Do When There Is Rework or Scrap?

Initially there will probably be scrap and rework issues. We must figure out how to deal with it. This is a difficult point in the project. The Lean answer would be to shut down the line and fix the problem, so it never comes back. However, we have never worked with an organization that is even remotely at the Lean maturity level to deal with this. If the stop the line strategy is employed at this stage, the line probably won't run for a week, month, or even a year. Many of these problems go back to the design or even the process capability. Again, it is not unusual to find lines where parts are still basically built by trial-and-error methods. Many times, engineering designed the product this way. So, the initial answer is to develop a countermeasure and work to figure out the root cause. The obvious danger is that once you work around the problem, the pressure to determine the root cause and fix the problem is now gone. So, it is a delicate balance at this stage.

If it is the first pilot implementation, we will keep the line running and address the rework. Generally, this means putting a rework station at the end of the line and making it very visible and painful. We assign the TL to fix the rework. Meanwhile, we call engineering and whomever else necessary to the spot where we are having the problem to start the root cause/PDCA problem solving process. If not, the line will not be viewed as a success. Being a Lean purest, this is difficult for me to admit but we have learned over the years that sometimes you have to compromise between theory and reality. It is better to compromise the Lean principles than to have the upper management kick you out because the Lean process in their eyes did not work. The argument you might make now is that we shouldn't have implemented it if the leadership was not ready or properly prepared for their Lean journey. However, we have found that if we compromise a bit and show the line is a success, we can start to make inroads to the culture piece. As my sensei once told me, "You have to earn the right to stop the line!"[9]

Lesson Learned: In the beginning, everyone will tell you that the 4.5 ft between the workstations is not enough and the machines need to be spread apart. Basically, when designing the layout, everyone keeps saying it is too small—we need more room. Ironically, once all the equipment is in place, the operators realize the errors of their ways. Now the 6 ft in between the workstations or the space between the machines is too far apart. They will start complaining they have to walk too far and too much. However, you tell them that this is what they wanted. But they quickly forget about that. Now, if you have not kept your utilities flexible, you have a big problem. The layout will never be as big as when it is first designed! After, it just keeps shrinking as we keep thinking up better and better ways to improve the process.

Action Item List

The hardest part about people generating ideas is getting someone to write them down. During our training seminars, we always assign a scribe to write down the ideas, and all too often, they forget, or everyone gets so caught up in generating improvements they forget to write them down and the improvements are lost forever or until someone remembers it again. We find that teams can generate 50–200 items or more after the first couple of days. Once you implement Lean, all the past sins become immediately visible. In addition, new ideas become obvious. Once we start to watch what is happening, we see the waste and the opportunities to change and improve the workstation design. Many times, this results in cutting down the size of the workstations. Action item lists become extremely important. They are the beginning of our CI culture foundation. Our goal is to get people to think, to challenge them to come up with ideas and implement them as quickly as possible.

It is important to have a flip chart at the site of the improvement area and instruct everyone to write down any problems or ideas they encounter along with their name. This is not the time to have people be anonymous. We must know who to go back to if there is a question about the action and many times even the person who suggested it does not remember they suggested it.

Someone needs to own the action item list. This person must be responsible to keep the list updated and make sure the items are reviewed at an agreed upon frequency. The goal is to implement as many good ideas as possible as quickly as possible to the extent it makes sense. Safety and ergonomic issues must be addressed immediately, and the HS&E people should be part of the improvement process and providing feedback and suggestions.

Lesson Learned: If you implement someone's idea right away, they will give you another one!

Author's Note: Remember, an action item must have a number, action, person responsible, and date to be completed. Also, make sure there is a good, detailed description of the action and that it is readable. Many times, we see actions get lost. When a day or sometimes a week goes by, and the actions are reviewed, no one understands how the action is worded. Everyone forgets what it was about, and it is never completed.

Lesson Learned: It is important to continue with the cumulative numbering of the action item list. As items are completed, one can determine how many actions have been implemented. If you continually start the action item list numbering over at 1, it becomes impossible to keep track of how many actions are remaining, implemented, etc., and actions get lost or forgotten.

The Chair!

Early in the implementation, the operators will complain about standing and walking. It is not unusual for a chair to show up later that day or the next day. What should you do? The first step is to examine the operation. Our rule for chairs is that if you must stay in the same exact spot for 10–15 minutes at a time every cycle, you should have a chair. Standing in one place all day is not good for you. However, if you must stand in one place for 5 minutes or less (which means the work may still not be set up properly) and you must move, every cycle to another station and back, you should not have a chair.

Set the Line Up Properly If Chairs Are Removed

At a company in South Carolina, we implemented a new Lean line. The line produced mixed model parts. Some models used the first, second, and third station, some used the second and third station, and some used just the second. When the operator only had to work the second station, they wanted a chair. We asked why. The operator said they had to stand in one spot every cycle for 35 seconds. This was due to a machine they had to assemble the parts on (we eventually split up the station). So, we asked the operator how the line would run if she had a chair. She said she would build the part and set it down and the other operator could come over and get it. Prior to this, she delivered it to that station as part of her standard work (1–2 seconds). The first operator said they didn't want to go to her station to get the part as that slows them down. Finally, we found out she had a true medical problem with her knee. So, we moved her to another area where she could perform a sit-down job.

In another case, the operator was standing in pretty much one spot. When we reviewed the situation with the operator, we found she had moved the parts around from the original order and they were now spread apart where the operator could not move–work–move–work. This meant that they were standing in one place. Once we rearranged the bins in the proper order, per the PFA, the operator could stand and walk, which resolved the chair issue.

Lesson Learned: You will find that there will be a temptation to give in to the operators wanting extra space or a chair. If you performed your analysis correctly and followed the process, trust your work product. Don't give in to the chair request unless they really must stand in one place for 10–15 minutes at a time. However, if that is the case, with rare exceptions, it probably means you did not design the work or set up the workstation correctly. An advantage of implementing bumping is that the operators must stand and walk.

Everyone Will Want to Start at Once

When we first start up the line, if you just let the team members go at it, you will find that despite their 2 hours training class, they revert to their old jobs and behaviors in the brand-new line. Some are naturally excited to start working and some of course are probably not as enthusiastic. They will start to create WIP everywhere because they want to keep busy and will think you want them to rush, even though you have repeatedly told them this is not the case. Therefore, it is imperative that the quick response team be at the line prior to its starting to start the team off correctly. If not, everyone will get confused and complain they were not given clear instructions.

Cautions to Consider When Implementing a New Line—Variation

Many times, batch lines are in place for a reason. Do not underestimate this! Remember one of the causes of batching is variation. We have occasionally run into lines where we don't get the results, we projected from the analysis right away. This is generally due to high variation in the line (our eighth cause of batching).

How to Handle Variation When Starting a New Line

We never seem to work with companies that have low-mix, high-volume, 55 seconds TT, car-like lines. So, we have had to learn to cope with variation whether it is in assembly, machining, forging, casting, etc. The variation exists in equipment designed for batch, unreliable processes, small lot sizes, over one million options, etc. To handle variation on lines, we must compromise the Lean principles. This is a dangerous practice and carries with it the potential for a lot of waste. It is normally the lesser of the two evils. Please keep in mind the fact that putting in Lean lines doesn't mean they are optimized and generally we must batch for some period. So, until we can solve the eight things that force you to batch, we still end up batching occasionally; however, we significantly improve productivity. We have successfully implemented one-piece flow on lines where many consultants before us set up cells but still batched at each assembly station because they couldn't deal with variation. So listed in the following are some methods we have used to cope with the variation.

Small Lot, Mixed Model, and Unlimited Options

Lean was designed to handle these types of businesses. Obviously, it is easier to implement on high-volume low-mix lines but most of the time product options and customization are not difficult to handle on a Lean line. It may mean more labor or SWIP on the line to balance it, or it may require an options station at the end, but we have never found a line where we couldn't make some type of Lean improvement or set up a line for it. Even the model shop cell can many times be set up to accommodate a similar flow of materials. There are times where some parts will cross cells that makes them more difficult to handle and will require batching from one-piece flow cell to another. The group tech matrix comes in handy for most of these applications.

Machine Reliability

In some cases, machines aren't designed to get it right the first time. At one company, if the machine didn't get it right the first time, it was programed to send it through another time because 95% of the time it could get it right by the second time. It would automatically unload the parts into a good bin or a bad bin. When it went into a bad bin, the first thing the operators would do was run it through again. We were now up to a 33% first time pass rate. When we implemented the new line, the first problem we ran into was that the cell was down every other cycle when this machine or the operator recirculated the part or it was just finally scrapped. To get around this, we had to run the machine one work order ahead in a batch mode.

In an electronics example, a lazy engineer designed a part that had a potentiometer that had to be tuned toward the end of the process to pass. We Kanban the parts prior to and after this operation and had one person (as an isolated island) who would sit there and tune/tweak the parts all day, but this allowed us to keep the line running.

Batch Equipment

One of our eight causes of batching is equipment. Sometimes, we cannot replace this equipment right away, so we must deal with it. Many times, we incorporate the cycles of the machine into the standard work. For instance, if a machine is set up to test 15 parts and the cycle time is such that we need to test three at a time, every cycle includes three cycles on the line. So, in the first cycle, I must unload and load the parts and it tests the first piece. I take one from the buffer of three pieces and continue to process it down the line. In the next cycle, I can't unload it, so I take one from the buffer (batch) and continue to process it through the line while the machine tests the second piece. In the next cycle, I can't unload it, so I take the next part in the buffer and process it while it tests the third piece. In the next cycle, I start over again. One cycle includes three cycles where one cycle has extra time to unload, load, and cycle three parts through the tester. This happens all the time in almost every factory. It happens with washing, ovens, etc. We create a buffer or SWIP to handle it until we can replace the machine with a one-piece flow machine. Remember: excess WIP is always the sign of a problem even if it is SWIP.

Lean Rework Lines

This is the worst solution one can have but I have seen companies implement it. They have a problem they haven't resolved due to cost. They know they will never fix it. There is no compelling need to change. They put rework lines in place and in some cases, companies will set up a one-piece flow rework line. So, if you are not going to fix the root cause, Lean out the rework!

At company in Maryland, they were making a small handheld computer. They implemented Lean and achieved a 50% productivity improvement, freed up 14 operators (without laying anyone off), and correspondingly increased their rework that was running about 20%. The contract only ran for a year longer, the root cause was in the design, but the customer controlled the drawing package, and to fix it was going to take several million dollars including requalifying the parts. If the company went for a deviation, they may not be considered for the next contract. We set up a Lean rework line. Not the thing I am most proud of in my career as a LP but when you are making 400 units a day and 100 need rework, it must be dealt with in some fashion and rather quickly.

While this may sound impossible with all the variation possible in tear down, lot traceability, etc., there are many remanufacturing companies which essentially repair and overhaul products and are reworking the original parts. Transmission, engines, and all types of other parts that are remanufactured or rebuilt lend themselves to Lean production techniques. Hospitals for the most part are repair and overhaul facilities for people.

Unreliable Test Equipment: Failures (Even When the Parts Are Good!)

Worldwide, we have run into test equipment that strangely enough will fail good parts and even worse will pass bad parts. This occurs when the parts pass one set of criteria, but the operator is forced to interpret a readout or graph to see if, even though the machine said good, the parts are bad. We have witnessed these phenomena many times at many companies. Many times, the data is also furnished to the unsuspecting customer. In the batch world, the operator loads the part, tests the part, and waits for the test to finish and the readout to appear. At this point, they have plenty of time to determine if the parts are good or bad. Once we set up a one-piece flow line, the operator is now multitasking. They are no longer just watching the test machine but may be running multiple machines or performing assembly operations in addition to running the machine. In both cases depending on an operator, to interpret screen results is at best wishful thinking (since we are humans and being such two to three sigma at best) but adds the complexities of running multiple operations, and the operator is bound to forget at some point. When this occurs, two things will happen. Either someone will find out and say we must go back to the old way, or no one finds out and a bad part ships to the customer. In either case, it is not an acceptable solution for us. We are almost always successful at getting engineering to figure out a way to have this be a go/no-go test to run the line successfully.

Lack of Jidoka

Whenever an operator must stand by and watch a machine, it is a visual signal that we need to implement jidoka. When operators must physically unload a machine, it is a lack of jidoka. Two button switches (for safety reasons) again are a lack of jidoka. The machine should protect the operator from injury. It should not require the operator to press two buttons. We would estimate the multiplicatively of this solution across the United States and Europe under the guise of safety that robs the United States and Europe of millions if not billions of dollars in productivity every year. Think of the idle time attributable to having to press two buttons at a time and stand and wait for the machine to finish its cycle. Instead, we should be creating a cage or installing a light curtain to free up the operator.

At an international company in the Netherlands, they had a machine that would "screw on the top of a rather large part." But the machine was less than one sigma capability, so the operator had to press two buttons for 3–4 seconds while the machine traveled to the part (possible pinch point) and hold in the button the entire time it screwed on the part. If the machine made a mistake, the operator would try to have the machine reverse itself and try again. The logic behind it was that if the machine screwed it in wrong and the operator could stop it soon enough, they could take their finger off the button and cause it to stop. However, in most cases, it was very difficult for the operator to stop the machine until it was too late, so it ended up being scrapped anyway. The operator before would queue up WIP there because he couldn't go any further. Between the 3 and 4 seconds (2% of the cycle time) to activate the machine and the 14 seconds (8% of the cycle time) to hold the button in and the additional rework time on the machine, we were losing more than 10% of our potential output on the line. In the end, we added a light curtain, eliminated the two-button switch, and added a resistance sensor and torque angle spec to the machine that immediately determined if it was cross threaded, in which case it would reverse and try again. The operator now only spent less than a second to press a button to start the machine and then moved to the next machine. We could deal with this variation because the operator was no longer tied to the machine, and it was not a bottleneck. This type of improvement was made throughout the line realizing an increase of 200% productivity on the line after one and one-half years.

Remember: Once you WIP the machine, it is no longer part of the cycle time (unless it runs longer than the cycle time on the line).

Poor Fixturing

The next cause of variation is poor fixturing. If the operator can't use the fixturing as intended or if it doesn't totally free up their hands, it is poor fixturing. If the operator must struggle with it, this causes variation and prevents standard work. We can still use baton zone balancing but it covers up the basic problem. We have seen very poor tools developed by engineering for team members on the floor. In this case, when we are allowed, we force the engineer to come use the tool for a day with the threat that if they don't fix it, we will bring them back every day until it is fixed. This generally creates a compelling need to change.

Poor Process Reliability: Process Capability Index (Cpk)

In the example earlier, normally, these test graphs are there to tell us we have a problem with the process and generally they give hints to where the problem lies. This means the operator must interpret the graph and normally it means a change a component, add a shim, or some other modification to the assembly. At most companies when starting a new model down the line we must gather three to five pieces for a first piece inspection. This means we can't start the line until a unit or enough units are reworked to pass the test setup. It is not unusual then to have quality or R&D involved to double-check the first piece(s) to start the production. This would work fine in a batch environment because we can work on other lots of material while we are waiting to hear back from R&D if the product is OK to build. However, in the Lean world, the line is down during this entire time, and everyone is idle. We witnessed one line that took 45 minutes waiting to hear back from R&D and meanwhile the line was down. Then we were told, "It looks like this Lean stuff is not working!"

Some processes just lack the capability to produce the product as intended or more likely as promised by the sales force. We have seen certain specifications promised to customers where a company had no way to even measure if they could meet the spec. Fortunately for them, their customers can't measure it either.

Cross-Training

We always ask if everyone is cross-trained. Oh yes, is normally the response. Why is it then that the first problem we seem to run into is that they are not cross-trained? It becomes obvious as soon as we ask each person to run the line by themselves. This creates all kinds of problems bringing up the line. Suddenly, one operator can only do one job. Now they are at one station the entire time and want a chair! It also leads to some operators having to work around others. This then makes standard work impossible.

The Importance of Cross-Training

While recently working with an organization, I was completing an initial observation of an operator who was performing a process off-line. We spoke during a moment over their break. During the conversation, I found out they were the only one on day shift who could do that job. Before taking any time off, they had to stay late and build parts for the coming day. The operator had not been absent in over two years. I spoke with the leadership and asked how they would handle an unexpected absence of this operator. You should have seen the panic in their faces. No one knew! Would you believe that cross-training began that same day? The organization has now begun looking at process versatility within the entire organization.[10]

Lesson Learned: One cannot perform standard work if the line is not laid out properly and all operators are not cross-trained. In addition, processes must be stable. For example, the parts need to all pass on the test set and be built correctly. This does not mean the line cannot run but it won't be capable of producing its maximum output and normally produces significantly less than the capacity at which it was designed.

Learning about Your Lack of Cross-Training the Hard Way

On a sad note, a very special operator was killed in a car accident the night before I arrived at the company. Of course, no one expected it, nor could they believe she was really gone. The manager talked with virtually every employee looking for anyone who knew how to do her job. They could not find anyone who knew or had ever even been exposed to the job. There were no drawings, and all the knowledge was in the operator's head, which unfortunately went with her. The company had to discontinue the entire product line!

Lesson Learned: This very sad but true story addresses a couple of issues many organizations face but may not realize. It illustrates the result of tribal knowledge not being shared, captured, or put into a standard with the appropriate leadership accountability in place to ensure compliance to the standard. We often joke around and ask operators what would happen if they were hit by a bus, God forbid. We hear the same answer over and over: "I don't know." I've been doing this job for 34 years. While no one expects or wants the worst to happen, we must cross-train to be prepared and flexible. It is not fair to deny an employee vacation or promotions, because we as managers were too lazy or unaware to cross-train someone to do their job.

Other Lines Utilizing the Same Equipment

The next variability issue is when the line or a station must stop because the equipment is shared. While it should not be in many cases, this is a new revelation. "Oh, I forgot to tell you about" is the normal response. In this case, we try to move those operations to an off shift, put it on wheels so we can roll it into the cell, or if we can, incorporate it into our walk pattern.

What to Do about Rework?

The standard answer is eliminate it. However, many times, this is not an easy solution. In the meantime, we still must make our numbers. Again, the Lean answer is twofold: stop the line when there is a mistake and don't build rework into the line. Occasionally, we must violate this rule to stay employed. Remember, a change agent is not any good if he or she is no longer working at the company. Normally, we want to make the rework obvious and as painful as possible. We also assign an owner to the rework. It can be a great way to introduce the A3 process. Generally, the line leader is assigned the rework and must note it on the day-by-hour chart. We suggest any scrap be reported up to the plant manager (like safety incidents should be reported to the CEO). In the line, if retesting must be done, we try to do it off shift, but in mixed model environments, this is not always possible. Again, one must be careful in that creating these workarounds takes pressure off finding a real solution.

Impact of Model Changeovers the First Week

The next glaring problem we run into with short runs of different models is changeover between models. These can be relatively simple part changeovers or complex machine changeovers, which vary from model to model. The first couple days experience long changeovers. This coupled with other line problems discussed earlier can lead to worse output numbers than in the previous batch environment. This is because the batching hid all these problems. Once the line stabilizes, then we start on the setup process.

For changeovers, on assembly lines, involving parts only we try to have the parts for different models on different shelves. This eliminates the changeover but sometimes there are too many models or too many parts and not enough space on the line for the parts for every model. In this case, the line leaders and water spiders need to prepare and organize ahead of time for the changeover. Sometimes, this can be anywhere from 15 minutes to a day or two ahead of time depending on the product line. We generally suggest the water spider be at least three orders (assuming these orders are an hour's worth of work each) ahead of the line and the TL one order ahead. The group leaders should be monitoring orders further out. In addition, we suggest that within the same day, we don't do two small orders back-to-back, that is, two 1–10-piece orders, as the water spider will not be able to have all the parts replaced in time. It is better to follow a small order with a larger one to give the water spider and TL time to properly prepare for the setup.

Many times, just giving each operator job duties during the setup (i.e., creating standard work for each) will speed up the setup. In the beginning, the operators are just not sure what to do or how to help. Watching video of the setups together and converting as much internal time (time the cell is down) to external time (things that can be done while the cell is running) is the goal. Pure assembly line changeover should take 0–3 minutes with cells containing more equipment having a goal of less than 5 minutes.

Trial-and-Error Building

While one might think this is uncommon, we run into it quite a bit. Many companies can't build a product right the first time. This is evident whenever the following applies:

- A first-piece inspection.
- Another department must double-check the settings.
- It must be tested to figure out how to tweak, shim it, or try out another version of the same part until it passes the test.
- It must be tested multiple times on the same tester.
- Engineering must change the tolerance for the part to pass (so they weren't bad after all?).
- We split the lot into parts that passed and parts that need to be reworked later.

Single Piece Flow Can Still Be Implemented if Trial and Error Building Still Exists

A company in CA had been manufacturing a product used in everything from commercial stoves to military aircraft for years. They were the most profitable line in the division, although recently not as profitable as they used to be. There were competitors with new technology in place, but their existing product was designed into so many applications with expensive requalification requirements and other barriers to entry for the competition that it would be many years before they had to worry about significant volume reductions. As a result, they had no compelling need to change but they wanted better productivity. Three consultants had tried and failed! We studied the line, filmed it, analyzed it, involved engineering (it had already been the recipient of several black belt projects to no avail), and determined several root causes of other problems which were not design related. Examples were test equipment incapable of measuring certain parts to the required tolerance and test sets that passed bad parts and failed good ones. However, we couldn't correct the root cause in the design that drove the balance of trial-and-error building.

To set up the line and be able to "bump," we had to introduce two extra stations in the line to handle the trial-and-error portion of the assembly build. We still lost the labor productivity, but we were able to gain the advantages of one-piece flow. However, it took three months to cross-train the operators on the line due to the steep learning curve associated with the knack or feel (see Figure 1.69) it took to assemble the parts. As a result, it was the first and only line we have ever implemented that took over three months to show any productivity improvement at all. At first, it was far worse than batching because batching could handle all the variation. It took a total of four months to see a positive increase in productivity and another 6 to finally realize the 50% improvement in productivity, which was waiting for us (Figure 1.70). We just had to go get it. Fortunately, the company had enough faith in the new system to persevere to see the improvement. Again, please keep in mind that the original waste from the trial-and-error build is still in the line and hidden again by two rework stations and additional labor and material.

Parts Reliability

Parts reliability creates variation as well.

Figure 1.69 Example of "knack" required to line up this water bottle in order not to spill water everywhere when using this machine. It had to be lined up exactly as pictured—see arrow.

Savings by Month Percents	Line 1 Percents Stand Alone by Month	Cumulative	Line 2 Percents Stand Alone by Month	Cumulative	Overall by Month Stand Alone	Overall Percents
Jan	(7.0)	(7.0)			(7.0)	(7.0)
Feb	21.4	9.4			21.4	9.4
Mar	15.0	11.4			15.0	11.4
Apr	8.9	10.7	(32.0)	(32.0)	(4.6)	8.4
May	24.5	13.2	(10.0)	(20.0)	10.3	8.9
Jun	39.7	18.1	(8.0)	(16.0)	22.7	11.9
Jul	30.1	19.8	(7.0)	(13.0)	15.3	12.5
Aug	31.9	21.3	(12.0)	(7.0)	22.9	14.1
Sep	52.5	25.1	3.0	(6.0)	36.6	17.0
Oct	55.5	28.6	36.0	2.0	47.3	21.2
Nov	45.8	30.8	29.0	7.0	38.2	23.7

Figure 1.70 Sometimes, it takes a learning curve before the results are realized.

Removing Incoming Inspection without Supplier Certification

Some companies for various reasons will implement dock-to-stock programs, sometimes believe it or not, unknowingly. For catalog items, we only need to make sure we received the right parts, but for parts requiring drawings, incoming inspection should not be removed until the need for incoming inspection is removed. The need can be removed by reducing your supply base to a manageable level to where you can certify your suppliers to meeting the drawing criteria.

A company we worked with had two plants using the same supplier. Plant 1 had an incoming inspection department that frequently rejected the supplier's parts for not being in tolerance. We found that plant 2 removed incoming inspection due to layoffs because the indirect people needed to go first! Where do you think supplier, one shipped their rejected parts? Plant 1 had less than 1% reject rate assembling their parts. Plant 2 had a 10% reject rate and couldn't figure out why. They called plant 1 to find out what they did differently and found out they inspected all their parts. However, since they were even using the same supplier, plant 2 looked for another root cause and could not find it. The problem went on for years until we had them start remeasuring the parts and discovered they were getting all the rejects from plant 1.

Lesson Learned: Just because you are using the same supplier doesn't necessarily mean you are getting the same parts. Don't get rid of inspection anywhere until you eliminate the need for it.

With the problems noted earlier, the LP will find that they struggle with the new process to meet the past production numbers or maybe even significantly behind. To make matters worse, companies will start to question whether Lean will really work in this environment. The LP must have a deep-seated belief that one-piece flow will work and persevere to figure out how to fix the problems and successfully implement the line. Resorting back to batching should never be considered an option.

Chapter Questions

1. What is the number one rule of layouts (you do not want to see)?
2. Why are there problems with isolated islands?
3. What is a block diagram? Why is it important?
4. Should you plan rework into a line?
5. What do you normally find when you first go to bring up a line?
6. Why is it important to have a flip chart out on the line when you first start to implement?
7. What does fit up mean? Why is it important?
8. Who should review the layout before it is approved?
9. Should we have walls in our layout?
10. What is important when doing workstation design?
11. What is a plan for every tool?
12. Are toolboxes good or bad? Why? Are there alternatives?
13. What should we do with fixtures designed for batching?
14. Should we have personal tools in a machine shop? Why?
15. What are four of the guidelines to layouts?
16. Why is flexibility important in a layout?
17. Should everything be on wheels if possible?
18. What is hanedashi?
19. What is the problem with the T-shaped layout?

20. What is a point-to-point diagram?
21. Is it worth the cost to install flexible utilities? Why?
22. Discuss the use of a chair as related to a Lean line.
23. What is a water spider and the value to Lean lines?

Notes

1. Author's Note: This section is different than Theory of Constraints (TOC).
2. *Sources:* TPS, Monden, TPS Shingo, Kanban Japan Mgmt Assoc.
3. University of Michigan training material and Demand Flow Technology based on the book Quantum Leap.
4. Leveraging Lean in Healthcare, Protzman, Mayzell, Kerpchar, 2011 CRC Press
5. Greg Washburn.
6. "Sitting time and mortality from all causes, cardiovascular disease, and cancer," Katzmarzyk P.T., Church T.S., Craig C.L., Bouchard C. Pennington Biomedical Research Center, Baton Rouge, LA. http://conditioningresearch.blogspot.com/2009/04/too-much-sitting-down-is-bad-for-you.html. It's Dangerous, Charles Osgood on the CBS Radio Network. The Osgood File. June 10, 2010; "Don't Just Sit There-It's Dangerous," Charles Osgood on the CBS Radio Network. The Osgood File. June 10, 2010.
7. Influenced by the Donnelly Production System and Toyota Training Manual.
8. Star Wars.
9. Mark Jamrog, SMC Group.
10. Story furnished by Professor James Bond in personal correspondence 2/2013.

Additional Readings

Bollinger, J.M. 1955. Trade Analysis & Course Organization. London, UK: Pitman Publishing.

Duggan, K.J. 2002. Creating Mixed Model Value Streams. New York: Productivity Press.

Hales, L. and Andersen, B. 2002. Planning Manufacturing Cells. Dearborne, Michigan: Society of Manufactring Engineers (SME).

Irani, S.A. 1999. Handbook of Cellular Manufacturing Systems. New York: John Wiley & Sons.

Irani, S.A. 2005. Facility layout design for hybrid cellular manufacturing system, International Journal of the Physical Sciences Vol. 6(1), pp. 355–3556, 18 y, 201.

Muther, R. and Wheeler, J.D. 1994. Simplified Systematic Layout Planning, 3rd edn. Kansas City, MO: Management and Industrial Research Publications.

Sekine, K. 1992. One Piece Flow—Cell Design. Portland Orgegon: Productivity Press.

Suri, R. 1998. Quick Response Manufacturing. Portland Orgegon: Productivity Press.

Suri, R. 2006. 2006 POLCA Implementation Workshop. Madison, WI: University of Wisconsin.

Chapter 2

Using Analysis to Create Standard Work

If you don't have a standard, you have chaos![1]

Unknown

The first step toward improvement is standardization; where there is no standard, there can be no improvement.[2]

Ohno Taiichi

Why Are Standards Important?

Imagine a world without standards! How would one measure an inch? A meter? How could you make any recipe without a cup? Or a gram? Without standards, we have nothing to consistently measure our progress or our results. In effect, we could have no quality.

Metric System versus Imperial Units

Whatever happened to the metric system in the United States? We were all taught the metric system in school and told the United States was going to switch over very soon. This was in the 1960s! We used the metric system in all our science and chemistry classes. But we are still on the imperial system. Think of the costs in the United States due to having to have two sets of tools, drawing conversion issues on shop floors—because some of the machine shop computer numerical control (CNC) equipment are metric and some are not.

This reminds us of the space vehicle designed by NASA that had problems because some engineers designed using the metric system where others used the English system of measure.[3] Worse still, the 1999 Mars Climate Orbiter ended in pieces simply through failure to spot a mix-up of metric and imperial units.[4]

DOI: 10.4324/9781003185796-2

Strange that we were all trained in grade school in the United States for the certain shift to the metric system in the country, which for some reason has never occurred, and there are no known plans to support the change to metric.

Standard Work

The Holy Grail of Lean is standard work. Without standard work, there can be no real improvement, flexibility, or guarantee of quality. If we are going to create a continuous improvement environment, standard work must be the foundation of every process throughout the organization.

Definition

Standard work is repeatable and defined by Ohno[5] as three items:

1. Cycle time
2. Work sequence
3. Standard work in process (SWIP) inventory

Standard work must be written based on the flow of the product and is not necessarily tied to an operator.

Levels of Standard Work[6]

We have broken standard work into five levels—where each level is more detailed than the next.

1. Standard work is for the group leader/supervisor
   This level is higher than the operator work instructions and should be posted in the cell or at each station in the cell (see Figure 2.1). It can take the form of a standard work sheet or standard operations routine sheet. It is a guide for the supervisor or anyone else who is observing or auditing the work performed in the cell that defines the order and timing for each major step. At this level, for example, steps may include the following:
   a. Walk to the machine—3 seconds
   b. Unload the machine—10 seconds
   c. Load the machine—5 seconds
   d. Cycle the machine—1 second
   e. Check part quality—5 seconds (adjust offsets if required)
   We include key quality points or characteristics or critical to quality (CTQ) points for each step in the standard work. These become visual checks that guarantee customers' expectations are met. This document can be used by all management levels as part of an integrated visual management system to evaluate whether a process is in a normal running condition or whether corrective action must be taken.
2. Work Standards are typically for tasks that are not repeatable but follow a sequence of steps or troubleshooting. It could be a checklist. The work standard should have the sequence of steps, but the cycle times may vary depending on the job or model produced.
   a. Walk to the machine
   b. Empty the machine

Section chief	Floor foreman	Group leader	Manual on work directions	Item number	4320½—86022	Required quantity	448 units day	Group's name	Worker's name
				Name of item	Steering knuckle	Breakdown number	1/3		

Revised Feb 5. 1975 — Page ___ of ___ Pages

#	Work content	Quality Check	Quality Gauge	Critical areas (right and wrong, safety and ease in operation)	Net operating time Minutes Seconds
1	Taking out materials			With the right hand	03″
2	CE–239 Detach, attach and start machine	1/50	Visual	If center is too shallow, dangerous for subsequent LA, CR processes	11″
3	LA–1306 Detach, attach and start machine			Both centers must be attached securely	11″
4	LA–1307 Detach, attach and start machine			Both centers must be attached securely	10″
5	LA–1101 Detach, attach and start machine	1/1	C	22.5 + 0.25 + 0.20 33.1 + 0.25 + 0.20 Remove scraps by derrick	12″
6	DR–1544 Detach, attach and start machine		Visual	Ascertain penetration from reverse side	09″
7	SP–101 Detach, attach and start machine			Clean scraps from attachment sides on M-22, P-1.5	09″
8	MM–122 Detach, attach and start machine				05″
9	HP–657 Detach, attach and start machine			When bush is let into orifice the top side where oil chamber is cut in the circumference of a circle	12″
10	BR–410 Detach, attach and start machine	1/10		Attachment sides must be cleaned	
		1/10	PS	Brightness over 80%	15″
		1/10	LF	+ 0.25 – 0	
12	Cleaning machine, remove attach, and start				
12	Attach the nipple			Tighten with the impact	
13	Stamping serial number, detach, attach, and start machine	1/1	Visual	Half full is not acceptable	17″
14	Finished products stand				
				Time total	1″ 54″

Figure 2.1 Example of standard work.

c. Clean the machine

d. Job breakdown/workflow analysis

Behind or underneath standard work (see Figure 2.2) are job breakdown instructions with detailed steps and times so anyone can perform the work (assuming proper training and certification dexterity, etc.; these instructions have their roots in training within industry (TWI)[7] back in WWII. We taught the Japanese and then seemed to have forgotten it.

In the BASICS® approach, we break down the job, to the second, as part of the workflow analysis (WFA). Included in the analysis are minor steps, key points for each step (how you do the work), and reasons for key points (why you do the work). This is the document we combine with a video of the operation and use it to train the operator. We call the video depicting the operator standard work the golden unit. This becomes the foundation for our cross-training program which then leads to creating a certification program for all the operators and staff in an office setting. This is just one of the areas where HR gets pulled into the implementation. When we convert this to supervisor level standard work, we combine some of the minor steps into more major steps.

This is the level of job instruction the supervisor/group leader uses to train the operators. It comes from the WFA videos as to how the operator performs each step to the second and should include key points and reasons for key points both from a process perspective and from your customers' perspective. At this level, the steps from the example earlier would be the following:

3. Work instructions—standard operating instructions SOPs

These instructions are very detailed instructions. They are typically for how to operate or maintain a machine or how to use a particular jig or fixture etc. These would only change

WORK INSTRUCTIONS				
Work Assembly Product(s)	Name: 'ASSEMBLY Part Number: N/A Product Name: .	Revision Level: 1 Rev. Date: 01-26-2012 Issued: 08-23-2011		
Op Step/ Time	REPRESENTATION	Major work Steps	Key points	Reason for Key Points
1 / 40-SEC		Assembler pulls order bin down on table. Pick up BOM and pull parts bins down from shelf as needed from BOM. Place them at point of assy with correct tooling.	PULL ORDER AND PARTS	water spider preps work, makes labels and puts on shelf ready to pull by assembler.
2 / 6- SECS		Remove shaft and frames from bin.		
3 / 32-SECS		Change over Collet for shaft size. Reach for collet wrench.Remove and replace desired collet size needed.	COLLET CHANGEOVER Only have to change if shaft size is larger than collet	approx 15 to 30 seconds when needed
4 / 3- SECS		Put rod in collet	PSA BUILD	
5 / 5- SECS		spray piston,shaft and fastener with primer #7649.		
6 / 5- SECS		apply loctite #263 to rod .	Serves as thread locker and sealing material	May leak if not enough
7 / 4- SECS		Place piston on rod,turn piston to even out loctite	Twist piston on shaft to smooth out loctite	Even flow of loctite
8 / 1- SECS		Pick up power tool	clutch setting #6	Keep battery charged,see battery level gauge
9 / 2- SECS		Insert screw on bit		
10 / 4- SECS		Add loctite to screw		
11 / 2- SECS		insert screw through piston into shaft.		
12 / 3- SECS		pull trigger until screw stops.		

Figure 2.2 Standard work instruction example.

if the equipment were modified or updated. These support the job instruction and standard work. For example, the standard work may say to unload the machine, the job instruction would say to open the door, reach for part, unload part, move to table, reach for new part, load new part, close the door, and start the machine. The work instruction would designate the location and machine number and go through the detailed steps of how to start up the machine, perform maintenance, etc. This would be step by step saying where the power button is located, etc. Think about a manual you may get with your car or on the Internet as to how to start the car, etc.

4. Motion study

Motion study is at the therblig level which is the 18 motions developed by Frank Gilbreth. At this level, steps from the earlier example would look like this:

a. Search for the machine

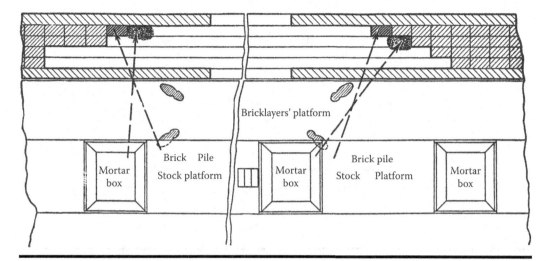

Figure 2.3   Gilbreth work instruction includes where to place your feet.

    b. Find the machine

    c. Walk to the machine with both arms transporting empty

    d. Search for the front door handle

    e. Find the front door handle

    f. Reach for the front door with right hand (left hand is reaching for air hose, grasping the handle, pulling the handle to the left while transporting air hose with left hand)

At this level, the standard work for the operator tells them where to place their feet, which hand to use, etc. You see this on the line at Toyota where there are markings for operators to place their feet. You also see it in the picture in Figure 2.3 from Frank Gilbreth's book <u>Motion Study</u>.

Goal of Standard Work

The goal is to standardize work by reviewing the analysis of the product, operator, and setup to simplify work methods. It becomes the baseline from which improvements can be evaluated and is the starting point for all improvements. Once we determine the work sequence, we can use the Omits process to eliminate, rearrange, simplify, or combine (ERSC) the tasks in such a way to eliminate waste.

Developing Standard Work

When planning standard work, it is important not to overburden (muri) or overwork employees and to work on leveling or creating an even pace (mura) for production (Figure 2.4):

Muri:

Overburden
Unreasonableness
Excessive workload
Difficult to do, see, hear, learn, train, remember, teach, reach, lift, or process
Beyond current capability

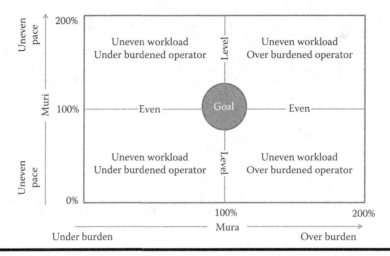

Figure 2.4   Muri vs. Mura.

Mura:

Unevenness
Uneven pace
Inconsistency
Instability

Fluctuation of quality, material consumption, production output, energy use, cost, orders, machines required, or manpower requirements, etc.

Once the waste is eliminated, the goal is for employees to work at a normal pace and create an environment where employees are able and look forward to learning and taking on additional tasks to become multiskilled and multi process capable. Employees will then become more valuable and more marketable fostering productivity increases without having to work harder.

A good analogy for standard work is a pass play in football (see Figure 2.5). Each time, the operator (receiver) must run the pattern (sequence of operations) in the same amount of time (cycle time) to complete the pass. If an operator does not follow the play or is too slow or too fast, they will not catch the ball (SWIP). As a result, football teams review the videos to look for improvements, and practice, practice, practice. The same is required to implement and sustain Lean.

Another good analogy is an orchestra. Have you ever heard of a fifth-grade orchestra play (see Figure 2.6)? How do they sound compared to a symphony orchestra? Let's look at our three components of standard work. What is the sequence of operations or steps? If you answered the music or each note, that is correct. Think about it. Every note must be played in the exact order and the right note needs to be played at the right time (cycle time) with the instrument being the SWIP. What if everyone in the symphony orchestra did what a lot of our employees do and decided to play the notes in the order they want to play them? Forcing them to play the music as it is written would make them robots, wouldn't it? What if each person in the orchestra believed they had a better way to play the music? What if they paid no attention to the conductor (supervisor)? What if they never practiced?

The differences between the fifth-grade orchestra and a symphony orchestra are that they don't always hit the right notes, miss the timing, and may not have exactly the right instruments. Like a symphony, standard work first must be created (i.e., the musical score or the football play). Then it takes training and education and lots of practice to make sure we hit the notes correctly and can follow the beat

Figure 2.5   Football play.

Figure 2.6   5th grade orchestra.

in synchronization with everyone else. The beat in our musical example is like the takt time (TT), which is comparable to the time signature of the score (i.e., 4/4 or 3/4 time). TT is the rate at which you need to complete a product to meet customer demand. In a perfect world, TT would match customer demand. The cycle time is the time we play the notes compared to the time we are supposed to play the notes.

Standard Work Drives Improvements

At Company X, I sat in the vice president's office and listened as he told a customer that he could not meet their lead time for welded parts and referred to his local competition. His current backlog was 37 weeks; thus, welding was the first line we tackled. Inventory was piled to the ceiling, and during the analysis, we discovered that the parts were washed seven times as they progressed through the process. We were told that it took up to four years to train a welder and we were also told it was impossible to weld standing up! After we started questioning the process steps and conducting a few quick pilots, we found that we could train a welder in only two to three weeks once the area was cleaned up enough to even weld. In some cases, after only a day, their work was sufficient for production. We found the weld area was spending an inordinate amount of time and money trying to maintain aerospace quality that was 200%–300% more than what the market wanted. We eliminated the costly steps and still improved quality. It took only four weeks to reduce a 37-week backlog to less than 19 weeks. By the fifth week, we shipped an order out two weeks early. By the eighth week, the area was building ahead of schedule. We also proved that sometimes hand welding is cheaper and better than machines, and by taking a new person who had never welded, we were able to prove that it could be done standing and the operator preferred it to sitting down.

Standard Work Components—Sequence of Operations

Each operator must be trained and must execute the process steps in proper order for each operation the same way, every time. Figure 2.7 shows a template which walks one through the thought process for creating the standard work. Standard work does not mean the operators are robots; however, it does mean that the operators will get into a rhythm as they perform standard work.

Lesson Learned: Standard work is a very inflexible yet flexible system. It is inflexible in that we want everyone to always follow the standard and do the work the same way; yet it is flexible in that we want everyone to constantly think about how to improve the process and then experiment with the improvements.

Policy and procedures are not the same as standard work. A policy and procedure dictates what we do and, sometimes, when it is expected and who is responsible. Detailed work instructions are also different from standard work. Work instructions don't have cycle time or SWIP. For instance, an operator job breakdown sheet may say:

1. Reach for part A with left hand—2 seconds
2. Grab part A—1 second
3. Place part A on to part B—2 seconds
4. Pick up tool 1 with your right hand—2 seconds
5. Tighten part A with tool 1 (25 ft - lb.)—3 seconds
6. Put down tool 1—2 seconds

The work instruction step might say:

Place part A on part B and tighten (25 ft lb) with tool #1

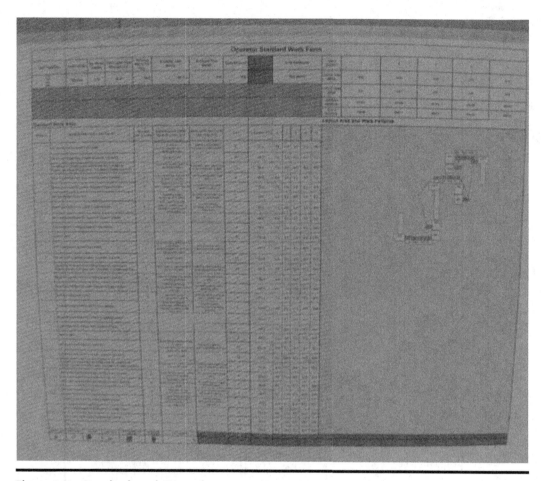

Figure 2.7   Standard work Example.

Standard Work Components—Cycle Time

The next component of standard work is cycle time. Cycle time is the time it takes to do each step in the sequence of operations. It is important to differentiate cycle time from TT. Standard work must be based on cycle time because to run to TT may not always be feasible. For example, TT may dictate that the line or area is run with 1.5 people, but we can't run with half of a person. Therefore, we must run with two people. This means that we must recalculate the time using two people, which yields a cycle time that is faster than TT. This means we will overproduce unless we stop the line when we meet the required output and then we find something else for the half a person to do each cycle. The amount of cycle time can also be driven by the difference in skill sets and the need to have additional people to run the area. Because there is so much variation, in some cases, we may have to have a range of cycle times in the standard work depending on the model of product being produced. Figure 2.8 is another example of standard work with the line balancing portion built into the spreadsheet and the actual picture of the cell with the location of each step noted.

Operator Standard Work Form

Product A	PART NAME	No. People Needed	Total Labor Time Secs.	Working Hours Per Day	Available Time (Secs)	Daily Demand	TAKT TIME SECS	Line Balancing	HEAD COUNT:	1	2	3	4	5
Assy Cells		2.17	228	7.5	27,000	257	105.1	See below	CYCLE TIME SECS	227.6	113.8	75.9	56.9	45.5
									CYCLE TIME MINS	3.8	1.9	1.3	0.9	0.8

Standard Work Area:

Station #	Operation Description (what they do)	Standard WIP Quantity	Who Does it?	Key Points and Quality Notes (how they do it)	Reasons for Key Points (why they do it)	Time	Cumulative Time	Line Balancing 1	2	3	4	5
	PULL ORDER, PARTS & PRINT LABELS	NA	Water Spider and Assembler	Waterspider pulls and verifies order. Assembler pulls in to form shelf and totes part number and BOM. Assembler pulls shaft endcaps, seals, rod tooling and place them on table at point of assembly.	Water Spider checks paperwork, pulls parts from bulk to reduce mistakes and maximize downtime for assembler. The assembler double checks what will be assembled with the BOM in order to pull material.	3.2		0.0	0.0	0.0	0.8	0.0
1	CHANGE OVER COLLET (IF NECESSARY)	NA	Assembler	Only have to change over if shaft size is larger than the collet.		0.1	0.1	1.0	1.0	1.0	1.0	1.0
2	PSA BUILD		Assembler	Assemble piston shaft / double shaft add grease and seals.	This step is first to start the flow of operation differently so the product should never go backwards. PSA added to reassemble parts efficiently and control cost.	49.0	49.1	1.0	1.0	1.0	2.0	2.0
3	PSA / END CAP ASSY		Assembler	Apply grease and seals to top endcap and place endcap on the PSA just assembled.	If any problems arise, it will be found on the first piece. Grease eliminates chance for parts to tear or leak and be work smoothly together.	30.0	79.1	1.0	1.0	2.0	2.0	2.0
4	PSA INSTALL IN FRAME		Assembler	Pick up frame and add grease in bore, insert PSA and endcap into frame put in holding fixture.	It is important to add the correct amount of grease	9.0	88.1	1.0	1.0	2.0	2.0	2.0
5	WIRE ASSY SIDE 1		Assembler	Press down on endcap and add wire to wireblue on frame, pull wire to hook. Pull up PSA using tool to cut seals until flush with frame. Be careful not to cut seals, pushing into frame.	Cut seals will make cylinder leak.	29.0	117.1	1.0	2.0	2.0	3.0	3.0
6	FLIP AND WIRE ASSY SIDE 2		Assembler	Flip frame over in holding fixture. Add seal and grease rear endcap, but in frame and wire to flush with frame.	Be careful not to cut seals, pushing into frame as leaking seals causes rework.	34.0	151.1	1.0	2.0	2.0	3.0	4.0
7	TEST		Assembler / Water Spider (REWORK Only)	Remove frame from holding fixture. Hook up water setting adapters to ports. Test top and bottom ports for leaks, test both ports for blow by. Look for bubbles. If any air bubbles are seen the cylinder must be marked at leaking point. Seal must be replaced and retested. Water spider will transform cylinder where leak is found and put back into one piece flow process. To minimize downtime for assembler.	If you see bubbles you have a leak and you put an X around the notch or outside seal or air's rest to the shaft so we know it is a shaft seal or air sleeve	26.0	177.1	1.0	3.0	3.0	4.0	4.0
8	DRY OFF UNITS		Assembler	Blow off all water with air hose along with mounting holes and air ports.	This prevents customer from getting products in with water to them.	15.0	192.1	1.0	2.0	3.0	4.0	5.0
9	ADD MISC HARDWARE TO UNIT PER BOM		Assembler	Add any hardware to cylinder called out on BOM. Check which loctite to use on hardware.	Choosing the right loctite is important as some types are permanent	33.0	192.1	1.0	2.0	3.0	4.0	5.0
10	CLEAN,LABEL, & INSTALL PORT PLUGS		Assembler	Make labels and apply to cylinder after cleaning with cleaning solvent.	Check to make sure labels are correct. Some customers order from these labels.	33.0	225.1	1.0	3.0	4.0	4.0	5.0
11	INSPECT AND PAPERWORK		Assembler	Fill out inspection sheet. Check culti options that you have applied.	This step is for inspection purposes.	2.0	227.1	1.0	2.0	3.0	4.0	5.0
12	DAY BY HOUR		Assembler	Record stats on hour to hour board and note any problems, countermeasures or ideas on chart. Then put parts on final inspection cart.	So Everyone can visually see output by hour attained and highlight problems as they occur.	0.5	227.6	1.0	2.0	3.0	4.0	5.0
	FINAL INSPECTION		Inspector				227.6	1.0	2.0	3.0	4.0	5.0

Layout Area and Walk Patterns

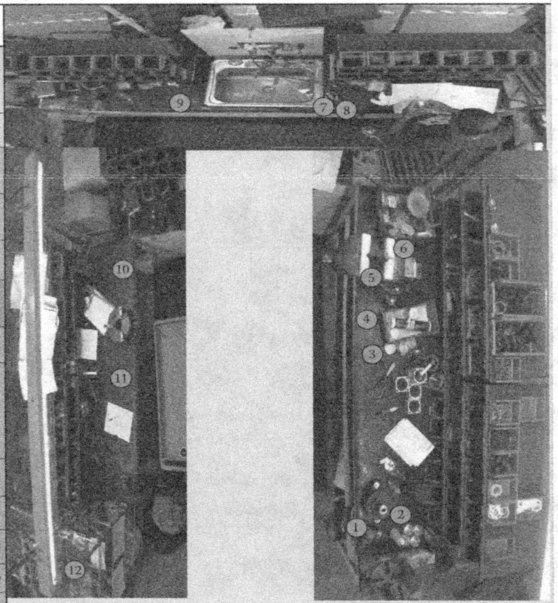

QUALITY CHECK	SAFETY CHECK	AIR CHECK	STANDARD CLEANLINESS	STANDARD WORK IN PROCESS
★	✓			

Note: Handoffs are based on no hardware and will vary based on parts per workorder, number of work orders, amount of hardware etc. This is why Baton Zone "BUMPING" should be utilized to maximize output.

Figure 2.8 Standard work example.

Standard Work Components—Standard Work in Process (SWIP)

SWIP is the amount of inventory necessary to meet the cycle time and perform the job safely. We can approximate the calculation of SWIP in the process using Little's law that is

$$\text{Throughput time} \div \text{cycle time} = \text{SWIP}$$

When calculating SWIP, we need to include the piece the operator has in their hands and then any inventory necessary for the machines or equipment in the process. For machines where the operator can leave unattended, we would keep one piece in the machine all the time. If the machine is a manual machine, the piece in the machine and the operator piece would be the same.

We then need to determine if the equipment is interruptible or uninterruptible. If it is interruptible, it means we can unload a piece and then load a piece and start the machine one-piece flow. If it is uninterruptible, we consider it a *batch* machine, which means we can't interrupt the machine cycle until it is completed. Example: an interruptible oven would be a conveyor-type oven or oven where we can open the door each cycle. To calculate the quantity, we need in an oven, we need to take the oven time and divide it by the cycle time. If the oven takes 60 minutes and we are running 20 minutes cycles, we would have to always have three pieces in the oven (60 minutes per piece ÷ 20 minutes per piece = 3 pieces) (see Figure 2.9).

Note: For SWIP, we need to use cycle time because the factory floor is almost always running to cycle time versus TT. We have run into very few companies where factories are running to true customer demand and not over or under producing.

An example of an oven that is uninterruptible or a batch oven is one where we cannot open the door for the entire 60 minutes until the thermal cycle is completed. This means we must always have three pieces in the oven. In addition, we must build up an extra three pieces while the three pieces are in the oven because we cannot open it. These three pieces are needed to replace the three that will be removed from the oven after the thermal cycle. We need a total of six pieces to manage the oven.

To carry this example through, let's show each cycle in the succeeding text. The first figure shows the three pieces in the oven while we build up the three pieces before the oven (see Figure 2.10).

In the next cycle, the three pieces have completed the oven cycle and are taken out. The three pieces in front of the oven are moved in. We then take one of the pieces we just removed to the next step, which we will assume is the cooling step. We call it cool WIP (see Figure 2.11). In the next cycle, we can't open the oven, so we remove another one to cool WIP and build up one more at the front of the oven (see Figure 2.12). In the next cycle, we are back to three before the oven and we take the last piece after the oven to cool WIP (see Figure 2.13).

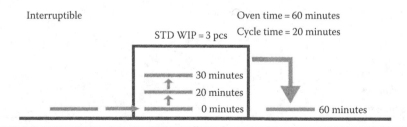

Figure 2.9   How to calculate interruptible standard WIP quantities.

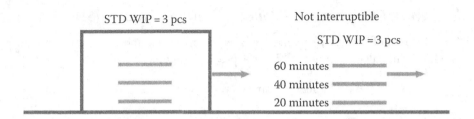

Figure 2.10   How to calculate uninterruptible standard WIP quantities.

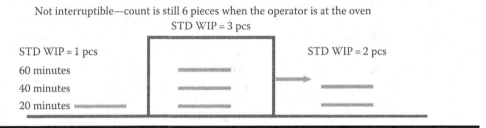

Figure 2.11   How to calculate interruptible standard WIP quantities.

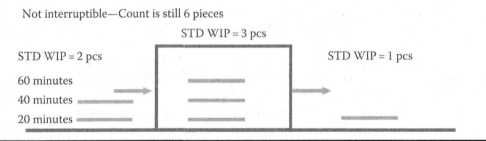

Figure 2.12   How to calculate interruptible standard WIP quantities.

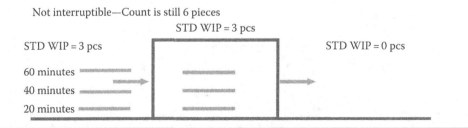

Figure 2.13   How to calculate interruptible standard WIP quantities.

SWIP is a very difficult concept to understand. We have had engineers take 2–3 days to figure it out on a line. So, it is no wonder that operators have a difficult time understanding the concept. Wherever SWIP is located on the line, it should be clearly labeled and should be at the labeled quantity all the time! No exceptions. This can get complicated with mixed models that have different oven temperatures and times.

How Do You Know When You Need SWIP?

When a machine or line is empty and has zero SWIP, we call it dry. Let's take an example of an operator running a machine that has a 50 second machine run time. The labor time to load and cycle the machine is 5 seconds. The operator has another 60 seconds of labor time in the cell to complete a fully machined part. First, we need to revisit our principle of separating man from machine.

Our assumption is we can load the machine; but we must wait for it to finish its cycle, because we are not sure if it is going to break down or crash. In this case, the operator would load and cycle the machine (5 seconds) and then must stand at the machine and wait for it to finish (50 seconds). The operator would then unload the part (5 seconds) and run the rest of the cell (60 seconds) for a total cycle time of 120 seconds. The operator is standing idle watching the machine every cycle for 50 seconds and we get a part every 2 minutes or 30 parts per hour—SWIP = 0.

Wetting the Line

Whenever we set up a line, we will have to wait to get the SWIP in place before the line can run properly (See Table 2.1). Let's assume that we have performed jidoka on the machine and can now leave it while it is running. In this case, we would load and cycle the machine (5 seconds). We must wait 50 seconds for the first piece to get done. Now we can unload, load, and cycle the machine—second piece (10 seconds) and then take the first piece and run the rest of the cell (60 seconds). When we get back to the machine, the second piece we left in it is completed. The total time for the first piece is 125 seconds. But each piece after that we should get every 70 seconds (10 seconds unload, load, cycle, and 60 seconds to run the rest of the cell). However, the part now waits in the machine, and the machine is idle for 10 seconds every cycle. Is this bad? How would we find out? We need to know our TT. If our TT is 70 seconds or more, it is fine if the machine sits idle and we only need one operator for the cell.

Note: Therefore, machine utilization is no longer a metric driver for us anymore. Machine utilization only becomes a driver when it is a true bottleneck machine. This is an area we must discuss with Finance in every Lean implementation. In this case, if we only cared about machine utilization, we would have to have a full-time operator on the machine building a bunch of WIP inventory, batching, which we don't need.

We would now label the machine with a sign that said SWIP = 1. Now, our total cycle time is 70 seconds which equals 51.4 parts per hour (except for the first hour where we lost one piece due to getting the SWIP in place). We call this first cycle, where we must wait for the SWIP, wetting the line. By adding SWIP, we have almost doubled our output and freed up the operator from having to watch the machine, not to mention having to pay him or her to watch the machine run for 50 seconds every cycle or 1,500 second/hour (41% of the operator's day!). Now that we know our times, we can turn that 50 seconds into true cost savings since we are getting more output, assuming we have other productive work for the operator to do. We get a part every 70 seconds or 51.4 parts per hour which is a 41% improvement in productivity compared to the operator standing there idle watching the machine.

Table 2.1 Wetting the Line Saves 50 Seconds Every Cycle

Machine 1—50 Seconds			Rest of Cell—60 Seconds		
Without SWIP			With SWIP Wetting the Line		
Step	*Time (s)*	*Clock Time (s)*	*Step*	*Time (s)*	*Clock Time (s)*
First Piece			**First Piece**		
Load machine	5	5	Load machine	5	5
Wait for machine time	50	55	Wait for machine time	50	55
Unload first piece	5	60	Unload first piece	5	60
Second Piece			**Second Piece**		
Load second piece	5	65	Load second piece	5	65
Wait for Machine	50	115	Wait for machine	0	65
Run the rest of the cell	60	175	Run the rest of the cell	60	125
Note: First piece is now completed			Note: First piece is now completed		
Third Piece			**Third Piece**		
Unload second piece	5	180	Unload second piece	5	130
Load third piece	5	185	Load third piece	5	135
Wait for machine	50	235	Wait for machine	0	135
Run the rest of the cell	60	295	Run the rest of the cell	60	185
Note: Second piece is now completed			Note: Second piece is now completed		
Cycle time is 120 seconds. Idle time cost = 150 seconds = .71 pieces lost each cycle			Cycle time after the first piece is 70 seconds. Idle time = 50 seconds but only on first piece after that idle time = 0		

Source: BIG Archives.

Trading Labor Efficiency for Output

This gets to the concept of what we call trading labor time for productivity. What if we now wanted to increase output in the cell? If our TT was 60 seconds, we could have two operators in the cell but how would they be working? One could run the rest of the cell for 60 seconds while one just stands at the machine and unloads, loads, and cycles it for 10 seconds each cycle. One would be surprised to learn we see this all the time! However, we are picking up the 10 seconds each cycle and getting parts every minute or 60 seconds versus every 70-seconds. However, one operator is going to have 50 seconds of idle time every cycle, or if they split the work between the two operators, we will still have 50 seconds of idle time. But if we split the work, it only works if one operator is always ready to unload and load the machine at exactly the time the machine stops!

Machine Runs Twice as Long as the Cycle Time

Next let's assume the machine cycle time is 100 seconds (vs. our 50 seconds before) and we can leave the machine running and we are starting with zero (0) WIP. Now we are going to load and cycle the machine (5 seconds) and wait for the machine to run one piece (100 seconds). Then we are going to unload the first piece and load the second piece (10 seconds) and cycle the machine (100 seconds), then we take the first piece and run the rest of the cell (60 seconds). Total time for the first piece was 175 seconds. The second piece still has 40 seconds to go (100–60 seconds to finish the first part). The operator will have to stand and watch the machine for 40 seconds before they can unload it. Our cycle time is going to be 110 seconds (40 seconds wait, 10 unload, load, cycle, and 60 to complete it in the cell). So, what are our options if we have a 70 second TT? We can add a machine, speed up the machine, or modify the machine, to run two pieces at a time.

Let's say we can modify the machine to run two pieces at a time and we start dry. Now the machine will complete two pieces in 100 seconds or a net cycle time of 50 seconds per piece. However, now, a cycle is going to equal *two* pieces. The machine is really batching the two parts, which makes figuring out the SWIP a little more difficult.

The first cycle will be to load and cycle both parts in the machine (5 seconds × 2 pieces = 10 seconds); the machine runs for 100 seconds and then we unload both parts (10 seconds) and load the third and fourth parts (10 seconds). Now we must finish the first part in the cell (60 seconds). The total time to get the first piece is 190 seconds. When we get back to the machine, the third and fourth pieces are still running; but remember that we got two pieces from the first cycle, so we can finish the second part in the cell (60 seconds). The total time for the first two parts is 250 seconds or 125 average seconds per part, which does not meet our TT; but now the line is full of SWIP or wet.

In our second cycle, we can unload the third and fourth and load the fifth and sixth pieces and cycle the machine (20 seconds). We take the third piece and run the rest of the cell (60 seconds) and then the fourth piece and run the rest of the cell (60 seconds). Our second complete cycle takes 140 or an average of 70 seconds per part which meets our TT. Cycle one is always going to take 80 seconds and cycle two, which is just running the second part around the rest of the cell, is 60 seconds. Our goal in this case would be to ultimately modify the machine to meet our cycle time.

In the first example, the operator waited on the machine. Then we WIP the machine and now the machine, after completing its cycle, is idle, waiting on the operator.

Lesson Learned: Once you WIP the machine, it is no longer a bottleneck or factor in the cycle time unless it is still running longer than the TT or total labor time (TLT).

This is a normal phenomenon for Lean. Let's say next we improved the labor time for the rest of the cell to 40 seconds and the machine cycle averages 50 seconds per part—now we are waiting on the machine again. As we make improvements, we should see this progression of man waiting on machine and then machine waiting on man. Therefore, separating man (or person) from machine is so important.

Drying Up the Line

What happens if we dry out the line at the end of each day? In other words, at the end of the day, on our last cycles, the operators see, for example, that they can get two more pieces completed by working off the SWIP waiting in an oven. Assuming we are running the same parts the next day, we are now going to have to wait to *wet the line* again and we will lose the output during the first hour. Think what would happen if you dried up an automobile assembly line every night! The next day, everyone in the line would be idle until the SWIP is built back up to the proper levels to allow the assembly line to run continuously.

If you don't supervise the operators the first week of bringing up a line, they will dry it out every day because they think they are being more productive (see Figure 2.14). If you are running a mixed model line, we still want to keep the line wet versus drying out the line for one model and then starting the next model and having to wet the line again. Sometimes, this is unavoidable, but it is the exception not the rule.

Variation and Standard Work

In almost all operations, we encounter substantial variation. Very seldom do we get a line where everyone has the same amount of work. Variation generally leads to overproduction, that is, batching and excess inventory. So, in many cases, we must first implement work standards (Figure 2.15) instead of, in addition to, or as part of standard work (work standards are described later in the chapter). Sequence of operations, SWIP, and/or cycle time may vary. Sometimes, in mixed-model environments, where the SWIP should be different for different models, we run with the max SWIP when we first bring up the line even though some models may need less to make it easier for

Figure 2.14 Operators will dry out the line if not trained and unsupervised.

Work standards are different than standard work. They are normally missing the element of cycle time and or standard WIP

WORK STANDARD

	DATE	SHEET NO. __ of __
	PREPARED BY	DATE
	APPROVED BY	DEPT.	DATE

	PRODUCT	Hourly Board
	AREA	All
	MACHINE NO.	
	OPERATION	All
	NAME	

#	WORK ELEMENTS	KEY POINT
1	Team Leader determines daily production needs and writes on hourly production board	Team Leader work with inventory control to determine customer needs
2	Team leader breaks down hourly production needs.	Make sure to subtract any planned downtime
3	Write hourly plan in lower right hand of box. Write accum in lower right hand box of hourly chart.	
4	Team member writes hourly and accum number in box hourly	Note any reason for not achieving target in the comment section.
5	Team member identifies any delta.	
6	Transfer daily production to schedule attainment chart.	If less than 80% of scheduled achieved note on the issue counter measure sheet.
7	Team Leader reviews hourly board hourly to determine if support is needed.	Initial board hourly.

SKETCH, DRAWING or PHOTO

#	WORK ELEMENTS	KEY POINT
1	Enter the name of the machine, tool, operation or the task being standardized	1.1 example: Mold # 5 startup
2	Enter the product, area and machine # in which the tasks takes place	2.1 example: Epic mirror, Area 2, machine # 5
3	Enter the sequence #	3.1 The sequence of operation required to complete the task
4	Enter the work element	4.1 The description of the work to be performed
5	Enter the Key Point	5.1 The description of any Safety, Quality or Ease of operation specific to the task being performed
6	Enter the sketch, drawing, or photo	6.1 The visual aid to help the operator better understand the task being performed
7	Enter all other information	7.1 The date the document was created 7.2 The sheet # 7.3 Who prepared the document 7.4 Who approved the document with the department they work in and the date the document was approved

SKETCH, DRAWING or PHOTO

Note: Numbers correspond with work element numbers.

Figure 2.15 Work standards may have a range of cycle times but the steps are in sequence.

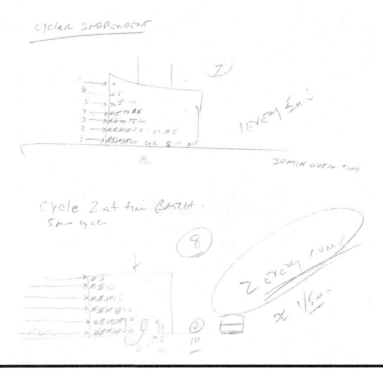

Figure 2.16 Hand calculations for WIP quantities.

the operators to get the concept. Then as they get more familiar, we will introduce the variation in quantity in the SWIP locations. This means that the operators must understand how to dry up one to several pieces of one model and then build it back up for another model (see Figure 2.16).

In-Process Assembly Kanbans Are Not Standard WIP

SWIP is defined as the amount of inventory necessary to meet the cycle time and to do the job safely. It is generally calculated by dividing the total throughput time by the cycle time (not TT). In some cases, this number is modified based on the number of operators, cycle time, and TLT of the units where there is a lot of variation. Remember, in-process Kanbans between operators are buffer inventory used to hide line imbalances and make it easy to balance a line. SWIP should be used only where a machine or process cycle time allows for a part to remain and be processed while the operator continues. If this process runs longer than the TT, more parts will be required in WIP for that machine or process. If the operator is tied to that machine, it does not make sense to use SWIP in the machine; his part which he stands there, and watches, becomes the SWIP.

An example of this would be a press operation where the operator can load the part, hit the button, and then move on to the next operation. The goal of the SWIP is to allow the operator to continue to produce the part just pressed while the press machine is working on the next part. In this case, when the operator reaches the machine, the next piece will be completed and waiting in the machine. The operator will unload the completed part, load a new part, start the machine, and continue up the line with the completed part.

Therefore, it is important not to tie operators to machines.

Work Standards

Work standards (see Figure 2.17) are different from standard work and are designed around jobs that do not repeat or only repeat every so often. In some cases, the work standard may have no times for each step or a range of times for each step because there is so much variation in the process. Remember that we can only implement true standardized work where we have constant repeatable operations with little or no variation. This means that all tools, materials, supplies, and equipment are ready in their proper locations and in the right amounts necessary and on hand exactly where and when they will be needed. The work standard is a way to document these non-standardized jobs and capture improvements as they are implemented. We find uses for the work standards in maintenance, office processes, healthcare, conceptual tasks, etc.

Standard Work Observations

- Most good operators will intuitively see the need for standard operations once you start to try to balance the line and bump.
- The line cannot be balanced without standard work.
- Standard work cannot be implemented until all the parts and tools are available in the correct order (process flow analysis [PFA] & 5S) for the operators to do their job.

An example of the above is from Company X. They had one operation where three wires were soldered on a board, black, green, and red. It didn't matter which one was soldered first. We standardized on soldering the black first, green next, and red last. When we ran the line, the line balance split was on this step. The operators chose not to follow the standard work and every time

WORK STANDARD			Date	Sheet No. ___ of___	
	Product		Prepared By		
	Area		Approved By	Dept.	Date
	Machine No.				
	Operation Name				

#	Work Elements	Key Point	Sketch/Drawing/Picture
1	Fill in the **Plant, Product, Location, & Processing Information**	1.1 Location refers to the specific area within the plant. Process refers to specific line or work center within the area.	
2	Fill out Operator ___ of ___.	2.1 Represents total # of operators in the cell or work area.	
3	Fill out TT and Cycle time. Go to Engineering or Lean area for information	3.1 For TT, P.C. or Eng. Can supply this # 3.2 Cycle time refers to elapsed time from completed part to completed part.	
4	List Major Operational Steps, including sequence and QC checks.	4.1 Seq. No. is simply the numbering of steps. 4.2 BNC and QC are identified by diamonds and should be strictly adhered too.	
5	Fill in Manual, Auto, Wait, and Walk times.	5.1 These times are calculated from the PPF or Eng.	
6	Fill in Total times at the bottom of each column.	6.1 Fill out total times at the bottom of each column.	
7	Sketch, draw, or insert a picture describing the work sequence in the space provided.	7.1 Show work sequence and SWIP. 7.2 Refer to legend for symbols used.	
8	Must fill out the "last Updated" section.	8.1 Make sure to place the name of the person who does the update and the date on which the update was done.	
9	Get approval signatures and submit a copy to the QS document control person.	9.1 Must be signed by the group leader/supervisor and Eng. 9.2 Must have appropriate QS verification.	

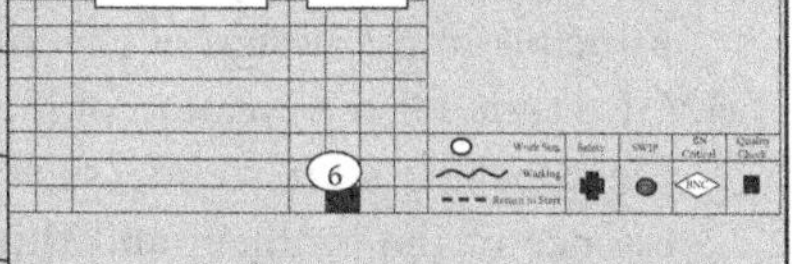

Figure 2.17 Work standard form example.

they handed off (bumped) at this step there was total confusion and sometimes one of the wires would not get soldered. The team leader met with both operators to discuss what was happening. The two operators now saw why standard work was so important and followed the standard work from then on.

Lesson Learned: The only way this system can work is if we give the team leaders or supervisors time to carry out the improvements and enforce the standard work.

It is not unusual to find operators still doing things their way. It is human nature to resist standard work and resist having to conform to the way everyone else is doing it. When we have a disagreement between two operators, or when one operator refuses to follow the standard work, we video them and then review the video to point out where and why they need to follow the standard work. It is a non-threatening approach with objective evidence to support the need to follow the standard work.

Professor Kondo's Four Points[8]

In his book *Human Motivation—A Key Factor for Management* published in 1989, Professor Kondo advocates that making work more creative is important for motivation. He suggests four points of action in support of such a process:

1. When giving work instruction, clarify the true aims of the work.
   Instead of explaining clearly what the aim of a job is, people tend to concentrate on the methods and means to be used for achieving that aim. However, every job has an aim, and it goes without saying that achieving this aim is the most important thing. Aside from mandatory restrictions related to safety and quality assurance, information concerning means and methods should be given for reference only, and we should encourage people to devise their own best ways of achieving the objectives. People must understand the why's of the job not just the how to's. This approach deepens the understanding and commitment to the job/process.
2. See that people have a strong sense of responsibility toward their work.
   This is related to the previous point. As we know well, human beings are often weak and irrational and tend to try to shift responsibility onto someone else, complain, or become evasive when their work goes wrong. It is, therefore, necessary to devise ways to quickly address such issues whenever they seem likely to appear. It's like peeling an onion. Each layer (excuse) is removed until the one reaches the heart of the onion (the goal) and a sense of accomplishment. The mandatory objectives, optional means' approach described in point one earlier that serves this purpose, and techniques such as the stratification of data, the correction of data by mean value or by regression, and the application of the orthogonal principle in the design of experiments[9] are all effective devices for putting a stop to excuses.
3. Give time for the creation of ideas.
   Once people start feeling such a strong sense of responsibility, they will go back to the essence of the problem and think about it deeply. This will result in flashes of inspiration and the creation of new ideas. Excellent ideas are most easily generated during those times when we have pondered the problem deeply and have arrived at a detached, meditative state of mind. An ancient Chinese proverb tells us that this kind of time occurs when we are horseback riding or lying down and relaxing. The times at which ideas come most readily are different for every individual; thus, we need to give people the time to be creative/innovative.

4. Nurture ideas and bring them to fruition.

Newborn ideas created in this way are extremely fragile. If ideas are examined critically with the intention of picking them to pieces or squashing them down, it is very easy to obliterate them completely; however, to find out whether such ideas are good or not, or to develop them in superior ways, they must be allowed to grow. There is no objection during this stage of growth to allowing an idea to change gradually from its original form into a better one as the main enemies of new product development are often found within the company itself. This means people are more concerned about going around stepping on new ideas than about encouraging their development. A newborn idea is like a newborn baby and raising it to maturity always requires someone to look after its interest and act as a loving parent. In most cases, those in positions of authority are the only ones who can play this role. Managers should embrace new ideas, should become their champions/patrons, and encourage their growth and acceptance. The manager should also involve the employee as their idea is matured and brought to fruition.

Professor Kondo concluded that only by addressing all four points will it be possible for work to be reborn as a creative activity. If ideas are created and fostered, those concerned will come to feel a real sense of self-confidence. This is an extremely valuable experience from the standpoint of motivation.

Eventually Standard Work Can Lead to Semi or Complete Automation[10]

As we standardize work and activities, we can now see opportunities to semiautomate or completely automate tasks. This concept, especially in the United States, is met with resistance. Yet, this is the nature of processes, equipment, and technology. Think about how fast technology is moving.

Some of you may be old enough to remember when we had people called operators. These women switched phone calls, by hand, all day long (see Figure 2.18). Would you want to do that

Figure 2.18   Telephone switch operators.

work when there are over 6 billion calls per day in the United States alone?[11] How many of you would be willing to give up your smart phones? People should not have to do mundane, repetitive, boring jobs all day long. If a machine can do it, we should let a machine do it. We cannot let the fact a person's job may be eliminated get in our way of improving a task. However, we need to make sure we don't lay anyone off due to continuous improvement and we invest in retraining those displaced for new or revised jobs.

Our experience is that jobs can be semi-automated (i.e., in its simplest form just in its simplest form just using a power screwdriver vs. a manual screwdriver) and realize 80% of the improvement for about 20% of the cost. It normally takes the other 80% of the cost to get 20% remaining improvement by fully automating tasks. Dr. Shingo's chart (Table 2.2) shows this path from manual to semi automation to full automation.[12]

Lesson Learned: Technology will never stop progressing. We need changes and we need machines to keep advancing. It is not until machines are doing tasks that we can start truly mistake-proofing operations.

True Standardized Work

Some make a distinction between true standardized work and standard work. True standardized work is obtained in the results and found by standard work audits, which means that we follow the steps in an exact repeatable sequence and hit the times with the right SWIP for each step every time. Another term for standardized work might be one-piece, balanced, synchronized flow. Standard work means that we follow the major steps, but because of variation in the process due to mixed model products as part of line balancing (heijunka), we don't always hit our times. Machines, for example, should do true standardized work. In some cases, if the line is set up properly, an assembly or semi-automated line can achieve true standardized work. True standardized work can be very difficult to obtain in some processes owing to the variation that exists.

Assembly Standard Work Form

The assembly standard work form is derived from the WFA we did earlier. After documenting the operator steps, key points, and reasons for key points, we go back and look for items to omit or items where we can save time through the improvements brainstormed during the omits process, that is, eliminate, rearrange, simplify, or combine. The steps not omitted are then rearranged into the proper sequence and become the basis for how to do the job. This becomes the basis for the operator standard work. As stated earlier, we then combine the steps to form the supervisor level standard work which is posted at the cell.

Figure 2.19 shows a standard work form. The standard work form is primarily designed for the group leader, supervisor, or anyone else observing the line. It is constructed at a higher level than the WFA (job breakdown). We have added columns for key points and reasons for key points, which were derived from the TWI.[13] We have also merged what is called a standard job sheet, which depicts a layout of the area. The standard job sheet is used to show the operator walk patterns and denote safety items, WIP storage, and number of operators, quality checks, and utility (electric, air, water, gas, etc.) locations. This form can be adapted to any area. We normally create standard job sheets to cover running the line with plus or minus one or two operators so the supervisor can run the process short or with additional staff (see Figure 2.20).

Table 2.2 Dr. Shingo's Model of Transition from Manual to Automated Operations

	Stage / Type	Hand Functions				Mental Functions			
		Principal Operations				Marginal Allowances			
		Main Operations		Incidental Operations		(Usual Method)		(Toyota Method)	
		Cutting	Feeding	Installation/ Removal	Switch Operation	Detecting Abnormalities	Disposition of Abnormalities	Detecting Abnormalities	Disposition of Abnormalities
1	Manual operation	Worker	Worker	Worker	Worker	Worker	Worker	Worker	Worker
2	Manual feed, automatic cutting	Machine	Worker	Worker	Worker	Worker	Worker	Worker	Worker
3	Automatic feed, automatic cutting	Machine		Worker	Worker	Worker	Worker	Machine that stops automatically (worker oversees more than one machine)	Worker
4	Semiautomation	Machine		Machine	Machine	Worker	Worker	Machine (worker oversees more than one machine)	Worker
5	Preautomation (automation with a human touch)	Machine		Machine	Machine	Machine	Worker	Machine (automation a human touch)	Worker
6	True automation	Machine		Machine	Machine	Machine	Machine	Machine	Machine

Source: Reprinted with permission from Table 3 on page 71 of A Study of the Toyota Production System by Dr. Shigeo Shingo, Copyright 1989 Productivity Inc., PO Box 13390 Portland, OR 97213, 800-394-6868. http://www.productivityinc.com.

Standard Work Form Line Group Leader/Supervisor

PART NUMBER:	PART NAME:	No. People Needed	Total Labor Time Secs.	Working Hours Per Day	Available Time (Secs)	Available Time (Mins)	Daily Demand	Line Balancing
		--	--	7.5	27,000	450	140	See below

PPCS Section

HEAD COUNT:	1	2	3	4	5
CYCLE TIME SECS:	0.00	0.00	0.00	0.00	0.00
CYCLE TIME MINS	0.00	0.00	0.00	0.00	0.00
HOURLY OUTPUT:	#DIV/0!	#DIV/0!	#DIV/0!	#DIV/0!	#DIV/0!
DAILY OUTPUT:	#DIV/0!	#DIV/0!	#DIV/0!	#DIV/0!	#DIV/0!

Standard Work Area:

Station #	Operation Description (what they do)	Standard WIP Quantity	Key Points and Quality Notes (how they do it)	Reasons for Key Points (why they do it)	Time	Cumulative Time	1	2	3	4	5
						0.0	###	##	##	##	##
						0.0	###	##	##	##	##
						0.0	###	##	##	##	##
						0.0	###	##	##	##	##
						0.0	###	##	##	##	##
						0.0	###	##	##	##	##
						0.0	###	##	##	##	##
						0.0	###	##	##	##	##
						0.0	###	##	##	##	##
						0.0	###	##	##	##	##
						0.0	###	##	##	##	##
						0.0	###	##	##	##	##
						0.0	###	##	##	##	##

Layout Area and Walk Patterns

STD Job sheet area inserted here is a picture of the cell and how it runs plus or minus one to two operators.

QUALITY CHECK	SAFETY CHECK	AIR CHECK	CLEAN HANDS	STANDARD WORK IN PROCESS	BOTTLE NECK OPERATION	TART TIME SECS	
★						193	TAKT TIME SECS

Line Balancing Section

Figure 2.19 Standard work form template with line balancing, PPCS, and standard job sheet.

Operator Standard Work Form XX Cell

PART NUMBER:	PART NAME:	No. People Needed	TOTAL LABOR TIME:		Available Time	Daily Demand		
123456	Adjustable	3.38	304		54,000	600		

HEAD COUNT:	1	2	3	4	5
CYCLE TIME:	304.0	152.0	101.3	76.0	60.8
CYCLE TIME MIN:	5.1	2.5	1.7	1.3	1.0
HOURLY OUTPUT:	11.8	23.7	35.5	47.4	59.2
DAILY OUTPUT:	177.6	355.3	532.9	710.5	888.2

Standard Work Area:

Job Step #	Operation Description (what they do)	Key Points and Quality Notes (how they do it)	Reasons for Key Points	Time	Cum Time	Baton Zone Map 1 2 3 4 5
1	Assemble shock tube and cylinder end assembly			11.0	11.0	
2	Install Shock Tube Assembly into Cylinder	Flat side of Retaining Ring faces outward	Retaining ring can jump out of groove	16.0	27.0	
3	Assemble Piston Head Assy and drop in unit	Throw out ball used to form seat	Ball can be damaged by Mecco press	40.0	67.0	
4	Assemble Piston Rod, Bearing, and Wiper Retainer Assembly	Cup side of Rod Seal faces down,	Unit will leak	33.0	100.0	
5	Install Bearing Assembly into unit	Don't fold or twist foam while inserting in Cylinder	Unit will not stroke properly	25.0	125.0	
6	Oil unit, assemble/install Fill Plug, set unit on "lockout", and wash unit	Verify unit was not oiled on "lockout"	Unit will not fill properly on "lockout"	60.0	185.0	
7	Paint, assemble/install knob, verify "lock out", install setting locking set screw, and torque fill plug			50.0	235.0	
8	Mark unit on Propen	Make sure unit sits flat in collet before clamping	Unit will not mark peroperly if sitting crooked	5.0	240.0	
9	Install Piston Cap and Cap Pad			14.0	254.0	
10	Test in Functional Test Stand			12.0	266.0	
11	Install red ball, gage threads, and crimp Bearing			19.0	285.0	
12	Roll unit in instruction sheet, bag unit, label, and box			19.0	304.0	

Layout Area and Walk Patterns

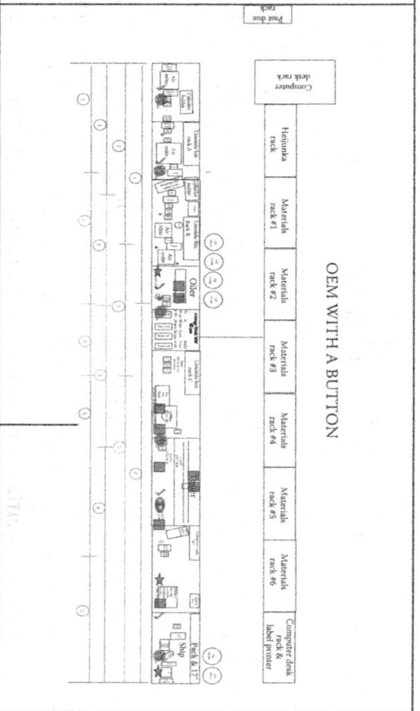

QUALITY CHECK	SAFETY CHECK	AIR CHECK	CLEAN HANDS	STANDARD WORK IN PROCESS	TAKT TIME	CYCLE TIME	HEAD COUNT	BOTTLENECK OPERATION
★	✓			■	90	76.00	4.0	●

	0.500	0.333	0.250	0.200
1	2	3	4	5
0.04	0.07	0.11	0.14	0.18
0.09	0.18	0.27	0.36	0.44
0.22	0.44	0.66	0.88	1.10
0.33	0.66	0.99	1.32	1.64
0.41	0.82	1.23	1.64	2.06
0.61	1.22	1.83	2.43	3.04
0.77	1.55	2.32	3.09	3.87
0.79	1.58	2.37	3.16	3.95
0.84	1.67	2.51	3.34	4.18
0.88	1.75	2.63	3.50	4.38
0.94	1.88	2.81	3.75	4.69
1.00	2.00	3.00	4.00	5.00

Figure 2.20 Standard work example.

Why Is It Important to Have Standard Work?

During analysis, we invite the operators to review the videos. At one facility, we asked each machining operator how often they inspected parts coming off their machines. Each one gave us different answers ranging from 5 to 50 pieces. Is it no wonder the assembly teams had trouble occasionally with the parts fitting? No statistical process control (SPC) was utilized. It turns out that much of the inspection was done on internal time when the machine was down instead of while it was running. Before we could figure out how to staff the cell, we had to standardize the number of inspections for each machine and make it external work. This eventually led to one operator running six machines.

If It Doesn't Fit—Hit It with a Hammer!

At Company X, we were videoing an operator when we noticed something strange. He was working on a very high precision assembly used in the aircraft industry. Suddenly, he pulls out a decent sized rubber mallet and starts beating the part which he had just added on to the product. We asked him if this was normal. He stated, "That is the way I was taught to do it!" (so now we know more than one person is beating this thing with a mallet). When we reviewed the video with the supervisor and some of the other more experienced operators, they almost had a heart attack, got quite animated, and immediately started looking for someone to blame. We stated that Lean is about the process not the person. They pointed out the actual process called for the part to be put in an oven for 0.5 hour to enlarge it and then the component part would easily fit, not mallet required fit. At some point, no one could figure out why the oven was abandoned in favor of the mallet, and no one was ever able to produce a procedure for us where the oven was even mentioned!

Lesson Learned: Every company has them… they just come in different sizes. If you get rid of the hammer, it will force you to fix the problem. Hammers should be outlawed at just about every non-carpentry related company. They are only there for rework! Every time I see someone pick up a hammer, I cringe. Remember the adage our fathers always taught us, you should never have to force anything, the old bull in a china shop mentality.

Separate Worker from Machine

It is important, during analysis, when operators interact with machines to separate the work performed by the machine from the person. We have run into several situations where people perform the work better than robots and others where the robots performed better than people. We apply all the same Lean tools to analyze robots and machines as we do with people. With the respect for humanity principle, human work should include the following[14]:

- Creativity—the joy of thinking
- Physical activity—the joy of working with sweat on the forehead
- Sociality—the joy of sharing pleasure and pain with colleagues
- Leadership—implementation of total quality management (TQM)

People need to be used wisely, have challenging work, and be taught to constantly identify problems and make improvements.

Machines should do the following work:

- Hazardous
- Dangerous
- Boring
- Repetitive

We break out machine time into value added (VA) and non-VA (NVA). It used to be just considered machine time. But we have always felt it is just as important to determine if machines are doing VA or NVA work as it is people. When operators interact with machines and the machines can be left alone, then the machine is physically changing the part versus the person. Remember, the person only hits a button to start the machine. So, the VA is considered the machine's work whereas the operator's work of unloading, loading, and cycling the machine is considered NVA.

An example would be milling a part. The preparation of the part, placement of the part in the mill, closing the door, and cycling the machine are all part of the operator's TLT and considered NVA. The 3 minutes the machine is milling, however, is considered machine time and not part of the labor time. This is because the machine is doing the work and the time for the machine is captured in the PFA. While the machine is working, the operator may be *waiting* for the machine to complete or, hopefully, performing another task in parallel to the machine running.

Author's Note: When you put the microscope on the machine, one finds not all the machine's work is VA either!

Sometimes You Have to Eliminate the Robots!

Sometimes, people are better than robots. Robots have their place. They are good for repetitive tasks, dangerous tasks, and for total automation. But if the robots just sit there and batch up parts, they are not very useful for Lean. Robots should do one-piece flow just like people. There are many cases where we have removed robots and found another home for them. In Figure 2.21, this robot

Robot marking machine

Marking machine in the cell

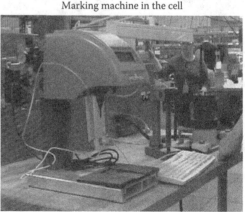

Figure 2.21   Sometimes humans are better than robots.

spent all day either idle or marking parts. Sometimes, the line had to wait for the robot to finish the batch. Other times, the robot was way ahead with bins of WIP waiting to be processed. We removed the robot and put the robot marking machine in the line. This allowed for the smooth flow of production, eliminated the batching robot, and improved the on-time delivery performance of the line. Robots should also displace a person or persons. If not, why are we adding the robot? At Company X, they replaced a person with a robot. However, the robot had much difficulty handling many of the various models, so a human had to be inserted for a large portion of almost every day. So, in the end, what did we save?

Standard Operations Routine Sheet[15]

This sheet is also known as the standard work combination sheet (Figure 2.22) and combines the PFA (product steps) and WFA (operator steps) generally at higher level time increments. We tend to use it the most when humans are interacting with machines. It can be used for assembly operations, but we find assembly standard work sheets work better.

The purpose of the sheet is to graphically depict the operator steps against the operational or physical machining steps that may be in a different sequence depending on how the work is split up between the operators. In the example (see Figure 2.23a and 2.23b), one can see that operator 1 may run machines 1, 2, and 3 or may run 1 and 5. So even though the process goes 1, 2, 3, 4, 5, it is possible for the operators to have different walk patterns. This is an advantage of a U-shaped cell. When one operator is running both the beginning and ending machines, there is no way the cell can start more than it finishes or finish more than it starts.

In the left-hand column of the standard operation routine sheet (SORS) are the operator steps. Generally, the walking is included in the time but sometimes not broken out. A straight line is

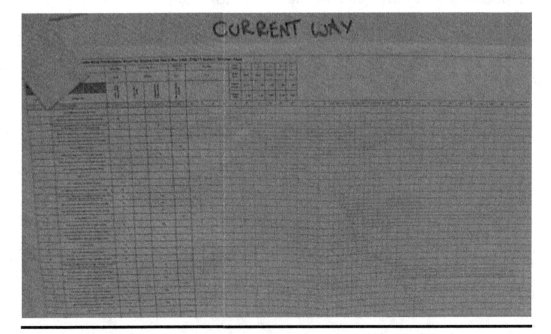

Figure 2.22   Hand drawn standard work combination sheet.

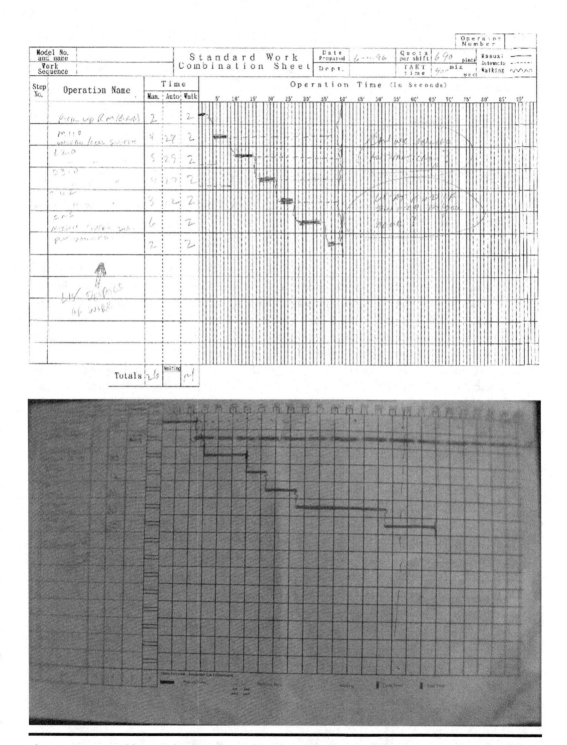

Figure 2.23 (a and b) Standard work combination sheet hand drawn.

shown for manual work and a dotted line for the machine work (to show how long the machine runs). A red line is drawn vertically on the page to show the TT. Very quickly one can determine if the operator has more work than the overall cycle time (or TT) or if a machine runs longer than the cycle time or TT.

Lesson Learned: It is not until the machines are doing the tasks that we can start truly mistake-proofing operations.

Capacity Planning and Analysis: Part Production Capacity Sheet

Ohno said that capacity is equal to work + waste.[16] Work + waste also equal throughput time. Throughput time is how long it takes for a product to get through the entire process. It is composed of process time (which contains some VA), transport time, inspect time, and wait times, none of which are VA.

We have another definition of time called complete time. This is equal to the sum of machine time (VA and NVA) and labor time (VA and NVA). It differs from throughput time in that the SWIP time is not part of the complete time. Lean has a tool called the part production capacity sheet (PPCS) (Figure 2.24 and Table 2.3). We have built this PPCS capacity information into our WFA, 10-cycle analysis, and standard work sheets. We also have a separate sheet called the PPCS[17] where we can capture this information separately. Once we have analyzed an area, if necessary, we use this sheet as the vehicle to pull all the previously analyzed data together. This PPCS is described in many books but is well documented in the book Toyota Production System by Professor Monden.[18]

The PFA is captured in the description of process boxes and listed in the proper order on the left-hand side and the labor times come from the sequence of operations on the WFA sheet. Setup times are also factored in the middle of the sheet and amortized based on the lot size across each part.

The next two columns are for labor VA and labor NVA time. These two columns sum up to TLT. The next two columns are for machine VA and machine NVA time (a new column we created back in the mid-1990s). These two columns sum up to total machine time. This is where we separate the operator (person) from the machine. The next column is complete time. This column

Part Number		Hours/day	Seconds/ day	Customer Demand	Takt Time	Total Labor Time	Number of Operators Required	Factory Demand	Factory Cycle Time	Variance to Takt Time	Head Count	1	2	3	4
Part Name															
						Time Distribution					Hourly Output				
Order Of Process	Description of Process (PPF Steps)	Station Name/ Number	Labor Non- Value- Added Time (s)	Labor Value- Added Time (s)	Machine Non- Value- Added Time	Machine Value- Added Time	Complete Time	Bottleneck	Tool Exchange		Production Capacity				
Totals							(s)		Units	(s)	Time Allocated	Daily Capacity	Hourly Capacity		

Figure 2.24   PPCS.

Table 2.3 Capacity Analysis Example

Savings Comparison Base to Lean Lines (Assumes Prices from Link to But Not Including Final Test + Capsule Weld) (Does Not Include Electricals)

Base	Current Cell Staffing Base (No Lean Lines)	Units per Person per Day	Units per Person Lean Lines	Working Days	Total Units per Day Produced Capacity Base	Total Units per Day Produced Capacity Lean	Units Needed per Day Based on End of Year	Takt Time (Minutes)	Units Produced per Year (Old Way)	Units Produced per Year (Lean)	Employees Needed Base Condition (No Lean Lines)	Employees Needed if All Lean Lines	Variance Lean Staffing to Current Staffing	Yearly Demand
Cell 20	8	5.31	8.70	236.00	42.50	69.59	97.74	4.45	10,030.99	16,422.89	18	11	3	23,067
Cell 30	5	9.75	11.70	236.00	48.75	58.50	59.59	7.30	11,505.00	13,806.00	6	5	0	14,064
Cell 40	5	7.8	9.36	236.00	39.00	46.80	54.81	7.94	9,204.00	11,044.80	7	6	1	12,935
Cell 50	4	3.25	3.90	236.00	13.00	15.60	22.78	19.10	3,068.00	3,681.60	7	6	2	5,375
Cell 60	1	3.25	3.90	236.00	3.25	3.90	8.34	52.16	767.00	920.40	3	2	1	1,968
Totals	**23**			**236.00**	**146.50**	**194.39**	**243.26**	**1.79**	**34,574.99**	**45,875.69**	**41**	**30**	**7**	**57,409**
					33%				# employees short		18	11	Savings	
												$ 37,000.00	Person worth per year	
													Savings per year	$ 404,982.75

Source: BIG Archives.

adds the labor and machine columns together to get the total time necessary for each step for one piece. The next column is called tool exchange time. This is where changeover information is entered if applicable. There are different ways to use this form and it can be modified to suit the project application. The tool exchange time contains a column for the lot or batch size utilized and the setup time column has the amount of time required for the changeover. The form then divides the setup time by the number of products run (lot size) to get an amortized run time per piece based on the changeover time. This is then added to the complete time for that step. Remember that this form was originally designed for manufacturing, but it is a powerful form. It can be used for any process in a variety of industries from banking, insurance to landscaping and hospitals.

The next column is capacity. But before we get to that, let's discuss the top lines. On the top is customer demand and available time. Once these are filled out, the form calculates the TT. There is also a block for factory demand (or transactional area demand) and once we have this number, we can calculate the cycle time we need to use. The next block is TLT. This block is the total of VA and NVA labor time. If we divide it by the cycle time, it tells us how many operators we need based on the demand we are going to run through the process versus the customer demand.

Now, back to the capacity column. Once we have the available time, we can divide it by complete time to determine our capacity. The lowest capacity number represents the bottleneck. Again, a bottleneck should never be a person because we can always add people. The longest complete time driven by a machine is the bottleneck operation (but keep in mind it may not be a true bottleneck). If there is a machine, we need to *WIP* the machine, which means that the machine always has a piece to work on while the operator is running the rest of the cell. The next step is to calculate headcount.

The cycle time with one person is always equal to the TLT with one person.

Even if a machine had a longer cycle time, the operator would end up idle waiting for the machine to finish. The cycle time with two people would be half of the cycle time with one person and so on. This assumes that the work is or can be balanced. The output per hour is determined by dividing the cycle time into one hour or 60 minutes; however, the output per day is determined by dividing the cycle time into the available time per day.

This is a phenomenal tool for the supervisor of an area to have at their disposal. Now, they have data with which to answer any question thrown at them from upper management at their fingertips. We have used this form successfully in many business applications. In some cases, it is difficult to use this form, so we have built our own models to determine labor staffing and capacity unique to those areas.

Part Production Capacity Sheet Real Life Example[19]

This PPCS sheet combines (see Figure 2.25) the product and operator or as Dr. Shingo called it, the network of operations. To create this sheet, one must list down the PFA steps in the left-hand column. We then enter the labor times (VA and NVA) from our WFA sheet. Notice in this example that the labor times are all NVA because the machine is doing the work. The labor times add up to 283 seconds. Next, we load in the machine times. These are all VA in this example because the machine is physically changing the parts, which the customer wants, and the machine is doing it right the first time. The machine times add up to 383 seconds. When we add up each row, we get the complete time. So, for step 1, the Mori, we add the 11 seconds it takes to unload, load, cycle, and inspect the piece from the Mori and 70 seconds to run the part and get a complete time of 81 seconds. When we first started with this shop, the operators each only ran one machine. So, in this case, think what this means. The operator would spend 11 seconds to load the part and then wait

Figure 2.25   Old ancon gear facility in Long Island NY.

70 seconds for it to run every cycle. So, over the course of a day, 86.4% of the time the operator was idle watching the machine.

Next, we fill in hours per day of available time. In this case, it equals 7.3 hours or 26,280 seconds. If we divide the 81 seconds of complete time for the mori into the available time of 26,280 seconds, we get our daily capacity, which is 324.44 parts per shift. This logic follows for the rest of the column. Once we calculate this information, we can determine that the bottleneck is the gear cutter at 191 seconds per cycle. Is it a true bottleneck? The answer is no because we are very close to our TT just running one shift.

Next, we fill in the head count information in the upper right. The easiest way to do this is to think about what happens in the cell logically. If one person is running the cell, how long will it take them to complete a cycle? The answer is 283 seconds, which is equal to the TLT of the cell. The only time the cycle would be longer is if it was paced by a machine. Do we have a machine that runs longer than 283 seconds? The answer is no. But if we did, the operator would be idle at that machine for the extra time and our cycle time would equal the bottleneck time of the machine. Since it takes 283 seconds for the operator to unload, load, cycle, and deburr the parts, then this is equal to the cycle time for one person, and we put that in the appropriate block. The hourly output would be equal to 3,600 seconds per hour divided by the 283 seconds cycle time or 12.72 parts per hour. We then use this as a basis to fill in our day-by-hour chart on the line. To calculate the daily production, we must take our available time of 26,280 seconds and divide it by the 283 seconds cycle time to get 92.86 parts per day.

Once we have this information, it is relatively straightforward to fill in the rest of the section. With two people, what should our cycle time be? It should be equal to the TLT divided by two people, assuming we can divide the work evenly. 283 seconds ÷ 2 people = 142.5 seconds per person. This calculates to 14.12 parts per hour or 184 parts per day based on available time. However, you will notice the sheet says 103.06 as the max output per day. How can that be? The problem is we have now been impacted by the bottleneck, the gear cutter, at 191 seconds (vs. our 142 seconds). When labor and machine times are included, the complete time is 255 seconds for the gear cutter, which means we would be running 255 seconds cycles. This means that between the two operators, 28 seconds are going to be idle spent waiting for the gear cutter. So, the most parts we can get out per day is the same as the daily production capacity of the gear cutter.

The first time we were asked to evaluate the cell, it had two operators. Does it pay to have two operators running the cell? The answer is no. If we take a step back and look back at the numbers, how far off the TT of 275 seconds are we? The answer is 283 − 275 or 8 seconds. Where could you take out 8 seconds of work? Take another look at the PPCS sheet. We would start with the 64 seconds of manual time at the gear cutter. If we can eliminate 8 seconds of labor time, do we need two people in the cell? The answer is a resounding no. The point here is once we get the data, we can easily figure out the cell.

Now, we have true numbers on the cell and know exactly what our output should be each day and our supervisor is now armed with this information. We also have all the data we need to start working on and measuring our improvements.

Consider another variable in the capacity calculation: that of machine change over (see Table 2.4).

Setup time is included by amortizing the setup time over the number of parts in the production run or lot prior to the setup. So, let's go back to the Mori. The Mori had 70 seconds of run time and 11 seconds of load, unload, and quality check manual time. The complete time for the Mori was 81 seconds. Let's assume that the changeover time for the Mori is 10 minutes or 600 seconds. If we run 300 parts in each lot, our setup time per part would equal 600 seconds divided by 300 parts or 2 seconds per part. We would then add these 2 seconds to the 81 seconds to get a new complete time of 83 seconds. By dividing this number into the available time of 26,280 seconds, our new capacity number is 316 parts versus 324 parts. So, the setup costs us eight parts on the Mori lathe per day.

To continue with our example, try out the homework listed in the succeeding text:

Homework: What options (good and bad) do we have if we really wanted to double the capacity of the cell? See the endnotes for some of the possible answers.[20]

In real life, they sped up the machine and *double hobbed* the gear cutter by adding another hob and making the gear cutter twice as fast. They then used the other gear cutter in the cell for *external setup* since the gear cutter had the longest changeover time in the cell. This way, when they completed a part in the cell, they could quickly change over to the next part. We then experimented with SWIP at various machines.

Table 2.4 Setup Impact on Capacity

Process No.	Process Name	Machine No.	Manual Time	Auto Time	Time to Complete	Interval Changes	Setup Time	Capacity ( )	Remarks
Basic Operation Time									
	Manual time—Total time required to complete process—could include load and unloading of machines, manual assembly, etc.								
	Auto time—Total time for machine to cycle								
	Time to complete—Manual time + auto time								
	Interval changes—Number of pieces run before tool is changed, i.e., replace drill, etc.								
	Setup time—Minimum time required to complete tool change $$\text{Process capacity} = \frac{\text{Total time to complete}}{\text{Total time to complete} + \dfrac{\text{Interval changes}}{\text{Setup time}}}$$								

Source: Professor James Bond.

Lesson Learned: The tools can be applied quickly, and once we have the data, it is very easy to put together risk mitigation plans or to answer customer inquiries as to what it would take to increase our output. All this information is now in the hands of the operators and team leaders or supervisors.

Ancon Gear Case Study

This is a real-life example from a company called Ancon Gear located in Long Island, NY (see Figure 2.25). Ancon was a small 6,000 ft² machine shop specializing in all types of custom gears and capable of holding 0.0003″ tolerance on these small gears. They were a job shop with high-mix low-volume orders. Ancon Gear at the time (back in 1995) had a 30% OTD but 100% quality rating. During my time as a Materials Manager, I was sent to stay with them until we received our delinquent parts. This was a common way of expediting parts back then. We would normally beat the suppliers into submission. But this time with my Lean knowledge I decided to take a different tack. I toured the facility with Joe, one of the owners, and we did a PFA together starting at the receiving door. About halfway through, Joe said, "can we stop now? I get it! We are really screwed up." Of course, I said no and forced him to walk through the rest of the process (building the compelling need to change). I explained Lean concepts to them that afternoon and less than six months later, they had created their first cell. The PPCS example earlier was based on that actual cell in February 1996 and Joe and Ed Markievicz (the owners) invited me to look at the cell they just installed. One day, I flew up to Ancon, videoed the cell, and reviewed the video with Ed, Joe, and John (their best operator). We did a PFA (see Table 2.5), WFA analysis (see Table 2.6), 10-cycle analysis (Table 2.7), PPCS (see Figure 2.26), and baseline standard job sheet (see Figure 2.27); brainstormed improvements; corrected the layout (see Figure 2.28); created a material plan (see Figure 2.29); created a SORS (see Figure 2.30); implemented the changes; experimented with SWIP before the gear cutter; and freed up an entire person. I flew back to Baltimore that evening.

Part No	Gear #12345	Hours/ Day	Seconds/ Day		Total Labor Time	Takt Time (s)				Head count	1	2	3	4	5
Part Name	Gear	7.3	26,280		283	275				Cycle time	283	142	94	71	57
Desc.	Gear	Time distribution								Output Hourly	12.72	14.12	14.12	14.12	14.12
Job Step	Process Step	Labor Non-Value Added	Labor Value Added	Machine Non-Value Added	Machine Value Added	Complete Time		Tool Exchange Time		Output Daily	92.86	103.06	103.06	103.06	103.06
		(s)	(s)	(s)	(s)	(s)	Bottle-neck	Units	(s)	Time Allocated	Prod Cap (units/ day)	Comments			
Cumulative times:		283	0	0	383	666									
1	Mori	11			70	81					324.44				
2	Lathe	27			31	58					453.10				
3	Gear cutter	64			191	255					103.06				
4	Inspection	17				17					1545.88				
5	Sand	50				50					525.60				
6	Deburr lathe	51				51					515.29				
7	Brush	16				16					1642.50				
8	Mill	47			91	138					190.43				

Figure 2.26 PPCS example.

Table 2.5 PPF Analysis

Summary	Baseline	Post Lean Projected	Reduction	Reduction %
Total steps	25.0	18.0	7.00	28
Orig S	28,232	13,308	14,924	53
Minutes	470.5	221.8	248.73	53
Hours	7.8	3.7	4.15	53
Days	1.1	0.5	0.57	53
Weeks	0.2	0.1	0.1	53
Distance	44.0	44.0	–	0
# of people	4.0	1.0	3.00	75
# of machines	6.0	5.0	1.00	17
Va %	1.8667%	3.02%	-1.15%	-62
NVA %	0.40%	0.46%	-0.06%	-16
Storage	97.50%	96.03%	1.46%	2
Inspect	0.12%	0.26%	-0.14%	-112
Transport	0.12%	0.23%	-0.11%	-93

No. of Steps	Omit (X)	Flow Code	Description of Product Step	Alt. Start Time (S) (optional)	Cumulative Time (s)	Baseline Time (s)	Post Lean Estimate Time	Distance (in Feet)	Distance Post (with Omits)	Machine	Person Who Touches it (Job Class)
1	x	RM	Parts sit as bar stock			14,400	0		0		
2		t	Move to mori			10	10		0		Eric
3	x	VA	Mori			125	0		0	Mori	Eric
4	x	B	Sits in parts tray in mori			16	0		0		
5		T	Move to hand to inspect			3	3	1	1		

Source: BIG Archives and Courtesy of Ancon Gear.

Table 2.6 Ancon Gear WFA

Each	Estimated Time	VA	Non-Value-Added but Required Work (RW)	Pure Waste–Idle Time (PW)	Material Handling (MH)	Inspect (I)	Unnecessary Work (UW)	Get Tools (T)	Get Parts (P)
Current TLT (seconds)	468		468			0		0	0
Current TLT (minutes)	8		8			0		0	0
Estimated TLT	283	0	283	0	0	0	0	0	0
Estimated TLT (minutes)	4.7	0.00	4.7	0.0	0.0	0.0	0.0	0.0	0.0
1 Open door Mori		Mori	RW 1	1					
2 x Press button			RW 2	0					
3 Pick up pliers			RW 3	3					
4 Pull out bar			RW 2	2					
5 Close door mori			RW 2	2					
6 Press start/cycle machine			RW 1	1					
7 Open part catch			RW 1	1					
8 Take out part			RW 4	1					
9 x Grab mic			RW 2	0					

Source: BIG Archives and Courtesy of Ancon Gear.

Note: This particular version of the form was developed by Mark Jamrog SMC Group and put into Excel by Dave Okoren and Charlie Protzman.

Table 2.7   Ancon Gear 10-Cycle Analysis

Step No.	Description		4.53	5.63	5.82	Max	Min	Avg	Std Dev	Std Dev	Cum Time	1	2	3	4	5
		Cycle Time (minutes)	4.53	5.63	5.82	401.0	255.0	319.7	41.6							
		Cycle Time (seconds)	272	338	349	401.0	255.0	319.7	41.6							
1	Mori	Alt. start time (optional)	0													
		Cum	23	601	1,146	28	21	24	4	15.0%	24	1.00	1.00	1.00	1.00	1.00
		Split time	23	21	28											
2	Lathe	Alt. start time (optional)														
		Cum	43	703	1,202	62	16	33	25	78.0%	57	1.00	1.00	1.00	1.00	
		Split time	20	62	16											
3	Wait	Alt. start time (optional)														
		Cum	54	738	1,312	70	11	39	30	76.7%	95	1.00	1.00	1.00	2.00	2.00
		Split time	11	35	70											
4	Gear cut	Alt. start time (optional)														
		Cum	152	831	1,405	58	53	55	3	5.3%	150	1.00	1.00	2.00	2.00	3.00
		Split time	58	53	53											
5	Inspection	Alt. start time (optional)	300													
		Cum	314	851	1,429	24	14	19	5	26.0%	169	1.00	2.00	2.00	3.00	3.00
		Split time	14	20	24											
6	Lathe and sand deburr	Alt. start time (optional)														
		Cum	438	1,009	1,559	90	78	84	6	7.1%	253	1.00	2.00	3.00	4.00	4.00
		Split time	84	78	90											
7	Mill	Alt. start time (optional)														
		Cum	540	1,118	1,707	69	62	66	4	5.7%	320	1.00	2.00	3.00	4.00	5.00
		Split time	62	69	68											

Source: BIG Archives and Courtesy of Ancon Gear.

Note: In cycles two and three, we were experimenting with SWIP. But we found adding the SWIP just moved the wait time from the lathe—62 seconds on cycle 2 to the wait time before the gear cutter—70 seconds on cycle 3. This particular version of the form was developed by Mark Jamrog, SMC group and put into Excel(R) by Dave Okoren and Charlie Protzman.

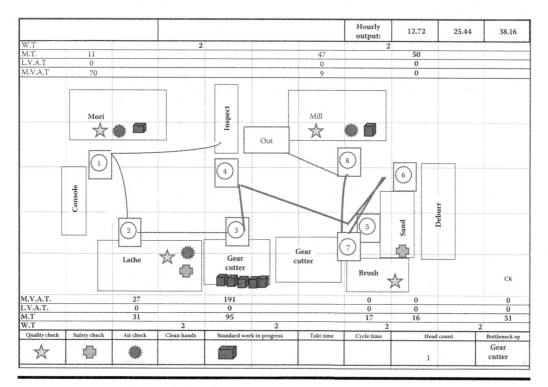

Figure 2.27   Standard job sheet. (Courtsey of Ancon Gear).

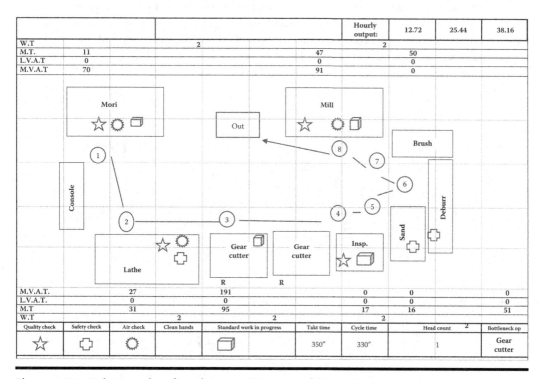

Figure 2.28   Point to point after changes. (Courtsey of Ancon Gear).

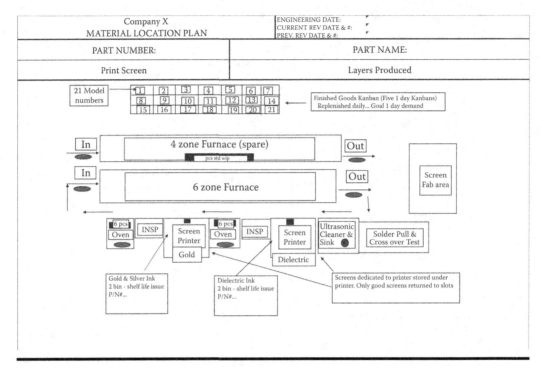

Figure 2.29   Material plan example.

Results: So, in one day, we freed up a person and were able to meet the TT on one shift with one person. The tools can be utilized very quickly once you have a good understanding and have some practice. So, what is the return on investment (ROI)? At the time they had literally a wall of parts that were delinquent and some orders were several years old, which their customers still wanted. This is not uncommon in batch environments—when you're batching, the "hardest to

Part Number		Hours/Day	SECONDS/DAY:	Total Labor Time	Head Count	1	2	3	4	5													
Part Name		7.30		26280	283.00	Cycle Time	283	142	94	71	57											
Part Desc						Output Hourly	12.72	25.44	38.16	50.88	63.60											
Process Flow	Description	Manual Times Increased Costs	Value-Added Times	Non-Machine Value Added	Machine Value Added	Output Daily	92.86	185.72	278.59	371.45	464.31											
		sec	sec	sec	sec	10	20	30	40	50	60	70	80	90	100	110	120	130	140	150	160	
1	mori	11			70																	
2	lathe	27			31																	
3	gear cutter	64			191																	
4	inspection	17																				
5	sand	50																				
6	deburr lathe	51																				
7	bursh	16																				
8	mill	47			91																	

Figure 2.30   Standard work combination sheet.

*Edward and Joseph Markiewicz, Ancon Gear &
Instrument with Alex Tentas, Sandvik Coromant
sales engineer. Working together, set-up times
have been reduced to levels which have allowed
Ancon to machine smaller batches and be more
competitive for JIT production.*

Figure 2.31 Inventory is evil article with Joe and Ed Markiewicz ancon gear.

make orders" get pushed to the side. Within six months after implementing Lean, the wall of parts was gone.

Joe and Ed took over the company when their father passed suddenly and were struggling to make ends meet. They were even talking about getting out of the business and going to work for someone else back in August of 1995 when we first met. Their stats are listed in the following text.

In August 1995:

- 34 years in business
- AlliedSignal *problem* supplier
- 15 employees
- Approx. $700K sales

In August 2000:

- 39 years in business
- AlliedSignal preferred partnering supplier
- 19 employees
- Approx. $2M sales
- 6 months 100% on-time delivery to AlliedSignal
- The entire shop was re-laid out and every piece of equipment moved and reorganized into cells based on a group tech matrix
- Air conditioning installed for the employees
- Bonus plan implemented for the employees
- Profiled in an article in *Metalworking World* ©2008 "Inventory is Evil" (see Figure 2.31)

Staffing Analysis and Plan

Unlike managing a line based on experience or standards that have not been updated in years, with a Lean line, once we have done our due diligence of the analysis, we will know in no uncertain terms what the staffing and capacity of the line should be. In assembly lines, the capacity will be determined by the number of people we have on the line and the number of people the line can physically support. There are rare cases where we will staff lines to get more output but sacrifice productivity. For example, in a machining line that was designed to run optimally with one person, we add a second person. We may not be able to keep the second operator busy the entire time, but we get more out because we have them in the cell. This situation is normally driven by some critical customer or perceived customer demand. This was discussed earlier in the chapter under Trading Labor for Productivity.

To staff the line, we take the TLT that comes from the WFA and divide it by the TT or cycle time we wish to run. In a machining line, this same formula will work if there is not a machine that runs longer than the cycle time in which case the operator will be idle at that machine. The capacity is then determined by how many people run the line and the cycle time of the machines.

The WFA now becomes the standard for the line and our goal from then on should be to strive to constantly improve the standard and to reduce the labor time and ultimately the head count. This is where ongoing kaizen events whether they be for hours, or weeks should be utilized to sustain continuous improvement in the line.

Determining the Number of Staff Required for the Process

Once we know the TLT, it is straightforward to calculate the number of staff required by dividing the TLT by the TT or cycle time. Dividing by the TT will tell you the staff required to meet the customer demand and dividing by the cycle time will tell you the staff required based on the factory conditions, attendance, or scheduled demand for the hour or day. This is because TT and cycle time are often different in most factories or office settings. This calculation is made to determine the required number of operators and is normally fractional, so we use the kaizen approach to eliminate the operator with the least or fractional amount of work (see Figure 2.32). We utilize baton zone or bumping to balance the fractional labor across the entire cell until we can eliminate it. This is discussed in more depth later in the book.

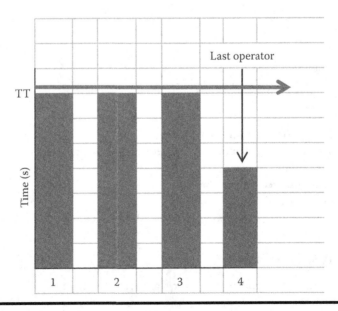

Figure 2.32   Load balancing chart.

Cross-Training Becomes the Initial Number One Obstacle

When converting a process from batch to one-piece flow, there may be some substantial time savings just from running one piece flow. Customer demand, cycle time, TLT, and standard work are directly related to one another. In some business environments, only certain people can do certain jobs. This creates complications when bringing up and trying to run the line. The key is to divide the work as evenly as possible and have the people in the areas flex to overcome minor variations in cycle times. If they can't flex then that person is stuck doing that job. This means they will end up batching and the other person(s) on the line will have to literally work around them to keep the line running.

Ohno uses the analogy between swimming relay handoffs and baton relay handoffs[21] to describe the differences in flexing. Swimming relay handoffs require the next worker to wait until the person prior to them completes their work, whereas a baton relay handoff allows work to be handed off before it is completed but requires the operator to be able to perform that work. In swimming relays, persons who have critical skill sets like butterfly stroke or breaststroke complete their specialty for their lap. The rest of the team is dependent on how well the *specialist* does their job. However, no one type of lap (i.e., breaststroke, freestyle, etc.) has the same cycle time. For example, freestyle is faster than all the other strokes, but it is person dependent. If the relay were to run all day, we would be able to predict the output based on the average of the sum of the laps swam. To get the average lap cycle time, we would have to divide the overall by the number of laps swum by each person, that is, if it was a 25 m pool and 50 m for each stroke, each person would be swimming 2 25 m laps or 8 laps total for the team. There is a drawback to this relay race. Assume the information in the following text:

Laps:

Butterfly lap	80 seconds
Backstroke lap	75 seconds
Breaststroke lap	65 seconds
Freestyle lap	60 seconds
Total	280 seconds

The overall cycle time (or throughput time) would equal 280 seconds. The average 25m lap cycle time would be 35 seconds. However, since the swimmers are not swimming simultaneously, each of the swimmers would have significant (up to 78.5%) idle time waiting for their lap to come up and for the other laps to be completed. In this case, each person can start immediately when the prior person touches the wall. The TLT across all four swimmers is 1,120 seconds of which 840 seconds are idle. In an individual medley, one person is totally cross-trained and can do all the strokes for the race and we have no idle time and a labor time of 280 seconds.

In the factory environment, if we have a machinist, welder, assembler, and tester that are not cross-trained, we run into the same problem as the relay race earlier with the labor times being the following:

Machinist	80 seconds
Welder	75 seconds
Assembler	65 seconds
Tester	60 seconds
total	280 seconds

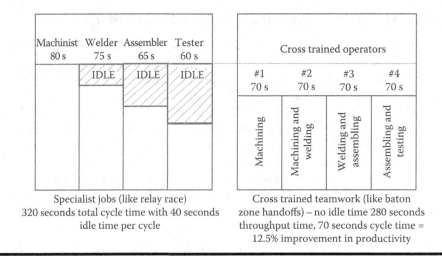

Machinist 80 s	Welder 75 s	Assembler 65 s	Tester 60 s
	IDLE	IDLE	IDLE
Machining	Machining and welding	Welding and assembling	Assembling and testing

Specialist jobs (like relay race) 320 seconds total cycle time with 40 seconds idle time per cycle

Cross trained operators #1 70 s, #2 70 s, #3 70 s, #4 70 s

Cross trained teamwork (like baton zone handoffs) – no idle time 280 seconds throughput time, 70 seconds cycle time = 12.5% improvement in productivity

Figure 2.33 Impact of cross trained operators.

In this case, the machinist will pace the line and assuming continuous production, we will not be able to get a part quicker than an 80 second cycle time. The first piece will result in the same labor and idle time as the swimmers earlier. However, once the line is wet and each person is working each cycle, our TLT is going to be 4 persons multiplied by 80 seconds (our constraint or bottleneck) or 320 seconds. The welder will be idle 5 seconds per cycle, assembler 15 seconds, and tester 20 seconds per cycle, or a total of 40 seconds of idle time per cycle. This means that for approximately every six to seven pieces we produce, we lose one piece to idle time. If every person could do every job, then each person would have 70 seconds worth of work with no idle time. At 80 seconds, our output per hour would equal 3,600 seconds divided by 80 seconds or 45 per hour. With cross-training, at 70 seconds cycle times, we get 51.5 parts per hour. Hence, we gain six to seven extra parts by capturing the idle time lost due to lack of cross-training (see Figure 2.33).

Lesson Learned: To eliminate idle time, we need multi skilled and multi process operators and layouts that support flexing.

The A or Act in PDCA = Sustain Which Requires Updating the Standard Work

Every time there is a change in demand, a change in products or services offered, a change in process, or new machinery introduced, it necessitates updating the standard work and recalculating all the numbers to rebalance the workflow. World-class companies see these changes as opportunities to improve and eliminate even more waste in the process.

Author's Note: Non-world class companies see this as a burden of extra work for which there is no time or resources!

Be careful with elements of a job that may have been categorized in the WFA as a group of operations with a large chunk of time. Sometimes, these must be split up to get the work to balance or even to update a new improvement. As a normal rule of thumb, we analyze operations down to the second to avoid this problem. Bottlenecks may also be caused by machines that require extended cycle times or have larger capacity to run multiple tests or processes. Ask yourself, what can be done to separate the machine work from the human work or to divide up the machine tasks across different machines where it makes sense to hit the cycle times or avoid batching within the machine.

Takt Time versus Cycle Time Examples

Cycle time is how often a part is completed by a specific process and TT is the customer demand calculation to determine how often a part must be completed by a specific process to match customer demand. Sometimes, we may be in a situation where we cannot run to TT (TT). An example of this might be if we had an employee out sick. If we could not find a replacement, we would run to a slower cycle time than TT and we would fall behind. The next day, we may add an extra person to the line to catch up by running at a cycle time faster than TT.

Lean and the Theory of Constraints (TOC)

Remember that any excess WIP or idle time is a sign of a problem within a Lean system. A bottleneck is the constraint (where the capacity of the machine cannot meet the demand) in any series of operations in a process. Per the theory of constraints, which is explained in detail in a book entitled *The Goal*,[22] the cycle time will always be equal to the slowest machine or slowest person in the process. We refer to these constraints as "Herbies." In theory, a person (Herbie) should never be a constraint as we can always add people to a line, but we cannot always add or immediately speed up machines. In essence, only machines should be bottlenecks in a process. This is a good and bad news story. The bad news is we have a constraint or bottleneck. The good news is, once we have our analysis data, we not only know we have a bottleneck (constraint), but we can also predict when the backup will start, how long it will last, and how many parts will queue up.

Types of Improvement

The term process improvement can be misleading. When reading Ohno and Dr. Shingo's books,[23] one will find that their approach to improvement is prioritized in the order listed below: The improvement starts with the work itself first. The reason is if one starts with equipment improvement, we may find as we improve the work, the equipment is not needed, it has too many features or the tooling needs to be modified:

1. **Operation/work improvement**:
   a. Manual operations: Should contribute to 1/2 to 1/3 of total cost reduction[24]
   b. Standardization: Study the process and establish sequencing of work, work standards, line balancing, and 5S
2. **Equipment/machine improvement:** "You must have the ability to tinker and improve the machines you have. If you buy the latest high-tech machines and use unskilled workers who become slaves to the machines, then you lose the sight of what will keep costs down"[25]

3. **Process improvement**: Refers to the order of processes (i.e., assembling a product and then inspecting at the end vs. inspecting after each operation or moving operations around in an order that makes more sense, i.e., running a part through a lathe prior to the mill vs. vice versa)
4. **Facilities improvement**
5. **Technology/information systems improvement:**
   a. Looking at the entire facility layout and potential improvements. Normally the costliest

It is important to do work improvement first, then equipment improvement, process improvement, facility improvement, and finally information system improvement. Most improvement comes from work improvement first for typically little cost. Once the work process is standardized and standard work is created, then we should look at how the task can be semi-automated. Once the entire process is standardized, then we should look at implementing software or information systems. If you add the equipment first, you may be adding equipment that is not even necessary or with features not necessary which result in waste for significant costs. If you implement the information system first, you are just automating the waste. If one starts with the facility first, we may find demands on the facility changed once we improved the work and equipment.

Walls—Up and Down

At Company X, new leadership came in and started with facility improvement first by installing a 20 ft floor to ceiling walls (see Figure 2.34) throughout the factory with the intention of improving the facility at significant cost and time. It was expensive construction, in that it had to be conducted on an off shift, paying time and a half, with the installation of huge plastic sheets to

	Jan	Feb	Mar	Apr	May	Jun	Jul	Aug	Sep	Oct	Nov	Dec	AVG
1999	23	24	28	23	29	24	29	31	22	33	27	27	27
2000	32	40	27	31	32	28	32	33	23	38	31	31	32
2001	31	31	23	28	34	33	32	34	29	29	30	30	30
2002	32	31	28	29	29	37	36	32	28	37	32	25	31
2003	32	30	27	23	26	27	36	34	26	35	22	39	30
2004	26	27	26	28	32	40	29	37	27	22	31	39	30
2005	22	19	23	25	29	31	28	25	28	31			26
	28	29	26	27	30	31	32	32	26	32	29	32	29

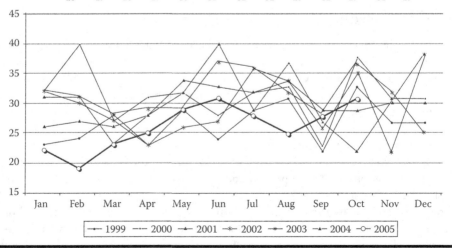

Figure 2.34 **Walls coming down.**

Figure 2.35   After walls came down.

prevent contamination of the circuit board areas. As we leaned out our work content and the lines over the next two years, the walls ended up being totally in the way of our one-piece flow efforts. We constantly freed up unusable space because of the walls. We ended up having to fight for over a year to get the walls torn down. What made the decision so difficult to rescind was because they had just spent all that money to put the walls up, so they didn't want to spend yet more money take them down (see Figure 2.35). After the walls came down, we redid the layout and were named a model Lean site.

Lesson Learned: Follow the order of the steps for improvement. With technology, if you automate or create a software solution for a poor process, you will still get a poor result. It is always important to improve the content of the work first. The analysis tools we have covered in this book are all geared toward work improvement. As you improve the work, the equipment improvement opportunities jump out.

True Bottlenecks

A true bottleneck is defined as a machine that runs 24 hours a day and cannot meet TT. How we handle a true bottleneck is different from other constraints. Other constraints can be made up with overtime, running multiple shifts, or speeding up the machine. But true bottlenecks must be managed intensely to mitigate any lost time. It is important during the analysis phase to look at the processes as an overall system and determine whether there are any true bottlenecks lurking. If one must manage a true bottleneck, one must develop backup and risk management plans to keep the machine running until such time as the bottleneck can be resolved. Sometimes this means we may have to have a person on that machine all the time, even though some of their time is idle (once again trading labor for productivity). Planned and unplanned downtime should be a metric on this machine. At one company, we had the machine programed to dial or text the maintenance person 24 hours a day in the event it sensed a fault or that a fault condition may occur. As one continuously improves the process, one will see the bottleneck rotate between person and machine!

Assess Roles and Responsibilities

Roles and Responsibilities Matrix

Once we have completed the analysis, we review the skill sets of the operators. In the Ancon Gear example discussed earlier, we needed an operator that could run every machine and operation in the cell. This cross-training is normally the first area to impact us when implementing one-piece flow. *We* quickly learn that we can't run the cell properly because not everyone is cross-trained. This applies in the transactional environment as well. Many times, in offices people are overburdened and the work not level loaded due to "specialist" skill sets and functional departments. In addition to the cross-training matrix, we use a roles and responsibilities sheet to define owners and accountabilities across functional lines. This makes it very clear as to who owns what in the organization. The format for this chart (see Table 2.8) comes from a book called Designing Organizations by Jay Galbraith.[26]

The most important rule is there can only be one owner per task. Someone can share the ownership but only one person is designated as responsible. This matrix lists all the employees in the cell/area/company and the skills they have acquired to date (see Table 2.9). The staff needs appropriate cross-training to perform the tasks and have a clear understanding of the benefits to the customer and the organization and to address "what is in it for me" as it relates to each person. Cross-training is normally the first thing needed to achieve the desired workload balancing. Staff members must be multi-process capable to fine-tune the work distribution. This necessitates that they learn more tasks or operations within a cell or work area. One way to facilitate this training is to use a cross-training matrix (see Figure 2.36) and post it on the team communication board to keep track of which staff members are trained up to what level in each task. The cross-training matrix shows the staff who trained for what process and how many team members are needed to be trained for the process.

How to Construct a Cross-Training Matrix

Each staff member that works in the area is rated based on a set of objective measures (0–4). These ratings should be continually monitored and revised. If a staff member has not worked in a particular area or performed the task for a given period (i.e., six months), they should either be recertified or lose their status for that operation.

Figure 2.36 Cross training matrix and training plan.

Table 2.8 Roles and Responsibilities Matrix

Decisions / Roles	Sales	Segment Marketing	Insurance	Mutual Funds	Marketing Council	CEO	Finance	Human Resources	Regional Team
Product price									
Package design									
Package price									
Forecast	A	R	C	C	C	I	I	X	X
Product design									

R = Responsible
A = Approve
C = Consult
I = Inform
X = No formal role

Product Teams versus Process Owners

Responsibility	Supervisor	Process Owner/Manager
Functional procedure and policies	A	R
Systems development	C	R
Function strategic plan	I	R
Budgets—Direct	R	C
Budgets—Indirect	C	R
Yearly vacation planning	R	A
Casual days	R	C
HR policy enforcement	R	R
Product audits	R	I
Process audits	I	R
Performance targets	C	R
Personnel assignments to teams	C	R
Resource allocation	A	R

Source: Designing organizations by Jay Gailbraith, John Wiley & Sons©2002.

Table 2.9   Roles and Responsibilities Matrix Example

	Tasks/Authorities Responsible (Can Only Have One Owner!) Approve Consult Inform Shares Responsibility X-None of the Above	Focus Factory Mgr	Buyer Planner Scheduler	Shipping and Receiving	Stategic Acquisition Manager	Water Spiders	Eng.	Shop Floor Team Members	Site Lead	Acctng.	Customer Service	Q.A.	Sales/ Product/ Project Manager	Shipping
1	Develop supplier statement of work	C	C		R		C		A			C		
2	Create customer RFQ				C		C				C		R	
3	Take the sales order										C		R	
4	Enter the sales order				I				I		R		I	
5	Field customer inquiries	C	C				C		I		R		C	
6	Develop vendor-managed inventory (VMI) agreement	C	C		R		C		A	I				
7	Develop long term agreements	C	C		R		C		A	I				
8	Negotiate blanket PO	A			R				A	I				
9	Enter blankets/VMI/ LTA into system	I			R				I			I		
10	Update approved supplier list		R		A				I	I		C		
11	Release against blankets		R					I						

Source: BIG Archives.

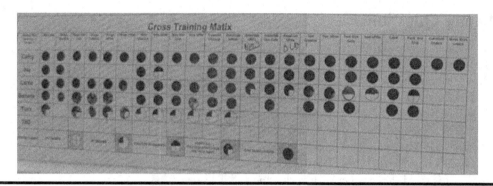

Figure 2.37 Cross training examples.

In an environment where continuous improvement is practiced, the tasks or operations will be continually improving and changing. This requires the staff to be trained on the latest developments and standard work in the area. The levels vary by company but generally follow:

1. In training
2. Can follow the standard at 50% speed
3. Can follow the standard and hit the cycle times
4. Qualified as a trainer

Note: Note everyone will be a good trainer.

The goal for the area should be to have all staff at a status *3* or *4* on all operations/tasks. This is just one example of cross-training matrices that can range from simple to complex. See Figure 2.37 for some other examples. In summary, we have prepared the flow for the overall chapter in Figure 2.38.

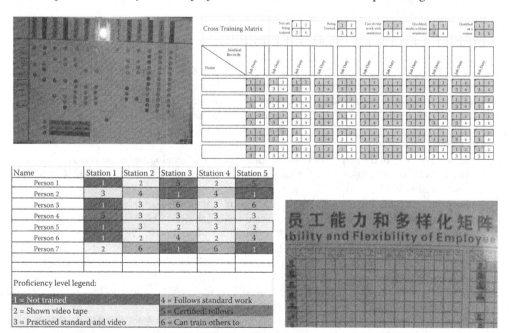

Figure 2.38 Overall flow of the chapter for standard work.

Chapter Questions

1. What is a cross-training matrix?
2. What is a PPCS?
3. Are robots always useful to increase efficiency? Why or why not?
4. Is standard work used for assembly lines only?
5. What does it mean to wet and dry up the line?
6. SWIP is used only on the manufacturing floor.
7. What is SWIP? Standard work in process (SWIP).
8. Discuss how to use Little's law. What is its relationship to standard SWIP?
9. What is the difference between cycle time and TT?
10. What is a work standard?
11. What is the difference between operator standard work and supervisor standard work?
12. What did Shingo mean by network of operations?

Homework Exercise

Create standard work for any process.

Notes

1. Dave Morrison.
2. Japan Management Association, *Kanban Just-in-Time at Toyota* (New York: Productivity Press), 1989.
3. http://www.airspacemag.com/flight-today/mayhem.html
4. http://www.popularscience.co.uk/features/feat21.htm
5. *Toyota Production System*, Productivity Press ©.
6. From the Art of Lean website: There are levels of standards and documents inside of Toyota just like in any company. There are governing bodies of standards and regulations inside the company known as Toyota Motor Regulations (TMR) and Toyota.
   Manufacturing Standards (TMS). Both sets together are about the size of 20 encyclopedia volumes and considered highly confidential and proprietary. When I started with the company in the 1980s, they were still mostly in Japanese and not very often changed (think of application of bearings, etc., where the laws of physics are constant or electrical power coming into the plant).
7. Donald Dinero, *Training within Industry and Training within Industry Manual* (New York: Productivity Press), 2005.
8. Professor Yoshio Kondo http://www.hk5sa.com/tqm/tqmex/kondo.htm. Professor Kondo was the author of the book, *Company Wide Quality Control* (Zenshateki Hinshitsu Kanri) (JUSE Press), Professor Yoshio Kondo, translated by J. H. Loftus.
9. Lawrence P. Sullivan, The Power of Taguchi Methods, Quality Progress, June 1987, p. 76.
10. Dr. Shingo's transition to automation. Reprinted from Table 3 on page 71 of *A Study of the Toyota Production System* by Dr. Shigeo Shingo, (Oregon: Productivity Press), 1989.
11. How Many Cell Phone Calls Are Made a Day?—DeadZones.com.
12. Shigeo Shingo, *The Shingo Non-Stock Production: The Shingo System for Continuous Improvement* (New York: Productivity Press), 1988.
13. Donald Dinero, *Training within Industry and Training within Industry Manual* (New York: Productivity Press), 2005.
14. Yoshio Kondo, translated by J. H. Loftus, Human Motivation – A Key Factor for Management published in 1989 (Zenshateki Hinshitsu Kanri) (JUSE Press) Professor Yoshio Kondo http://www.hk5sa.com/tqm/tqmex/kondo.htm

15. *The Toyota Production System*, Monden, first edition, industrial engineering, and management press, ©1983 pp. 89–91 and *Kanban JIT at Toyota*, Japan Management Association, Ohno, Productivity Press, ©1986, pp. 111–116.
16. Taiichi Ohno, *Toyota Production System, Beyond Large-Scale Production* (New York: Productivity Press), 1978.
17. This sheet is described in many books but is well documented in the book, *Toyota Production System*.
18. *Toyota Production System*, Yahsiro Monden, Engineering & Management Press, 1998.
19. This PPCS is based on an actual sheet used for Ancon Gear's first Lean Machining Cell in February 1995.
20. Answer:
    We could add a gear cutter machine (however, there already is an extra one in the cell).
    We could run the entire cell for two shifts with one person.
    We could run just the gear cutter at night and batch up the parts for the first shift and then run with two people.
    We could work two people overtime.
    We could speed up the machine.
21. Japan Management Association, *Kanban Just-in-Time at Toyota* (New York: Productivity Press), 1989.
22. Goldratt, Eliyahu and Cox, Jeff. *The Goal* (Great Barrington, MA: North River Press), 2004.
23. *Workplace Management*, Ohno, Productivity Press, ©1982, pp. 122–128.
24. *Toyota Production System*—Ohno, Productivity Press, ©1978, p. 67.
25. *Workplace Management*, Ohno, Productivity Press, ©1982, pp. 122–128.
26. *Designing Organizations*, Jay Galbraith, John Wiley & Sons, ©2002.

Additional Readings

Byham, W.C. 1988. Zap the Lighting of Empowerment. New York, NY: Ballantine Books.
Dinero, D. 2005. Training within Industry Manual. Portland, OR: Productivity Press.
Galbraith, J.R. 1995. Designing Organizations. San Francisco, CA: Jossey-Bass Inc.
Gordon, T. 1977. Leader Effectiveness Training. New York, NY: Wyden Books.
Johnson, S. 1998. Who Moved My Cheese? New York, NY: G.P. Putnam's Sons.
Team Editor 2002. Standard Work for the Shop Floor. New York, NY: Productivity Press.
Wheeler, D.J. 2000. Understanding Variation. Knoxville, TN: SPC Press.
Japan Management Association 1989. Kanban Just-In-Time at Toyota. Portland, OR: Productivity Press.
Monden Y. 2011. The Toyota Production System, 4th edn. Portland, OR: Productivity Press.

Chapter 3

Lean Material Basics

It ain't what you don't know, it's what you know that just ain't so.

Mark Twain

This chapter explores components of the supply chain, noting that the important thing to remember with Lean supply chain management is not to make it harder than it is and yet don't underestimate the ongoing effort required. In this chapter, the terms supply and materials are used interchangeably.

Inventory: Lean Materials and Supplies

When redesigning your value stream, we need to understand what and how many supplies are needed to perform the activities/operations within the process. For example, where Lean has not been fully implemented within your organization, we can review any area and find the same supplies in multiple places throughout the area. These supplies will not be where they are needed and there will be many more than needed. In redesigning the work area or administrative process, we need to ensure the right supplies and equipment are located at the right place at the right time to perform the activity.

Recognizing Waste for What It Is—Waste

Batching systems result in lots of work in process (WIP) materials. When you have so much inventory that it forces you to walk around it then you have too much. Many times, when doing layouts in batch environments, it often results in employees putting the equipment in the wrong place creating long travel distances, which leads to even more batching. Typically, after a physical inventory, we end up explaining the inventory shortages as variances to management. Equipment can also be considered inventory. We often find old equipment no longer in use, taking up space. Sometimes the equipment should have been used; however, for unknown reasons, they stopped using it. We have witnessed some companies continue calibrating equipment that was no longer needed. Supplies and equipment in the wrong place cause constant searches for materials, which is a clear waste of time; yet we see it all the time. Remember "Excess inventory is always the sign

DOI: 10.4324/9781003185796-3

of a problem." This is obvious when too many parts overflow the bins, or the door on a cabinet, or the drawer can't close. Richard Schonberger's book *World Class Manufacturing: The Next Decade* suggests inventory turns be utilized as one of the prime measures to rate companies on the ability to sustain continuous improvement.[1] Do you have:

- Equipment on the floor no longer in use?
- Do you have cabinets full of old parts and equipment?
- What does your maintenance area look like?
- How much space is your WIP consuming today?
- If you were Lean, how much space could you free up?

We were working with Company X on their materials process. One of the steps in the process was to double-check the count of the inventory (spot check) prior to releasing the order to their supplier. This is in addition to the cycle counting they were already doing. We asked if this was a value-added step. Everyone said yes because we have to do it. We asked why they have to do it. They said they can't always be sure the count in the perpetual inventory system is correct. I asked why this was. They said it was because people were too lazy to scan out the material they needed or didn't have time to scan in the materials. We asked again, "Is this really value added?" The answer was, "Yes, everyone who has this perpetual inventory system has to do it."

The point is no one looks at or sees this as waste. But in reality, the only reason we have spot checks in our process is because we can't trust the system to be correct with regard to what inventory is really in the bin, so we inspect the bin to see how much is there. Remember inspection is waste.

Lesson Learned: Continuously performing a process doesn't make it value added. We must be able to see and recognize waste in our processes for years and have the discipline and fortitude to call it what it is … waste or Muda.

Some Inventory Is Required: Too Much Is Evil

Too many supplies and/or inventories consume valuable space and consume cash, which creates waste. Companies with excessive inventories deplete funds that would otherwise be available to fund other activities beneficial to the stakeholders. Remember the two main rules in Lean:

1. Excess inventory is always the sign of a problem.
2. Idle time is always the sign of a problem.

Consider batch environments that are full of WIP inventory.

Too Many WIP Baskets

Company X in Ohio had large (4′ × 4′ × 4′) baskets of inventory everywhere throughout the plant. When we first toured the plant, they asked what results they could expect with Lean. "How about a 50% reduction in space?" When we completed implementing the new master layout, we saved in excess of 50%. The free space allowed the company to move all of their raw materials and finished goods from another building into their old facility and still have 20% of the space for growth. They saved the leasing and utility cost of the other building. In addition, when we left, their parking area was full of the old baskets no longer in use. We suggested they sell them or better yet give them to their competition.

Exercise: How much inventory do you have? If your answer is below 60–100 WIP turns, you still have much opportunity.

Problems with MRP Systems

In its simplest form, we manage our personal supply chains all the time. For example, we go to the grocery, department, or hardware stores in search of goods and services. We find something on the shelf and buy it or place a special order and have to wait for it to be delivered. The Internet has changed how we purchased goods and services as we can buy directly online and, with overnight delivery, have it the next day. But, when we go to the store, we sometimes can't find what we need: either they don't carry it or they are out of stock. The places we visit all the time are our first-tier suppliers. Each of these places must order their supplies unless they make their own. For instance, the supermarket is dependent on the farmer or distributor and the hardware store is dependent on either a manufacturer or wholesaler. The more levels to the supply chain adds complexity resulting in more opportunities for process errors. We are dependent on the supply chains of our first-tier suppliers. If a store constantly disappoints us, we create a mental report card deciding we will no longer use the store (supplier) and we go to their competitor.

Businesses are no different. They all have supply chains, but many times, their problems are more complicated due to the sheer number of parts and/or suppliers. We now have very sophisticated material requirement planning (MRP) and enterprise resource planning (ERP) software systems to help manage our purchases of goods and services and tie all our plants and suppliers together across the world. There are Internet-based supply chain services and who knows what the future will hold (see Figure 3.1). ERP and MRP tend to be very nervous systems. The systems can't plan to the hour, often lack data accuracy, and require large investments. Some new systems offer Kanban modules but it takes a lot of labor to keep the data fed.

Many companies end up working around their MRP software to get their procurement systems to work. This is a major flaw as it should be the other way around. The problem is most software, despite their claims, is not Lean and cannot keep up with hourly or daily demand requirements. Many companies run their MRP systems two to three times a week. By default, if the systems are not real time, they become batch-based systems, which means you have to have at least 2–3 days of inventory on top of the time it takes to replenish it. As a result, companies end up constantly rescheduling their suppliers and become their own worst enemies in terms of on-time delivery (OTD), but they tend to blame it all on the supplier. As a supplier, the further you are down the supply chain, the more variation exists and you tend to feel a loss of control and you experience constant expediting in the trade, we say, the further down you are in the supply chain, the more nervous the MRP system.

Implementing a New Materials System

At Company X, we spent several weeks working to implement a new materials system. In the past, it had worked literally from tribal knowledge. They never used the MRP system correctly or had accurate data loaded in the planning parameters. When they received a new order, they just intuitively knew what orders to place for component parts. However, when a new product line was introduced into the plant, from another division they were closing, they started experiencing serious problems. The tribal knowledge, now lost from the plants that were closed, created a serious

Overview logistics systems

	Deliveries to point of use			Deliveries to receiving point		
	SmartBin	2Bin	Code	SmartBin	2Bin	Code
Automatic recognition of inventory levels	•	•		•		
Manual recognition of inventory levels		•	•		•	•
Automatic transmission of orders	•	•		•		
Manual transmission of orders					•	•
Express processing	•			•		
Constant monitoring of inventory levels	•			•		
Periodic monitoring of inventory levels		•	•		•	•
Automatic monitoring of cycles	•			•		
Shipping in original boxes					•	•
Shipping in standard bins	•	•		•		
Deliveries to receiving point				•	•	•
Deliveries to point of use	•	•	•			
Return of empties	•	•		•		
Automated physical inventory counts	•			•		
Online overview	•			•		
Online reports	•			•		
Reports on orders	•	•	•	•	•	•
Monthly invoice	•	•	•	•	•	•

Innovation creates new standards in inventory management

Needed parts are automatically ordered online and delivered to the customer on time.

The supply cycle is simpler, quicker, more reliable and, of course, more cost efficient.

SmartBin consists of a combination of normal bins and scales.

The scales, specially developed for Smart-Bin, constantly check current stock levels. The gathered data is sent to Bossard each day. When the minimum stock level is reached the predefined order quantity is shipped automatically.

Bins have sensors which monitor weight and when triggered notify the company over the internet

Figure 3.1   Internet-based VMI two-bin system at Honeywell.

void, in that no one at Company X knew what component parts to order. This put them seriously behind schedule with their new customers. We asked the materials manager what he thought we should do. We developed a three-pronged strategy. First, we had to train everyone in their existing ERP system and fix the inventory status records and bill of material (BOM), and then create and develop a plan for every part (PFEP) and, finally, realign the organization to support the new materials effort.

We worked with their procurement manager to create an initiative we called "twice as fast" in which we used a lot of the strategies defined in their "to be" vision[2]:

- We developed and executed the purchased product twice as fast
- Incorporated a lead-time reduction strategy that resulted in 41% improvement
- Improved supplier OTD performance from 54% to >99% and improved material availability to >95%.
- Improved supply demand alignment from 72% to 87%.
      Note: We stopped letting things come in when we did not need them.
- Reduced supply base from 545 suppliers to 364.
- Implemented supplier performance index (SPI) and online supplier report card
- Improved production price long-term agreement (LTA) utilization from 1.6% to 50%
- Increased production purchase order auto-release utilization from 0% to 40%
- Improved LTA auto-release utilization from 35% to 78%
- Reduced head count by 6% with no disruption in customer service

True Partnering with Suppliers

The goal of true partnering is to move suppliers from the typical antagonistic environment to one where the supplier becomes a true partner or an extension of your facility. The goal with Lean is to develop and nurture a partnering supply base, which means the supplier literally becomes an extension of your company similar to any internal manufacturing or transactional area. Picture a fast-food company in a college or gas station. True partnering is managed differently than non-partnering suppliers. For instance, they don't need report cards as they are receiving constant feedback from their customers. They share the same systems and update their customers immediately if any problems surface. True partnering is getting your suppliers involved early in the design phase to suggest cost-saving ideas for materials used, labor required, setup time reduction, and standardized tooling requirements. Suppliers can suggest, for instance, off-the-shelf materials they currently stock or material substitutes that may be cheaper. Suppliers should be given target costs for delivery, schedule, and quality with a predetermined sharing formula when they can beat the targets. Truly partnered suppliers do not cut margins but work with their customers to reduce their costs. The goal is to keep your partners as viable sources by maintaining reasonable profit margins. Partnered suppliers will respond immediately to production problems. They work together to secure and maintain the business of the end customer.

Partnering with Suppliers

A Toyota supplier had a bad fire and was going to take several weeks to get back up and running. Some of Toyota's other suppliers banded together and made the parts until the other supplier was back on their feet.[3]

We find most companies don't have true partnering supply bases, even those that claim they partner with their suppliers generally do not have true supplier partners. Most can't conceptually visualize the concept. When we ask what they mean by a partnering supplier, it is normally a supplier who has a blanket or LTA. The mere presence of an agreement does not make them a true partnering supplier. The test for a true partner supplier is what happens when the supplier has a problem. It could be a pricing issue, quality issue, or delivery issue. How does the company (their customer) respond? Most companies are not willing to spend the time or money to work with the supplier to help them overcome the problem. Many times, unless they are a sole source, it is easier just to find another supplier.

Supply Chain Management

It is surprising how many companies have a totally reactive supply chain. They do not actively manage their suppliers or supply base and switch suppliers to achieve a better price or delivery. Many use auction buying where they constantly compete with suppliers against each other. As an example, a US government contract was in the bidding phase and a first-tier supplier was bidding on systems with drawing packages, which did not include the drawings (since the drawings were proprietary to the incumbent). This strategy may yield the lowest price but at what cost. Can you tell when companies buy toilet paper from the lowest price supplier?

Reverse Auctions Should Be Outlawed

One of the worst systems we have seen was at a Fortune 50 company, which put all its parts out for bid. Any company could bid on them, and many new companies went in at low-ball prices in an attempt to win the business. Their existing suppliers were frantic and extremely frustrated as they saw the online pricing going lower and lower in real time. They were continually reducing their prices and profit margins as much as they could, but most of them ended up losing all their business. At the same time, Company X increased the length of their payment terms, on remaining orders, to 90 days or more, forcing their existing suppliers to establish expensive lines of credit (ironically, one of these companies' major competitor's financing arm provided net 10-day payments in exchange for 3%–5% of the payment). Eventually, this strategy resulted in disaster. Many of the low-ball suppliers could not meet the prints, or their parts were of poor quality or required more labor to inspect the parts or created problems on the shop floor during installation. They eventually abandoned the practice and returned to most of their existing suppliers, but not before many of them were financially strained and some went bankrupt. The ill will it created is still felt by many of their suppliers today.

Supplier Report Cards and the SPI[4]

A common tool for managing suppliers, which assumes the company is managing its suppliers, is the supplier report card. Suppliers shouldn't need report cards. If they are doing a good job, they get the orders; if not, their competitors win the orders. Good suppliers will ask for feedback from buyers on how they can improve and service them better. Many companies have Lean assessments for their suppliers. The ironic part is that most companies that survey their suppliers can't meet the criteria themselves (with the exception of Toyota and Honda). However, since most companies are not as Lean as Toyota, many buyers operate in a silo (functional organization), which means their metrics reflect a silo organization. This is when we recommend the use of a tool called the supplier price index (SPI). The formula is:

Supplier price multiplied by a factor based on their quality and delivery performance.

SPI helps the buyers adjust the supplier pricing to compensate for those with poor quality or delivery and drive orders to the right suppliers with the lowest total cost even though their price may appear to be higher. The inherent problem is most purchasing departments are measured on the cost of the part (purchased price variance), or service, and have no method to capture the entire cost to the company (to include rework, extra inspection, and missed delivery dates).

Point of Use

The term POU (point of use) means exactly what it says. In a POU system, the parts or tools are exactly where they are needed when they are needed. It means excess reaching, walking, and/or searching have been eliminated. The operators are not leaving the line to obtain the kit of parts on the shelf or to the pallet full of parts in the aisle. They are not checking the kit part quantities, measuring the parts, taking parts out of bags, or disposing of papers in the kits. Parts and tools need to be placed in such a way that the operator doesn't need to think about where they are located. The operators simply reach down or over, and the part or tool is right at the POU where and when they need it (see Figure 3.2). Sometimes this POU process will require parts, tools, or equipment to be duplicated on the line.

Stockroom Materials

These materials at first include raw materials and at some company's subassemblies. Many stockrooms have carousels that we work to eliminate over time. We also work to eliminate traditional

Figure 3.2   5S Labeled tool in POU location.

Figure 3.3 Carousel.

types of kitting of parts. Carousels (see Figure 3.3) while sold as efficiency improvements actually reduce efficiency but generally do free up space because all the material is now stored vertically 15–20 ft high. Some are even called Lean Lift®.[5] The problem with carousels is that there is normally only one operator, it can only be operated from one position, and the software is slow. Our goal is to eliminate the carousels and even the stockroom over time. This requires a phased-in plan with two components:

1. Kitted parts must be eliminated. This means BOMs must be flattened with the parts now assembled in the cells, in the sequence they are required.
2. Raw materials and components must be moved next to or near the lines where they are used. In this way, the team leader or supervisor can visually determine the status of their parts.

This strategy eliminates the constant searching for parts on the floor, having someone assigned to locate the information in the computer to see if they are available in the stockroom, then filling out a stockroom request, having someone remove them, and finally take them to the line. This process can take from hours to days! Meanwhile, the line is waiting, is shut down, or has to convert to another model. The time to change over was wasted and team members became very frustrated.

I recall a shopping experience at Walmart where I was told, what's on the floor is what's in the store, because their trucks come in and replenish the stock each night. Similarly, as we remove parts from the stockroom to the floor, the traditional kitting process is eliminated along with the labor that went with it. Phasing out a stockroom can take from months to years. As the stockroom is emptied, it is amazing how many parts are found, which were lost or scrapped because no one could find them. Many times, the parts become part of E&O because we have already purchased them again. We have seen companies where it was literally easier to requisition a new part than to look for it in the stockroom or throughout the plant. We have found that the size of the stockroom many times will indicate where a company is in terms of its Lean Maturity Path.

Levels of Kitting

- **Traditional Kitting Work Orders:** Typically used with batch systems or bumping the part. Parts are individually counted or weighed and bagged based on the picklist and trip around the stockroom.
- **Kitting Work Orders with Bins versus Counting:** Bins or boxes, etc., of parts are picked and kitted eliminating need to count and bag individual parts.
- **Production Kanban Kitting (SPS):** Kits are made of sheet metal and follow unit down the line.
- **Centralized Supermarket Kanban:** No picklist. Empty bins are replaced via withdrawal, production Kanban or vendor-managed inventory (VMI). Typically use some type of tugger system. May still use MRP for low frequency. Parts may be sequenced in the supermarket or by supplier delivery.
- **POU Supermarket:** Supermarket is located next to the line and empty bins are replaced via withdrawal, production Kanban, or VMI. May still use MRP for low frequency.

Pros of Traditional Kitting

- If parts are counted properly, can serve as a mistake-proofing system to ensure all parts are accounted for at the end of the build.

Cons of Traditional Kitting

- Kitting is a process where we pull various parts for a sized lot of an assembly or subassembly. The lot size might be based on a work order or an economic order quantity anywhere from one piece to 1,000 pieces or more depending on the batch size being built. Kitting is normally, but not always, associated with batching. Most batch companies use some form of kitting. As companies move down the Lean path, POU Kanbans replace traditional kitting.
- The kitting process can be performed by an internal stockroom or an external supplier. The process begins with a BOM, which is part of the product design cycle developed by engineering. The purchased and in-house manufactured parts list is developed from the BOM. The parts' list has the part type and quantity of parts to be pulled based on the lot size and it should also have a work order allocation along with a location for the parts. However, if there is more than one location for the part, most MRP/ERP systems can't determine the EDD or earliest due date. This designation has replaced first-in-first-out (FIFO) since most items now have some type of manufacture or expiration date. The parts are then pulled from the stockroom by hand via a carousel or shelf and put into some type of container or bag. The kit is often pulled with shortages and staged on a shelf or cart or sent to the floor until the missing part(s) arrives. Many times, there are layers of pulled kits of parts waiting for assembly or assemblies built shortly because the wrong parts were in the kit, they were missing parts, or the kit did not arrive in time.

■ Managing throughput in this environment is difficult and labor-intensive and involves tracking parts from work center to work center. In addition, production control tracks how many assemblies were built each day and, in some cases, creates a line of balance chart (see Figure 3.4) to determine the predicted output on a given day, assuming the needed parts arrive. Sometimes, kits have more parts than needed, and there's no easy way to restock them, so they end up in the trash. When parts are scrapped, many times, they are trashed with no record in the MRP system. Thus, the MRP system shows these WIP parts in stock that do not exist. Many shortages end up taking weeks or months to procure.

■ Some companies may be forced to kit, particularly in aerospace applications where lot traceability and serialization are required. But in many cases, we have been able to work around this with Kanban systems. The very nature of Kanbans and one-piece flow makes kitting and serialization much easier than trying to manage it in an environment where there are three to four inventory turns a year. For some reason, it is human nature to think that kitting parts is the most efficient way to handle materials. We have even seen Lean companies go down this path. Why does this occur? Listed below are some of the problems with traditional kitting.

■ At Company X, even though they made sure all the parts were available ahead of time; the operator had to retrieve the kit, which means he or she was not working on assembling

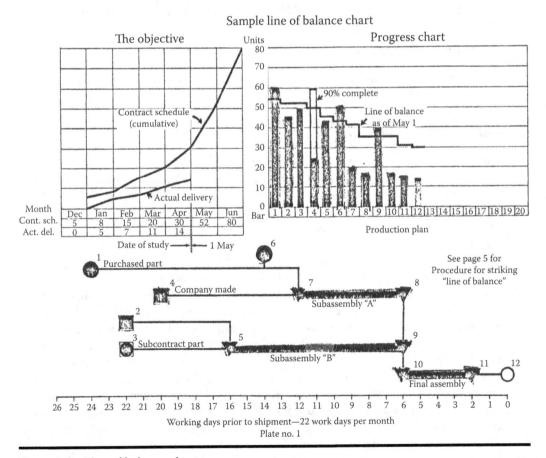

Figure 3.4 Line of balance chart.

units. This led to higher direct labor assembly costs, often providing the cost basis to support outsourcing.

■ Many times, operators must wait for the next kit. Sometimes, there are many kits for the same assembly on the floor at the same time, so if a part is scrapped, operators or production control may take the part from the next kit. The process will lead to future kits being short of the part we scrapped. A phone call goes to the stockroom telling them they sent the kit short to the floor and didn't label it. The stockroom personnel become frustrated because they know they didn't send the kit to the floor short. We used to have 20 people in the stockroom every day, doing nothing but counting and kitting parts. There were carts of kits everywhere. And of course, no one picked an entire kit. It had to go from person to person and floor to floor before the kit was completed. And of course, every time we received a shortage request, we had to stop working on the next kit to pull the shortages. When the parts were scrapped, they were never entered into the system. This meant eventually, we would end up with another shortage down the line. We had military programs where the final set of units couldn't ship for 10–12 weeks due to all the shortages that accumulated over the life of the contract due to the robbing of other kits.

■ Even though companies try to make sure there are no shortages, if there are shortages, they put them on order and mark the kit short. Of course, the kit will normally go to the line short where now we build it short and have to put the assembly aside until the parts are received. This can also be the beginning of one of the thousands of vicious expediting cycles that occur over the year.

■ We make sure the parts are of the right quality and meet the specs. Normally, this is the job of the supplier, and internally, we may have an incoming inspection department, but with many dock-to-stock or floor programs, we still actually see the operators measuring and checking the parts. So again, this is waste as the operator is not assembling the product.

■ It is now easier for the operator to obtain parts since they are all right there in the kit. But what about when the kit is on several pallets or a small kit is all mixed up inside a large bin, or the parts are mixed up on the tray or the wrong parts are pulled?

■ By having the kit ready, the operator can assemble it right away. However, the parts are normally still in their original packaging, and the operator has to stop to remove and trash the packaging, which is waste.

■ Very seldom are kit counts accurate. Why? Because we have humans counting them for the kits and humans taking the parts off the kits. Humans make mistakes. Humans always tend to take the path of least resistance, so if there is a part within their grasp, even though it is for another job, they will grab it! Everyone is fundamentally trying to do a good job.

Lesson Learned: All the problems listed previously are embedded in the system of kitting.

Point of Use Billing

POU billing is a system where the supplier does not invoice for the parts until the product is shipped or their component is physically used in the product.

At a former Allied Signal (now Honeywell) location we manufactured surface-mounted circuit boards. We contracted with a local distributor to have them on site which supplied the reels of components as manufacturing needed them and owned the inventory until the entire reel of chips was consumed. Once the component reel was depleted, the supplier would invoice for the reel. We did not pay for the parts until the system was shipped to the customer allowing them to completely reduce our inventory while increasing our cash flow.

Lesson Learned: Although there may be many versions of a product, there is normally a common material base or flow that exists. Many times, people will continually bring up a couple of cases where they think Lean would be difficult to implement in hopes of stopping the effort. Organizations should focus on the 70%–80% where Lean can be successful first and then deal with the low runners and exceptions. Don't let the exceptions dictate or constrain how or if you implement Lean.

Work Orders "Short Materials" Shut Down the Lean Line Every Time

If we negotiate with the supplier to deliver parts to the POU, all the expenses and problems associated with kitting can be eliminated. In many cases, the suppliers (vendors) will manage the inventory as part of a VMI system. The VMI system allows parts to be brought to the line, in the order needed, which provides immediate visibility to shortages. It no longer makes sense to start a job (work order) that is short parts, and you shouldn't. Companies will continue to violate this rule because they think it will help them make the end-of-the-month quotas; however, when a subassembly or assembly is built short and you are working on a Lean line, the people working after the shortage will be idle until the next unit reaches them. Another disadvantage is that production control needs to find a place to store the half-built part, which requires a label to identify what is missing. The production control and shop floor control teams must meet every day to determine when we (manufacturing) can finish the job, which requires the supervisor to pull someone off the line to finish it. What a mess! These problems are all system induced and are a result of kitting. Clearly, a Lean management system that utilizes a VMI process will provide significant benefits to the manufacturing and operations teams.

Lesson Learned: If you try to run the new system with the old batch behaviors, the new system will not work.

Supplier Kitting

Supplier kitting sounds good at first glance but takes a tremendous amount of work to make it successful. It is an easy sell to the customer because they no longer have to pick their own kits or carry the inventory, but the costs and systemic problems associated with third-party kitting are still in the value stream regardless of who is doing the kitting. The first problem companies find is the transfer of the BOMs to the suppliers. Upon the first kit supplied, we normally find that there are parts missing or wrong quantities. The root cause was the BOMs were not correct when transferred to the supplier. Changes to the BOM, such as typos and incorrect quantities or duplicates with different part numbers, occurred over time, which were never documented or corrected. The next problem is the drawing package. Suppliers would furnish us with the parts which met the specification but didn't work in the units. Once again, changes made over time on the manufacturing floor were either red lined or never updated or the drawing revision levels given to the supplier were not correct.

At Company X, they found out their kitting supplier had a more advanced drawing revision than even Company X had on file. It came from an engineer who hadn't updated the BOM. The other problem is the logistics associated with the process as it takes a full-time person to coordinate the supplier kitting. Once the kit comes in, we need to receive it, inspect it, and then issue it to the floor.

On the other hand, Kanbans are significantly easier to manage because they eliminate both the internal and external kitting processes. The operator simply picks up the parts in the order needed and assembles the product. The empty bins are then replenished by the supplier. Basically, the kitting is done via POU because the materials are laid out in the order they are used. Lean lines also allow the operator to continue walking and working versus having to get parts. There is no removal of packaging, no sorting of the parts, or searching or checking to make sure the kit is correct.

A Materials Case Study

At Environmental Technologies Group (ETG), starting in June of 1999 (see Figure 3.5), we worked for several years to implement Lean across multiple lines. We started the two-bin system for the line and the lineside warehouse with POU materials on the first pilot line freeing up several racks of shelves in the stockroom. The more lines we implemented, the more the stockroom shrunk. By

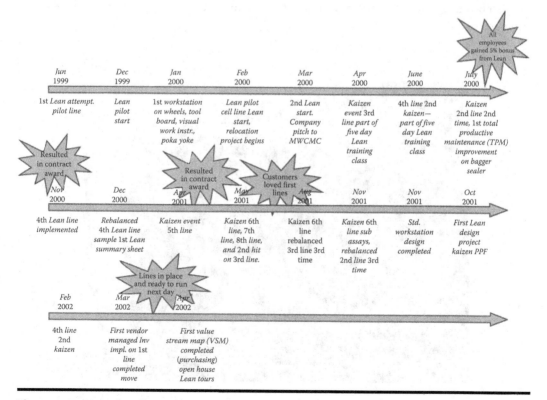

Figure 3.5   Lean time line example.

the end of 2002, we were able to completely eliminate the need for a stockroom. There were no walls and no fences. By 2003, VMI was in place for all "C" items along with two-bin Kanbans for all the lineside and material warehouse parts. On one of the lines, when they switched to VMI, they found they had enough hardware in house to last two years. The supplier took it back, gave them a credit, and then reissued it as needed. Inventory turns were approaching 60 turns per year (from less than 4) with most of the parts going directly to the lines. A certified supplier program was initiated and instrumental in reducing the need for incoming inspection and allowed critical material to go to the lines once it was received. Their Lean practitioners had eliminated virtually all the material packaging coming into the plant. Packing was now done at the end of the Lean line and the shipping department only had to move the box to the dock and enter it into the system. This eliminated most of the reliance on and most of the water spiders. The union even worked with the company to modify and eliminate many of the job classifications. Every employee received a yearly incentive bonus based on overall company profitability and taught all the employees open-book management. No one was laid off! Employees were retrained and redeployed as necessary increasing their marketability (provided professional employee development) as well. Employees that retired or left were not replaced.

Every line was made with catalog bought workstations (see Figure 3.6), which were modified in-house to add wheels for flexibility and ease of movement with daisy-chained electric connections. The lines included tabletop two-bin Kanban storage racks with colored clips used as replenishing signals, 5S tool holders, rightsized equipment and tools, visual assembly aids, and visual subassembly WIP. VMI was stored lineside for Kanban replenishment by the water spiders and was billed monthly by its VMI suppliers. Tools were available on the line in a location easy to reach by the operators. Standard work was attached to each workstation, utilizing a number of photographs.

Figure 3.6 Flexible workstation design.

In late 2002, we had to move the factory from one county to another approximately 30 mi away. We were able to move the entire factory in 8 hours with essentially one lost day of production as the move occurred over the weekend, shutting down at the end of Thursday and up and running on Monday. The wheeled workstations and line flow configurations were a major factor, which was attributed to easily relocating the production lines. The workbenches were wrapped, wheeled onto the moving truck, and then wheeled off at the new plant. Company X had resided on 4.2 ac comprising six different buildings. The six buildings comprised approximately 359,000 ft². The new facility was a total of 86,000 ft² and had 9,600 ft² of space available (unused) at move in time. The average office in the old building was 144 ft², with two visitor chairs and three four-drawer file cabinets. In the new facility, the average office was 80 ft² and set up within a bullpen of four. Most of the office walls were removed in the new facility. Each office (cubical) had one two-drawer rollaway file cabinet, and there was a meeting table for up to six persons within each bullpen area.

For the years, the Lean lines were in place and stockroom eliminated; we had no issues with missing inventory, tools, or equipment and were billed monthly by the VMI suppliers. Quality, cost, delivery, safety, and morale were high, continuous improvement was embraced by all employees, and life was good. In July of 2000, employees received their first bonus (5%), and yes, this was in a union plant, and additional salary increases for union employees could occur if certain Lean training modules were taken and completed successfully. On one line, after Lean was implemented, the company made so much additional profit that it had to refund the government $500,000.

Then in 2007, management turned over and they hired a new director of operations. The director of operations couldn't believe we had all this material on the lines with no accountability. We explained the supervisors were accountable for the inventory on the lines. This was not good enough for the new director of operations as they wanted total control over the inventory. The new director of operations resurrected the cage for the stockroom. It started out small and over a couple of years grew even beyond where it was when we started. During this transition, the company quickly reversed course on its Lean journey and reverted back to the old ways.

Now that there was a stockroom, they went back to kitting parts. Just makes sense, right? Kits were put on carts, which were rolled to the work cells. The stockroom attendants who delivered the parts refused to stock the line because it wasn't their job. So, the operators then had to stop their work, go to the carts, sort out their parts, put them on the line where they belonged, etc. "The bigger the back log … the bigger the rush to get it through."

The interesting part is their inventory variances continued to grow even though now the CFO had total control over all the parts. They also suffered from lost, misplaced, and stolen material, which again was the opposite result from what the total control was supposed to enforce. Back when the material was on the line, it was visible and accounted for by the supervisor and the folks that worked on the line. Over time and with new supervisors, they started to consolidate the parts in the workstations. Since there was no longer any Lean training, it didn't make sense to have more than one set of bins for a part. So, they started combining the parts and changing the workstation layouts.

Then someone suggested it would be much more efficient if they just started batching the sub-assemblies since the carts didn't come in complete sets any longer. The conventional wisdom of it being more efficient to pre-build always wins out. So over time, product flow was lost, the operator piece was lost, standard work was lost, and the stockroom continued to grow. As a result, costs went up and they started losing new proposals. The interesting part is their inventory variances continued to grow so much for "total control" over all the parts.

They stopped using their visual management systems. Actual touch labor hours per unit increased as the day-by-hour charts were abandoned. Whiteboards, which listed all program-specific production data, problems with due date and person responsible, and delivery dates with unit(s) status, were abandoned as well. Production data drifted back to being invisible and employees were no longer tapped for ideas. The bonus system was eliminated due to the reduction in profitability.

The time frame of beginning their Lean journey until the factory move described earlier was four years and then another two years of Lean advancements before accounting reversed everything. The managers driving Lean were released and replaced with managers from a factory the company was closing due to consolidation efforts. The fall from a Lean environment took place over four years (2007–2011) and was quite complete.

Then in 2011, the company had an audit performed over the entire global system[6]; the report was dismal, claiming if the company did nothing, they would not be able to continue in business longer than two years. A new global operations director was hired that had experience training in the Toyota manufacturing system and who ran General Motors factories globally. After a six-month evaluation, he systematically released all factory-level operation management and replaced them with people that had Lean training and would lead in that direction. Factory consolidations commenced and many people lost their jobs as he rightsized the factories to the level of the business. Since then, new Lean tools and controls have been rolled out. A business process development (BPD) board displaying all the company goals and objectives, which were tracked monthly for progress and problems, was implemented. The BPD board metrics were used to track progress and correct behavior and were reviewed globally each month during video calls. In many cases, accounts payable benefited because they returned to VMI suppliers that did a consolidated monthly billing. This meant, once again they only had to process one payment versus numerous invoices, which had to be matched up, etc. The stockroom still exists today but it has shrunk significantly.

Lesson Learned: Lean takes so much work to implement but can be undone so quickly! The process to implement Lean is often difficult, and without the vision and leadership needed to sustain Lean, the risk is that high levels of batching and non-Lean behavior will return. Leadership must embrace Lean and continuous improvement; otherwise, the Lean journey could be short-lived. One could postulate from this case study that the size of the stockroom can be correlated to some extent with where the company is on its Lean Maturity Path. It would be interesting to do a regression analysis across many companies to see what percent of the R^2 could be explained by the stockroom/size of the company versus their progress down the Lean Maturity Path.

PFEP (Plan for Every Part)

During a tour at Company X, we suggested modifications to a line. The immediate response was that it is impossible. We need room for all these parts. Our first question was "How many days' worth of parts does each bin hold right now?" They thought about it for a moment and said they really had no idea but probably at least a month. We said what if they only had a days' worth of parts? How big would the bins have to be? We freed up 20% of the space when we completed phase I of the Lean line implementation just by reducing the size of the raw material bin.

PFEP is an acronym for plan for every part. For an example of PFEP, see Table 3.1. This term was first coined in 2003 in the book Making Materials Flow[7]; however, the process has been used for a long time in the industry but never really had a name. The basic idea is to literally plan each

Table 3.1 PFEP Example

Item	Item_Status	Prod Line	Description	Make Buy	Stock on Hand	Cost Date	Frozen Cost	Date	List Price	Kmax	Kmin	Planned Type	Annual Usage	Daily Usage	Days on Hand
–23005	LADSCRUB	420	WASHER .140 ID .093T .312 OD	Buy		10/27/2010		10/27/2010	$-			MRP			
003002	Active	440	Bottom case 7pol.	Buy		10/31/2010	$3.07	10/31/2010	$10.50			MRP			
A01-15093	LADSCRUB	420	NC3, LABEL FOR CARTRIDGE DOOR	Buy		10/31/2010	$0.00	10/31/2010	$0.11			MRP			
A01-15160	Active	430	NC, DRIVE PINION GEAR, STEEL	Buy		10/31/2010	$24.21	10/31/2010	$72.81			MRP			
A01-15368	Active	430	TIMING BELT PULLEY, 24 × L037	Buy	439	10/31/2010	$8.76	10/31/2010	$29.00	81.20	44.20	Kanban	10234	40.936	10.72
A01-15369	Active	430	TIMING BELT PULLEY, 30 × L037	Buy	8	10/31/2010	$16.97	10/31/2010	$57.83			MRP			
A01-16098	LADSCRUB	420	STOP, DOOR NC5	Buy		10/31/2010	$11.56	10/31/2010	$48.94			MRP			
A01-16109	LADSCRUB	420	FISHPAPER, FAN HOUSING, NC5	Buy		10/27/2010		10/27/2010	$10.22			MRP			
A01-16164	LADSCRUB	430	COUPLING ENCODER TO RESOLVER	Buy		10/31/2010	$45.80	10/31/2010	$143.97			MRP			
A01-16357	Active	430	TIMING BELT PULLEY, 20 × L037	Buy	1000	10/31/2010	$10.08	10/31/2010	$23.00	71.45	39.45	Kanban	14256	57.024	17.54

(Continued)

Table 3.1 (Continued)   PFEP Example

Item	Item_Status	Prod Line	Description	Make Buy	Stock on Hand	Cost Date	Frozen Cost	Date	List Price	Kmax	Kmin	Planned Type	Annual Usage	Daily Usage	Days on Hand
A01-16361	Active	430	TIMING BELT PULLEY, 28 × L037	Buy	3456	10/31/2010	$10.33	10/31/2010	$31.00	81.20	44.20	Kanban	12345	49.38	69.99
A01-16362	Active	430	TIMING BELT PULLEY, 30 × L037	Buy	0	10/31/2010	$10.74	10/31/2010	$29.00	74.39	41.39	Kanban	17342	69.368	-
A01-16456	LADSCRUB	430	GEAR, SPUR, 36TEETH, 14.5PA, 24DP,	Buy		10/31/2010	$169.04	10/31/2010	$415.44			MRP			
A01-16514	LADSCRUB	420	ADAPTER PLATE, BURNY 2.5 TO	Buy		10/31/2010	$6.76	10/31/2010	$57.04			MRP			
A01-21755	Active	420	INSULATOR FOR RS232/422	Buy		10/27/2010		10/27/2010	$9.93			MRP			
A01-21961	LADSCRUB	450	BOOT, VINYL .75 × 1.25 × 1.00	Buy	345	10/31/2010	$0.33	10/31/2010	$1.82	74.39	41.39	Kanban	12345	49.38	6.99
A01-22150	LADSCRUB	450	GASKET, 1000 SER. TRANSFORMER	Buy		10/31/2010	$0.91	10/31/2010	$4.31			MRP			
A01-22188	Active	450	BOOT, 1.610 DIA × 1.25 BLACK	Buy	58	10/31/2010	$0.30	10/31/2010	$1.54	32.14	17.14	Kanban	13489	53.956	1.07
A01-22189	LADSCRUB	450	BOOT, .675 × 1.00 × 1.00 BLACK	Buy		10/31/2010	$0.13	10/31/2010	$0.66			MRP			
A01-22190	LADSCRUB	450	BOOT, .75 × 1.25 × 1.75, .30 WALL,	Buy		10/31/2010	$0.35	10/31/2010	$2.10			MRP			

Source: BIG Archives.

part in terms of usage, locations, replenishment quantities, container sizes, and supplier information, and in many companies, we add how the part is planned if it is in MRP. We only utilize the data necessary for the implementation. The vision for the PFEP is to create a pull system from the customer through the supply chain where we have the following:

- Level loaded demand
- All parts vendor managed and at POU
- Shop floor control system removed from MRP
- All material triggers come from Kanban

There will always be some parts that do not fit this vision and still have to be managed by MRP. The PFEP requires us to literally look at each part to determine the triggering strategy whether it be

- Kanban
- MRP
- Min-max/Reorder point
- Other

It is about getting all the information about each part in one spreadsheet. In the past, a multitude of screens or reports had to be run to glean the same data we now have in one row on the PFEP.

The PFEP can be created with pencil and paper but is easier to manipulate in an Excel spreadsheet. The PFEP involves literally listing every single part used in the process or area utilizing information from various databases in the MRP system, so the user has at one glance the status of any part. The PFEP provides a mechanism to track and determine the parts needed, the current demand, and the current state inventory information. We need to know where they are located, how many will be replenished, and a buffer plan to ensure that supplies will be available to meet peak demand.

Author's Note: Peak demand is extremely important to consider especially if your sales teams have promotions or large lot discounts, etc., all the things that get in the way of level loading. Our experience is that it is better to err on the side of too much inventory in the beginning and then to wean yourself off it rather than trying to cut the turns so low that you run out. If the Kanban runs out, the "I told you so's" will surface and the effort may fail. Until you can get rid of the peaks, you must consider them in the demand and Kanban sizing.

Each part is reviewed to determine the last 50 weeks of usage history (or better yet the next 50 weeks of forecasted usage) along with the lead time, average daily usage, days of supply on hand, safety stock, and appropriate Kanban sizes. The large spreadsheet is dynamic and needs to be maintained at the appropriate frequency because the volume or mix of models can change, thereby impacting the minimum, maximum, and reorder quantity levels. The manager or supervisor should have the final approval on the minimum, maximum, and reorder quantities.

The quantity at the workstation at the right place is generally based on the demand for the supply, how long it takes to replenish it, supplier minimum ordering size, supplier quality issues, and demand or coefficient of variation (CV). We create a beta or risk factor associated with the supplier's ability to consistently resupply the part. We generally add a small buffer of supplies called safety stock to cover this risk (see Figure 3.7).

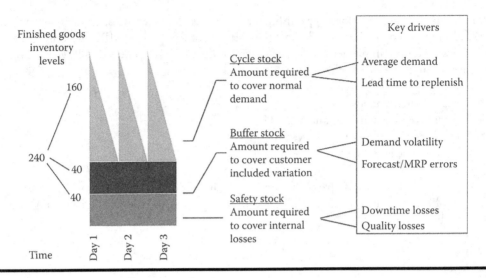

Figure 3.7 Finished goods inventory levels.

Initial replenishment of parts can be performed at time intervals from another location such as a stockroom. Each product line should determine the inventory of supplies on hand and how much they use based upon their demand (daily). In addition, for each part number, they should understand the replenishment process from the supplier, including how it is supplied to them (i.e., by box and the number in the box). The supervisor should also understand the lead time to obtain additional supplies. The supplier information will impact how many of each type of part is needed in the material warehouse next to the line or within the department.

The number of supplies, bins, and containers and the size of the equipment will all impact the layout. We need to make the bins or containers rightsized with the parts sized to the demand. If the containers or bins are too large, the tendency will be to overstock the bins. This can lead to organizational cash flow issues with money tied up in excess inventory. In addition, overordering and overstocking raise the potential to purchase supplies, which could expire.

PFEP is very time-consuming but so worth the effort. One can have IT set it up to feed monthly or more frequently by MRP system. We utilize the PFEP to integrate the Kanban information for each line as well as highlight where adjustments are required due to changes at the master schedule level or customer demand. It is important to have an owner assigned to the PFEP updating process to ensure the Kanban sizes are adjusted based on changes in mix or demand.

The goals/benefits of the PFEP are to:

■ Decrease lead times by 80% or more
■ Decrease inventory throughout the plant and increase turns
■ Free up cash but can impact short-term profitability
■ Free up warehouse space
■ Reduce purchasing labor (could increase short-term sourcing labor)
■ Treat suppliers as partners
■ Suppliers participate on kaizen teams with us
■ Eliminate any chance of rusted parts in the shop

Functional PFEP Roles

- Sales: Eventually the PFEP can be used to help forecast finished goods. Sales should own all finished goods inventory turns. Sales also helps with scrubbing data in the PFEP, works to standardize parts, helps us level load demand, and helps to create joint customer, company, and supplier value stream maps. Sales provides voice of the customer—immediate feedback to shop floor and suppliers, works to develop customer VMIs and supports supplier cost reductions.
- Logistics: Manages incoming deliveries, water spiders, and suppliers.
- Sourcing: Negotiates LTAs with Lean and productivity targets and incentives and removes triggers from MRP.
- Finance: Needs help to scrub data in PFEP, defines ABC codes, sets up monthly supplier billing, expenses as many parts as possible (normally all C's and some B's), and implements audit controls for suppliers.
- Production: Follows PFEP procedures.
- IT: Supports system changes for coding parts from assets to floor stock (expense parts), flattening BOMs, supplies help to scrub data in PFEP, develops data tool necessary to feed PFEP spreadsheet, helps with a way to forecast demand, and turn it into average future daily demand. In the future, IT helps us with electronic Kanbans/electronic data interchange with suppliers/Internet-based Kanban systems, developing triggering systems to suppliers, and help with supplier cost reductions. Initially they may have to find computers with enough horsepower to work on the large spreadsheets if there are thousands of parts.
- Supplier quality: Helps with transitioning suppliers to and certifying partnering suppliers as dock to floor, helps suppliers get Lean and ensures adequate process capabilities are in place, helps with supplier report cards (which should eventually become unnecessary), works with sourcing to dual source components, conducts vendor Lean audits, conducts root cause corrective action as needed, and helps with supplier cost reductions.
- Production quality: Ensures in-process quality controls are at or exceed expectation and control plans are in place.

Author's Note: Do not let the sheer number of parts keep you from creating the PFEP. It takes time to work through, but many times, formulas can be developed to help determine which parts lend themselves to Kanban. However, regardless of your formulas, at some point, you still have to review each individual part to make sure it is planned properly. We have done PFEPs with over 85,000 parts.

Rules for Kanban Parts

Our rule is, as long as a part repeats at some frequency and is not targeted for obsolescence, it can be considered a candidate for Kanban. Every company is different and every company has different rules for determining Kanban parts. Some companies use the CV where the CV must be less than 2 or 1. Obviously, the lower the CV, the better candidate the part is, but even if a part repeats quarterly, you are still at four turns with the Kanban, which in most companies is higher than they are today. Our recommendation is to start small with a pilot supplier and parts. Work up the procedures, etc. Below is an actual pilot plan:

1. Finance to review parts chosen for Kanban.
2. Label bins for pilots with different color labels.

3. Start the two-bin Kanban pilot with the local supplier:
   a. Document the new procedures.
   b. Call the supplier in for a meeting to review and agree to the procedure.
   c. Make any necessary changes to the procedure.
   d. Start the pilot.
   e. Record and fix problems as they arise.
   f. Make any necessary changes to the procedure (standard work).
   g. Look into future bar coding strategy and transmission to suppliers electronically.
   h. Develop lessons learned as you go.
4. Identify the next five local supplier candidates.

Consigned Inventory

This inventory is located in the manufacturer's or customer's facility but is still owned by the supplier. Sometimes the inventory is owned by the customer but in their supplier's plant, normally fenced in. This inventory can also be tied into flex fence management.

Vendor-Managed Inventory

This inventory is located in the manufacturer or customer's facility but still owned by the supplier or manufacturer, respectively. The difference between this and consigned inventory is this inventory is physically managed by the supplier. There is normally one invoice per month, and usage is determined by breaking a bag, resupply of a Kanban bin, or another agreed to signal.

In the VMI system, the vendor, external or internal (such as a machine shop), will totally manage your inventory to include filling the bins or breadman requirements as needed, typically daily or weekly. Most vendors supply parts in plastic bags. The customer does not pay for these parts until the seal on the bag is broken. Most suppliers will turnkey the operation, including supplying bins and bar coding the bins. VMI systems can decrease your overall costs.

Materials and Tool Presentation to the Operators

Gilbreth said, "Time is a shadow of motion."[8] This should be our guiding rule when working with operators to improve their assembly capabilities. Motion is directly correlated to time. The less motions the operator has to perform on the assembly, the quicker it will go together and the easier it will be for the operator to assemble it, which also supports the mistake-proofing process by standardizing the work. We can't standardize the work until every part and tool is exactly in the proper location every cycle.

Gilbreth revised the traditional presentation of bricks (see Figure 3.8) and cement to his workers and created standard-size pallets of bricks (like raw material for machining or parts in assembly) and organized the material presentation (see Figure 3.9).

Good operators will show you through observation firsthand or on video where they need their parts and tools. If the operator incurs excess reaching for parts, we need to move the parts closer. If they are putting the parts down next to them, we need to move the parts closer. Our objective is to have them pick up the part and place it immediately in the unit. Anything short of this is not acceptable, wastes time, and causes operator fatigue. Common bins of parts should repeat as necessary down the line to ensure the operator develops a routine walk pattern and further develops a

Figure 3.8   Brick presentation early 1900s.

Figure 3.9   Brick presentation after.

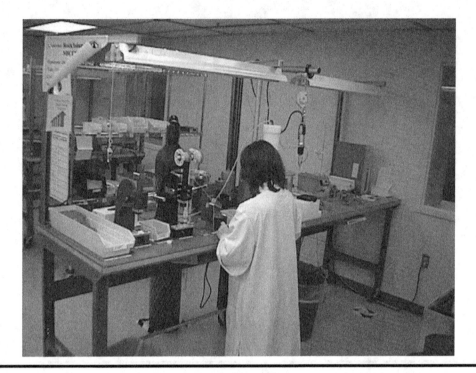

Figure 3.10   ETG cell design with tool balancers and parts and tools at POU.

rhythm. Containers or bins should be sized such that parts can be obtained with either the entire hand or the first two fingers. Normally screws should be picked up one at a time. It generally takes more time to grab a handful of screws, orient them, and try to position them to put the first one in the unit than to pick up one screw and place it on the unit. There are few exceptions to this where individuals have an unusual amount of dexterity and can do it faster.

At Toyota, as part of team members' initial orientation, if they are handling screws, bolts, nuts, clips, etc., they are trained by key trainers who will teach them the knack required to pick or orient the parts properly to make the installation of it easier.

The best way to determine the most efficient method is to video both processes. The tools should be hung with proper orientation on balancers (see Figure 3.10) or immediately available in the proper position to minimize motions.

Supplies Needed and Placement

The supplies needed to perform a task and the placement of the supplies is determined by videoing and observing operators performing their task. A good operator will show us how to design their workstation. Then during the video analysis, we hold discussions to determine why each part is used, what it is, and how it is used. Is it used daily or less frequently? We ask how and how often it is replenished. The quantity needed may impact the location and/or timing of the replenishment of the supplies. There should be an agreement across all parties that share the workspace as to the locations and quantity required. All shifts should have input to the workstation layout and design. Since many workspaces are personalized even though they are shared, there may be some resistance but this is normal. In addition, there are techniques utilized in Lean to help sustain workstation design such as labeling and outlining where supplies and equipment should be located to provide visual cues when equipment is misplaced. This was discussed earlier in the book. Supplies that are needed all the time should be at POU. Supplies needed once a day can be further away and supplies used once a week or month further away.

Never Enough Space: Mezzanines

This company in South Baltimore had so much inventory that they ran out of floor space. So, they only had one place to go—up. They installed 14 mezzanine units across the plant and filled them with inventory (see Figure 3.11). They shut down the plant once a quarter to do a physical inventory and counted all the parts in the mezzanines. The problem was when an operator needed a part, even if they could see it, no one ever felt like climbing up in the mezzanines to get the part or see what was up there. Over time, many of the parts became obsolete; however, they still counted them! As we implemented Lean, all but one of the mezzanines (the team started calling them "mezaleans" as a joke) was eliminated. The one that wasn't held a functioning motor used for a machine located underneath. Think of the waste incurred first

Figure 3.11 Mezzanines with inventory and smiley faces.

by having the inventory stored up there, the inventory having birthdays each year, and then shutting down the factory four times a year to count it. Things were so bad prior to Lean that when they brought in purchasing agents from Ford Motor Company for a plant tour to secure a $2 million order, they lost it because the factory was such a mess. But in their eyes, that's how it has always been done.

Materials Phases

As a company transitions from batch to the Lean, materials replenishment systems go through phases:

1. Supplier to stockroom and stockroom kits to floor or assembly bays; operators obtain parts from kits and put in line, and operators use parts to assemble. They may have some consigned inventory.
2. From the stockroom, it moves to material warehouses on the floor; water spider stocks from material warehouse to lineside location; Kanbans are established on floor and line; and consigned inventory and VMI begin.
3. Supplier stocks material warehouse on floor and water spider stocks from warehouse to lineside.
4. Supplier stocks to lineside and VMI, water spider moves to new role, and lineside inventory is minimized from day(s) to hours.

ABC Classification

Parts can be classified into various types, which is called ABC stratification. Companies have different definitions of what ABC should stand for. Since driving out excess inventory is a major goal of Lean (not for cash flow reasons but for exposing problems in the system), it is important to understand the consumption of inventory usage to manage and improve inventory turns. Experience has proven over and again that the Pareto rule applies to parts classification. We have found that typically 20% of your parts account for 80% of inventory dollars, usage, and suppliers. By examining and understanding this distribution, we can implement phased-in strategies to manage and lower our inventory costs.

ABC analysis can be performed using either dollars or usage as a criterion or a combination. We normally build both usage and dollar analysis into the PFEP. Parts are generally classified in two ways: either by individual part dollar value or overall part usage by volume or by total dollar value. The difference is listed as follows:

1. By price
   a. "A" parts are any part over $1,000 per piece.
   b. "B" parts are any parts that range between $25 and $99.99.
   c. "C" parts are any parts below $25.
2. By volume
   a. "A" parts are any individual parts that constitute 70% of our volume.
   b. "B" parts are any individual parts that constitute 20% of our volume.
   c. "C" parts are any individual parts that constitute the last 10% of our volume.

3. By total price
   a. "A" parts are any individual parts that constitute 70% of our dollars.
   b. "B" parts are any individual parts that constitute 20% of our dollars.
   c. "C" parts are any individual parts that constitute the last 10% of our dollars.
4. Some companies use "D" parts, which are generally very low-cost hardware-type items.

These can provide very different looks at your part stratification and management thereof. In the first example, we are looking at the individual part unit price. This strategy works well to manage your most expensive parts and the overall dollar value of inventory. The second looks at parts that make up your total volume and the third looks at parts that make up your total dollars. The differences in these strategies emerge when you review a very low dollar part (perhaps a $1 each) with a very high volume. In the first classification earlier, it would fall into the "C" parts category. In the second classification, it would fall into the "A" parts category, and in the third classification, it may fall into the "B" parts category. The strategies and percentages are determined by each individual company. Prior to ABC analysis, we find most companies rarely review part types; however, there is a drive to lower their inventories. Finance normally wants to account for every single part regardless of cost or volume, which creates extra work for minimal, if any, return.

In general, the first stratification is preferred. We start out managing "A" parts down to the week with a goal to manage them down to the day or hour. This is easy to do as there are relatively few parts and suppliers. We start managing "B" parts for two weeks with a goal to move toward one week and then days (and eventually hours). We like to look at "C" parts as parts initially at the one-month level and move toward weeks, and then days. If you are using the second or third stratification, it tends to skew the parts, and you can end up managing parts literally less than a penny where the cost to manage easily outweighs the benefits.

We then work toward moving the "C" parts from capital to expense, which removes the "C" parts from MRP pick lists and treats them as floor stock or expense parts. The parts still appear on the router. The "C" parts are normally screws, fasteners, wire connectors, etc., and are prime candidates for breadman and later material warehouse or lineside VMI. Once off MRP, it is important to continue to manage these parts internally by using VMI or a Kanban system.

Breadman Systems

Breadman is a term normally applied to parts consigned or vendor managed and centralized in one or several locations within the plant and taken to the lines by operators, supervisors, or material handlers. They are a good first-time pilot for beginning to convert the finance system thinking from capitalizing everything to expensing the parts. It is still important to have financial auditing systems in place for consigned inventory or VMI with a rigorous check and balance system on the suppliers. We have found that some suppliers will try to leave more inventories at the end of the month to make their quota and will even leave extra boxes of parts in addition to filling up the bins.

MRP/ERP Systems

MRP and ERP systems can interfere with Kanban implementations. For some reasons, companies tell us they want to live or die by the system, and, unfortunately, most tend to die by the system unless you are truly a class A user. However, keep in mind, if someone scraps a part but doesn't put it in the MRP system, it (MRP) still thinks it has the part so it doesn't trigger the reorder quantity. This is an overarching problem with MRP systems, which often results in running out of the parts you need and having too many of the parts you don't need. MRP systems cannot plan for the day or hour unless they are real time. It is their lead time offsets that are their Achilles heel when trying to support Lean. There are ways (and books written) that show how to merge Lean and MRP, and these are not bad strategies especially if you are in a very low-volume, high-mix business where 80% of the parts do not repeat. We are not proposing companies eliminate MRP entirely. We still need MRP for the BOM, parts lists, supplier forecasting, to manage non-Kanban parts, etc.

Some companies will try to use Kanban and MRP together in the beginning. We support this approach, if we have to, but now the company has to manage two systems. What companies find is the Kanban bin almost always triggers before MRP. If they continue to let MRP trigger, we find the lead time offsets are so bad that they normally end up with a bunch of excess materials on the floor.

Class A MRP Systems[9]

Class "A" performance in a business resource management program is based on meeting 50 measurement criteria (see Figure 3.12) that are composed of operational and behavioral measurements. Behavioral metrics deal with doing the right things, while operational measurements assess doing things right. If you are not a class A MRP or ERP user, you will always incur part shortages.

CLASS "A" BUSINESS RESOURCE MANAGEMENT CHECKLIST
1. Documented Business Plans are communicated throughout the organization
2. Sales Forecasts relate to meaningful manufacturing groups.
3. Sales Forecasts are updated by Sales prior to the Sales And Operations Planning Meeting.
4. Sales Forecast Horizons permit Capacity Planning beyond aggregate lead-time.
5. Sales Forecast Quantities are realistic.
6. Sales And Operations Planning is accomplished monthly with senior management from Engineering, Finance, Manufacturing, Materials and Sales.
7. Product Family Sales and Operations Plans support Master Schedule function,
8. Product Discontinuance Reviews are held to minimize obsolete inventory.
9. Master Production Schedules are re-planned at least weekly.
10. Master Production Schedule Quantities tie back to the Sales And Operations plan,
11. Master Schedules are not overloaded.
12. Master Schedule Demand and Planning time fences are honored.
13. Rough Cut Capacity Planning is part of the Master Scheduling process.
14. Material Requirements Planning information is used by Planners and Buyers for Material Scheduling.
15. Work Center Capacity is planned using date affectivity.
16. Schedules which can be produced are released to Manufacturing.
17. Daily Shop Schedules have accurate priorities.
18. Capacity Planning uses current Routings.
19. Outside Suppliers are included in the Capacity Planning process.
20. Low Performance business metrics have documented recovery plans.
21 Slow Moving and Obsolete inventory is regularly dispositioned.

22. Product/Process Rationalization is performed.
23. Safety Stocks are minimized or eliminated
24. Supplier Rating Systems are in place.
25. Cycle Counting has replaced Annual Physical Inventory.
26. Back Scheduling is used to schedule routed operations.
27. Business Management Groups operate as a team.
28. Facility appears CLASS "A"!
29. One Official Bill Of Material exists for active products.
30. Bills Of Material are maintained by an Engineering Change Control system.
31. Item Master planning data is reviewed at least semi-annually.
32. Return On Assets is 90% of planned R.O.A
33. Sales are 90% of Sales Forecast.
34. Production is 95% of Production Planned.
35. Units Completed are 95%of units scheduled.
36. Schedules released on time are 95% of schedules released.
37. Hours Completed are 95% of hours scheduled.
38. Bills of Material are 98% accurate of Bills audited.
39. Inventory location balances are 95% accurate of locations counted.
40. Routings are 98% accurate of Routings audited.
41. Supplier Schedules received on time are 95% of Schedules due.
42. Shop Schedules completed on time are 95%of Schedules due.
43. Customer Schedules completed on time are 95% of Schedules due.
44. Customer Schedules processed on time are 95% of Schedules received.
45. Top management has approved complete business management policies.
46. Procedure Manuals have been developed for all implemented business management modules.
47. Procedures are reviewed at least semiannually.
48. Users follow procedures.
49. Education and Training programs are in place.
50. Participation in relevant Professional Organizations is encouraged and supported

Figure 3.12   MRP class A requirements.

Electronic Kanban Systems

Min/Max: Replenishment Pull

Min/max is a system available on Oracle MRP software. Once a part is planned as min/max, the system will manage the part for you. When the system shows the min level is reached, it will automatically order the planned replenishment quantity. There are several issues with the system. In our PFEP, we include columns for min, max, and reorder quantity; thus, for example, if we have part A with a min of 25, max of 50, and reorder quantity of 25:

> In a true Kanban system, we would trigger the reorder with the first empty bin of 25. We then will cut into the second bin of 25 until the parts are replenished; thus, our max would never go over 50.
> The min/max system has characteristics which must be understood. As soon as the quantity drops below the max, it will trigger a reorder quantity to reach back to the max. So, if your quantity drops to 40, it will order 10. Makes sense, right? However, because it doesn't trigger at the min, your inventory doesn't average 25 pieces anymore. You now average closer to 50 since it keeps driving the inventory toward the max.
> If you have a minimum lot size requirement of 25 pieces, the min/max system will drive you to more than 50. So, when you hit 40 (below 50), it triggers the reorder of the minimum lot size, so now if you don't use any more parts and the new lot comes in, you have 65 pieces! So, the new max quantity is really 49 + 25 or 74 pieces.

Lesson Learned: Kanban is a powerful method for material management. Rarely do plants using Kanban run out of parts. There is evidence that plants using Kanban systems will have overall lower total material costs (including labor and overhead to manage the material).

Internet-Based Systems: Nocturne[10]

Nocturne™ is an example of a software program that optimizes the supply chain management process by enabling the effective management of costly inventories and vital production and shipping functions. Nocturne™ is a proven Internet-based system designed to easily integrate with an existing ERP or inventory control system. Nocturne™ delivers a proven and significant return on investment (ROI) with a typical user reducing costly parts/supplies inventories in excess of 30% while delivering a corresponding increase in inventory turns. Nocturne™ is easy to implement and use and can be functional in a matter of days. Nocturne™ is currently being utilized by mid-to-large-size companies worldwide. Nocturne™ delivers an expanding list of system capabilities to include the following:

- Demand forecasting
- In-transit inventory tracking
- Supplier rating system

Scrap, Excess, and Obsolete

What is the value of your E&O? Do you wonder how we seem to always end up with so much? There are several root causes of E&O:

1. Batch production systems
2. The MRP system has the wrong data

3. The only person who knew why the inventory existed and its original purpose left the company
4. Engineering changes
5. Lack of phase-out transition plan for old parts
6. Technology changes forcing lifetime buyouts.
7. Machine shops or internal departments need to make internal quotas.
8. Parts misplaced or in a drawer or file cabinet.
9. Product discontinued.

The list is large and can almost always be summed up as the result of violating our number one waste—OVERPRODUCTION! Plans should be in place, independent of the system you utilize, to avoid excess inventory and obsolescence.

Expensing versus Capitalizing Parts

Our accounting friends like to capitalize everything. This forces us to track every part of the company, which can be a very expensive proposition. But these costs are hidden. Our goal with Lean is to move more parts to "expense" and manage them via Kanban versus in an MRP system. Once the parts are on or near the line, keeping track of them or even inventorying them every day is part of the Lean system. Because the system is designed to be visual and to minimize or eliminate counting, it is very easy to keep track of parts (see Figure 3.13). If parts disappear, there are normally three main reasons:

1. Someone borrowed the parts.
2. We are using more than the plan.
3. Someone is stealing them.

The first two causes should be managed internally as it is not unusual to set up a Lean line and have parts common to other lines disappear. If parts are walking out the door, this is a different problem and must be dealt with accordingly.

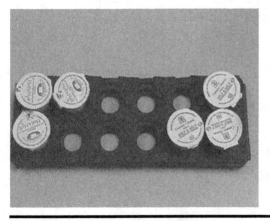

Figure 3.13 Visual systems that don't require counting.

Robbing Parts from the Lean Line

Each morning and throughout the day, at a plant near Columbia MD, mechanics used to wait in line at the stockroom to get their parts. We set up a Lean line with a two-bin Kanban system on the line and a two-bin system material warehouse next to the line. This eliminated the line at the stockroom. However, after a couple of days, we started hearing about parts disappearing on the line. It turns out the second shift was stealing them because the stockroom wasn't open on the second shift. The worst part was that they were taking the parts from the second bin; therefore, when the first bin emptied out, the second bin slid down and was also empty. The machine shop started complaining because they were only supposed to receive one bin at a time and were now receiving two bins at the same time and being rushed by the first shift supervisor because the Lean line was out of parts. There are two ways to handle this. Either we open the stockroom on the second shift or add more parts to the Kanbans on the Lean line and always pull from the first bin. We ended up adding parts to the line.

Recycling Containers

Using recyclable containers makes sense (see Figure 3.14) and is more than just friendly to the environment. The recycled containers eliminate all the packaging, which used to come with the

Figure 3.14 Kanban systems examples with recyclable containers.

parts, and allow for the containers to be used multiple times. Think of how much time and money is wasted each year, packaging up parts in bags, then small boxes, and then larger final shipping boxes. The receiving company also wastes time unpackaging the parts. Many times, the parts end up on the line in the plastic bags in which they were shipped. What does this do to efficiency? The first thing the operator must do is remove the parts from the bag and dispose of the bag. They will normally batch this task versus doing it in a one-piece flow, so the line shuts down. Then there is normally searching for a trash can and time to walk to throw away all the packaging. We once spent 4 man-hours unpacking just one order of 250 bearings for use on one product line at a plant in South Carolina.

All kinds of arguments will be heard as to why the parts have to remain in bags such as they are lubricated or will become contaminated. The key is to develop methods to remove all obstacles as there are covered recyclable containers that can be used. It is very rare we find an application where recyclable containers cannot be introduced. The money saved in labor time, Mother Nature's raw materials, as well as minimizing the impact on landfill capacity should make recyclable containers a primary goal of any purchasing department while embracing the green strategy of the companies. There are companies that now have zero landfill waste. Lean is green!

Chapter Questions

1. What is the difference between VMI and consigned inventory?
2. What are some advantages of recyclable containers? How are they green?
3. What impact do MRP systems have on initial Lean implementations?
4. What does POU mean?
5. What is a class A system?
6. What does it mean to have true partnering with suppliers?
7. What is a PFEP? Why is it useful?
8. Where should supplies be placed?
9. What is a breadman system?
10. Why is looking at peak demand important for Kanban sizing?
11. What is ABC analysis? Why is it used?
12. Is there a correlation between the amount of inventory in the plant and where they are on the Lean Maturity Path?

Notes

1. *World Class Manufacturing: The Next Decade*, Richard Schonberger, The Free Press, a division of Simon Schuster, 1996.
2. Results furnished by Jane Fitzpatrick.
3. Toyota suspends production due to fire, http://ask.elibrary.comlprintdoc.asp?querydocid=3100524@urn:bigchalk:US;Lib&dtype=O...8/2512002, Author not available, Toyota suspends production due to fire, Reuters, Business Report, January 3, 1997.
4. Contributed by Jane Fitzpatrick.
5. http://www.cisco-eagle.com/material-handling-systems/industrial-carousels/vertical_lift_modules
6. GMS—Global Manufacturing System—which is an exhaustive survey of Lean tools and principals audited by top management creating a baseline for each factory; no matter the starting score, each factory has been given 2 years to get to 85%. A plan was made and is tracked every 3 months at the factory site reviews.

7. Making Materials Flow.
8. *Motion Study*, Gilbreth, 1911.
9. *Alban Associates 10616 Beaver Dam Road*, Hunt Valley, MD 21030 (410) 771-3031.
10. https://www.healex.com/nocturne Nocturne is an example of an Internet-based system we discovered some years ago in use at some of our clients. This is not meant to be an advertisement for this company and no fees were received. It is merely a reference for the reader. There are other companies of this type.

Additional Readings

Japan Management Association 2002. Kanban for the Shop Floor. Portland, OR: Productivity Press.
Gale, B.T. 1994. Managing Customer Value. New York: The Free Press.
Harris, R. 2006. Making Materials Flow. Brookline, MA: Lean Enterprise Institute.

Chapter 4

Lean Materials: Strategic

> Inventory is a substitute for information: you buy them because you are not sure of the reliability of your supplier or the demand from your customer.
>
> **Michael Hammer**
> *The Economist, 2000*

In Lean, we recommend that materials organizations shift to a strategic materials focus (Figure 4.1). This requires the materials or operations organization to create a position that will look at the overall materials plan by commodity by program. A review is made of all materials (PFEP) across all programs or product lines in the site or sites. Again, the Pareto rule applies. All level "C" parts and maintenance, repair and operations (MRO) consumable items, which typically account for 80% of the parts and 20% of the dollars, are provided to suppliers on annual or multiple-year contracts who manage the inventory at the sites. These materials are expensed when received, and the costs are part of the material burden overhead. Suppliers are audited to ensure compliance, and companies do not pay for items until they are delivered or in some cases used. Some suppliers will manage the inventory for the company, and for others, replenishment is triggered by a fax, e-mail, Kanban container, Internet signal, or from the user via some type of visual control system.

Strategic materials manage type "A" and "B" items by commodity by program/product line. Annual or multiyear requirements are packaged, quoted, and negotiated with suppliers. If necessary, company-owned tooling may be moved to a new supplier. Pricing is negotiated with any tooling amortized into the individual unit price. Each supplier and site are provided a list of what parts were negotiated at what price with each supplier. These suppliers eventually become partnering suppliers.

The strategic materials group is responsible and accountable for managing the partnered suppliers. The strategic group is responsible to send the suppliers one-, three-, and six-month forecasts of upcoming requirements and negotiate flex fences to cover surges or decreases in demand.

One of the main goals is to reduce and localize the supply base. It is much easier to manage a small number of high-quality and value-oriented suppliers than a large number of mediocre suppliers. The closer the supplier facilities are to the plants, the easier it is to set up milk runs. Milk runs are named after the old-style milk delivery trucks where each truck has a route with

DOI: 10.4324/9781003185796-4

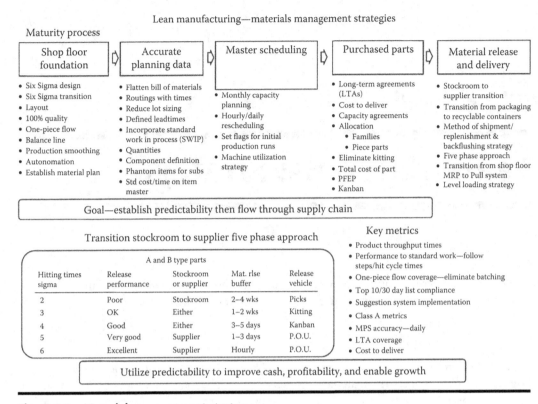

Figure 4.1 Materials management strategy.

designated number of stops within a certain time which is similar to school buses today except, they are dropping off empties and picking up full containers of parts versus school children. In some cases, where volume and profitability justify it, suppliers rent space next to a plant and set up a dedicated cell for just that supplier. Some automotive suppliers have partners in the building with them similar to a Starbucks® located in a hospital. At AlliedSignal (now Honeywell), electronics distributors were in the surface-mount technology (SMT) circuit board production area restocking SMT parts cartridges. Our suppliers at the time (in the 1990s prior to electronic data interchange [EDI]) placed their own orders on our material requirement planning (MRP) systems at a desk in our purchasing department.

The sites/plants are strongly encouraged to buy from the partnering suppliers. In some cases, partnered suppliers may need to be added to drawings or briefed on specific program requirements, or they may supply non-franchised parts. A common method to encourage interaction among the suppliers, engineers, and purchasing agents is to hold periodic conferences or calls to flow information. In the event, the site chooses to buy from a non-partnered supplier, the site is then responsible to manage that supplier.

In this scenario, the need for the typical buyer who receives MRP requisitions and negotiates and places requisitions all day long is virtually eliminated. In a Lean environment, replenishment requirements are now generated from the floor via Kanban. An empty bin is used in place of a MRP generated requisition. The empty bin triggers replenishment by an external supplier (internal consignment or external via email, text, or fax etc.) or by a withdrawal or production Kanban to an earlier process within the plant. If the bin is filled by a supplier, the quantity is deducted and credited to the long-term agreement (LTA) quantity. Today, there are companies such as Menlo Worldwide Logistics[1] that will manage your supply chain for you.

Buyers Assigned by Commodity versus Program: Which Strategy to Pick?

Those with material backgrounds know there has always been a struggle between commodity and program (value stream) buying.

Commodity Buying

When buying commodities, the buyer gains a certain amount of expertise within the industry main sources, brokers, delivery expectations, and amount of negotiation possible. The other advantage is that only one representative of the company contacts each supplier. However, if a buyer is behind in placing requisitions, the buyer can negatively affect every program in production. When incurring a problem, the floor doesn't know who to call, so they escalate the problem to manufacturing or operations management who calls the materials manager, who then communicates the problem to the proper buyer. In addition, the buyer never learns about the overall programs or product lines for which they are buying. They become a "specialist" where they tend to get pigeon holed in that commodity and it is difficult to get cross trained on other commodities. Back in my buyer days, I knew buyers who purchased the same commodities, that is, steel and metals their entire careers. This type of strategy also lends itself to more temptation to accept gifts, etc. when one is dealing with the same sales persons and companies their entire careers.

Program or Product Line Buying

When materials are changed to a program or product line focus, each buyer places all the orders for their program or is assigned to a product line or value stream. The buyer gains expertise in the buying requirements for each program. The buyer is forced to learn about each commodity as they proceed, so they become cross trained. The buyer is held to a budget for the overall program and can play a purchasing program management-type role as to the delivery of the material. The buyer becomes an expert in the needs of the program, is many times then co-located with that program, and can make suggestions that can save the program money. This type of organization is more aligned with Lean or value stream thinking. The Lean organization is aligned with the customer and can react to customer suggestions or complaints much quicker.

When the floor has any materials related problem, they now know who to call. This sets the stage for product teams within a company (Table 4.1). The negatives to this approach are it takes longer for the buyers to become experts in the commodities and they do not always have the necessary background to obtain the best pricing. You miss opportunities to package parts up for pricing that could be spread across different programs. You can also end up with ten buyers at a company calling the same supplier.

However, there are strategies to deal with all the drawbacks. It is possible to get the benefits of commodity purchasing while buying by product (value stream). For instance, you can assign each buyer as the main contact for your largest suppliers. You can also still assign commodity specialists (i.e., each program buyer learns one or two commodities) who can train and answer questions

Table 4.1 Materials Roles and Responsibilities Matrix

Tasks	Goal	Resources Required	Material MGT Policy Council	Model Business Team	Product Teams	Corp Commodity Team
		Material Strategies/Role Assignment				
LTA penetration	90%					
Aspire	$1.7M					
Cost take out	$3.3M					
Direct to floor	40%					
Pours set up	40%					
Supplier reduction	−35%					
Comins saving	$4.9M					
DOS reduction	60					
Inventory/ right level	4.1Turns					
PPM qual level	625					
On time delivery	95%					
Material floor	90%					
MPS performance	95%					
MOH reduction	6.80%					
Outsourcing	N/A					
Material availability	95%					
Cycletime reduction	25%					
Supplier certification	50					

Source: BIG Archives.

Legend: O, Owner; S, support; P, policy driver; 2L, secondary lead; I, Inform.

for the other buyers. We have much experience with companies that have converted to purchasing by value stream. It takes a lot of communication and hard work, but in the end, it works out best for the company and the customer. It's interesting, when you are a small business since there are normally only one or two buyers, they have to buy both by program and commodity, so it is a normal course of doing business.

Total Cost Materials Management

Strategic buyers review the total cost of material throughout the value stream, not just price variance or history. Total cost includes the cost of the raw material, operator labor, setup times, supplier inventory on hand, replenishment frequency, nonrecurring, ownership of tooling, overhead elimination, engineering support to the supplier, cost of receiving and inspection, defects and scrap in manufacturing, response time to engineering, recurring and nonrecurring tooling, shelf life, warranty, and the requirements imposed on the supplier's vendor. Strategic buyers or corporate commodity teams must remember the same part at one site may require additional selection (sorting) or testing criteria at another site as the design requirements might be different.

At Company X, there is an ongoing corporate-driven metric to reduce historical price variance. This metric is calculated by subtracting the current price paid for a component from the last price paid. We have found this to be a very dangerous metric for the following reasons:

■ It is a results-focused metric and encourages short-term solutions independent of what other departments are impacted. We have seen many times where reductions in price resulted in additional labor and frustration on the shop floor (which firms rarely measure!).
■ It generally is forced down to the supplier and discourages supplier partnering.
  – Note: There are other ways to encourage suppliers to work to increase their productivity and reduce their costs annually.
■ It can result in procuring substandard components that take longer to assemble.
■ It can result in changing suppliers and bringing in new parts that may meet the spec but do not work as well in the product.
■ The metric itself does not necessarily drive or reflect an overall strategy to meet the goal.

A better metric is to focus on reducing the number of components in an assembly or to reduce the overall cost of materials by a significant percentage.

Annual or Multiple-Year Contracts, Long-Term Agreements

Use of Commodity Teams

Commodity teams is a strategy that may be utilized in larger companies to consolidate the individual plant's purchasing requirements to obtain better pricing and supplier partnering. The commodity teams are responsible to manage their suppliers and work to value engineer their parts and help their suppliers with their Lean journey. Some companies have incorporated this approach into an overarching logistics strategy to purchase for other organizations.

Materials Implementation

It is not unusual for a site to resist the commodity team approach. Taking the best buyers from several sites and using them to form commodity teams is a normal approach to implementation of this strategy. It can take months to years to put this process into place depending on the size of the organization, existing supplier bases, and complexity of the purchased requirements.

This is a very difficult process to implement. The sites are required to submit all of their purchase requirements with drawing packages, any special test procedures, and existing suppliers to the commodity teams. The commodity teams are responsible for advising all existing suppliers of the new process, quotation of the items, and final negotiation and selection of the new suppliers. The sites should be continuously informed and involved as questions from existing suppliers arise. The commodity teams are responsible to survey each supplier prior to any awards and review their financial viability and physical capacity to handle the requirements. The delivery and quality history should be reviewed from each site for each vendor, and the vendor should initially receive a report card showing their performance.

When commodity teams are utilized, the plants manage their purchased requirements by program since the program versus commodity split is now at the top level. Each plant may have a strategic materials group (SMG) to handle local (or "off contract") parts. These are parts that are not given to the commodity teams. The SMG is now responsible for the local long-term agreements, supplier quality, and their continuous improvement goals. The traditional buyers move to the floor and become buyer/planner/schedulers who are now responsible for the PFEP input for their programs and ensuring the parts supply JIT (just in time). Any major quality problems are handed off to either the commodity team or SMG depending on whether it is a local or corporate LTA supplier. The strategic materials group (or commodity team(s)) is responsible to notify the supplier and site of the awards made to each supplier. In some organizations, IT is required to make this process seamless with the sites by structuring a database for both the corporate LTA and locally managed SMG LTA, including: parts, prices, suppliers, and supplier metrics. This database should link to existing sites, and processes should be put in place where site orders and forecasts can be automatically issued to partnering suppliers via EDI.

Negotiation

Many companies don't realize how important the skill of negotiation is for their bottom line. The push to meet MRP demands often places purchasing agents so far behind in their requirements they end up settling for a higher price to obtain the parts. These are hidden costs seldom tracked. Just asking the question "Is that your best price?" can typically yield some savings. At AAI (now Textron Systems) in Hunt Valley MD, we always had the last three prices paid on the bottom of the requisition. A higher price than history required a sign off and encouraged buyers to push to beat the history price. In a true supplier partnering arrangement, books are opened and target costs disclosed to provide a win-win relationship. Many times, buyers will negotiate a package price with a supplier only to be undone when someone finds they can purchase one of the parts cheaper somewhere else. However, this is the nature of the packaging arrangement. One can always cherry pick a better price, but the company then loses in the overall savings opportunity.

Lesson Learned: Negotiating to obtain the best price does not always outweigh dependability. The long-term total acquisition costs must be kept in mind when negotiating. It pays to send your materials people to negotiation classes and to give them targets to meet for both pricing, delivery and quality.

Long-Term Agreements

LTAs are annual or multiple-year contracts with suppliers. The goal is to lock in the best pricing with a long-term quantity and quality commitment but only take material as it is needed. LTA may have any of the following components:

- Can range from a year to five years.
- A fixed price is the norm; however, time and material contracts can work for some services but are a last resort.
- Some escalation factor built in, that is, price of precious metals pegged to an index.
- Continuous improvement requirements.
- Lean assessment components.
- Rebate if certain thresholds are met.
- Options for pricing for additional years.
- Flex fences.
- Shipping terms.

Flex Fences

Flex fences is a concept that provides flexibility to an LTA. Flex fences examine the overall horizon of the agreement and build in risk mitigation plans in the event the projected volume was to increase by 10%–30% or reduce by 10%–30%. For example, we may pay the supplier to keep extra raw materials on hand so we can increase our volume by 30% over a specified period of time. We may arrange with our supplier to have 10% of the material just about completed all the time in case our volume increases rapidly (see Figure 4.2).

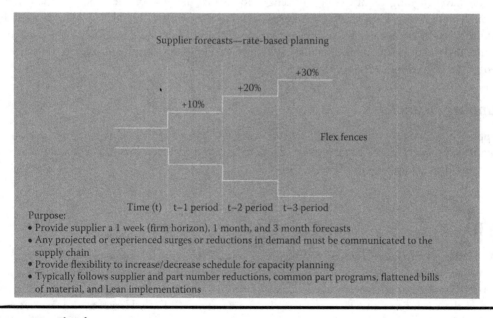

Figure 4.2 Flex fences.

Forecasts

Forecasts are a necessary component of any materials system. However, we always say an accurate forecast is an oxymoron. The problem with forecasts is the longer the forecast horizon, the less accurate it usually is. The goal of JIT is to reduce the cycle time to allow a forecast in days or weeks versus months.

Early Supplier Involvement

Engaging suppliers early in any of your Lean initiatives, with the goal to decrease inventory, can save significant dollars and should be a part of the overall materials cost-reduction strategies. Once suppliers are engaged and partnering with your facility, they should receive feedback (sometimes in the form of report cards) on their progress for quality, cost, delivery, and service (QCDS) improvements. Early supplier involvement (ESI) is also tied into 3P. This process involves the supplier very early on but generally after the concept phase. These suppliers are true partners working with design-to criteria with cost and value engineering targets set by their customer.

Supply Sequencing

Part of LTAs may involve sequencing of parts to fit the supplier's assembly line. This typically involves loading the parts in reverse order, so when they are offloaded, they are in the correct order. Supplier sequencing is generally supplied to the automotive industry where delivery is measured to the hour.

LTA Metrics and Enforcing Quality with Suppliers

LTAs should have built in quality requirements with the ultimate goal of zero defects. Suppliers should have ongoing requirements/challenges to reduce the cost of the product whether it is through design or taking waste out of their processes. Suppliers should have stipulations that require them to implement Lean sigma programs. Delivery should be on time to the customer's requirements, not to the supplier's ability to deliver. Service should be rated based on some agreed-upon criteria up front in the contract.

Supplier Financials

Supplier financials are an important part of any LTA. Most suppliers have a rating that can be obtained through Dun & Bradstreet or other credit rating agencies. It is important to make sure your suppliers are financially viable.

RFID[2]

The ability to track an item or specifically, a radio-frequency identification (RFID) tag, in free space, with very accurate location precision has traditionally been exclusive to the active RFID technologies. Ultra-wide band (UWB) and Wi-Fi systems are the most precise and common of these solutions known as real-time location systems (RTLS). However, in recent years, a small company[3] out of St. Louis, MO, has shown it is both possible and viable, from a business perspective, to track ultra-high frequency (UHF) passive RFID tags to within 18 in. in most environments. The company RF Controls has developed a system known as the intelligent tracking control system (ITCS). This system can locate and track UHF RFID tags within specific areas of coverage with high levels of location accuracy. An active phase array, called a signal acquisition source locator (SASL), provides the ITCS system easily accessible, real-time location information on tagged items. This technology can be directly applied to a loss prevention solution, which will track tagged items in a retail environment. The most effective loss prevention configuration with minimal cost uses a single SASL (Figure 4.3) installed directly above a doorway. ITCS processes information gained by the SASL and reports detailed locations and movements of UHF RFID tagged items, indicating any specific items leaving the store.

ITCS provides much more than just tag identification data. By installing ITCS smart antennas, you can illuminate an area (or volume) in which tagged items move or are stored and achieve real-time, perpetual monitoring of an area of interest.

For example, in a retail setting, you could install ITCS (Figure 4.4) back-of-store and thereby achieve knowledge of what items of inventory you have on hand and exactly where those items are presently located, leading to improved replenishment process efficiency.

Add to this the fact that ITCS keeps a time-sequenced record of the locations of tags (tagged items) as they are read, and you achieve the ability to track the movement of tagged items, automatically.

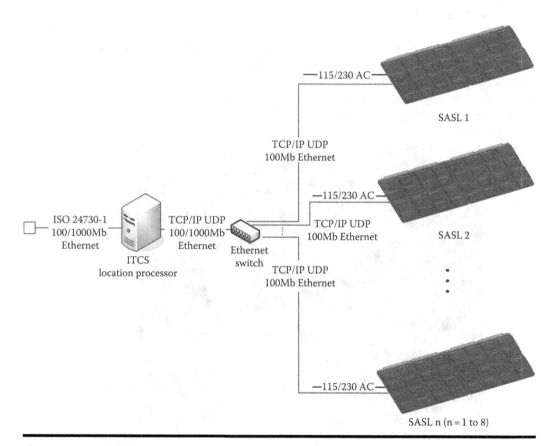

Figure 4.3   SASL RFID.

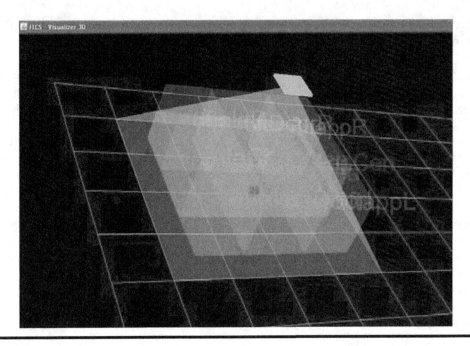

Figure 4.4   ITCS RFID.

The RFC SASL (Figure 4.5) smart antennas are at the core of ITCS, which are installed well off the ground and typically attached to building infrastructure out of harm's way. These antenna arrays leverage the same bidirectional electronically steerable phased array (BESPA) technology that is used by target acquisition systems and radar control systems; however, they have been modified to work with UHF RFID technology.

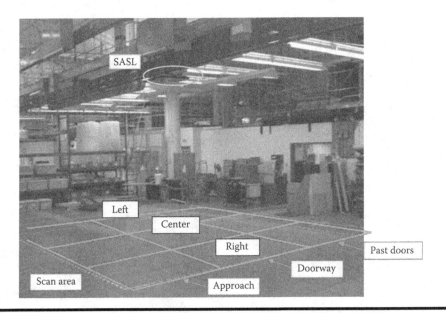

Figure 4.5   RFC SASL smart antennas are at the core of ITCS.

EDI

EDI and refers to the ability of supplier and customer computer systems to talk to each other. It eliminates the need for paper purchase orders or other paper-based transactions. EDI systems will allow the supplier to see the customer's part usage. There are also electronic and Internet-based Kanban systems available in the market today.

ISO 9000

There are many books written on ISO 9000, which, in a very simplified view, profess the following:

1. Say what you are going to do.
2. Do what you said you were going to do.

Despite what some may believe, ISO 9000 doesn't necessarily guarantee quality or improved quality or better processes. ISO 9000 is often given as a reason why a company can't make Lean changes. In this case, all that is necessary is to change your documentation to reflect what changes are needed for Lean. The big advantage to ISO-based systems is they establish a quality system and infrastructure. Without this infrastructure, we would have no system to incorporate our new standard work procedures, control plans, etc. Lean, ISO, Baldrige award criteria and SHINGO award criteria, all work very well together.

Lean and Government/Military Contracting (CPSR, DAR, FAR, and DCAS)

Lean works very well with government requirements; as long as they are documented properly and supported, we have never had any issues. In most cases by incorporating standard work into operations management (includes materials and manufacturing and sometimes IT), it becomes easier to meet all the requirements and audit criteria.

Electronic Drawing Capability

These are systems that communicate between suppliers and customers via engineering systems where supplier drawings can be integrated seamlessly at the customer. There are also rapid prototyping systems and systems that can share drawings from one supplier to another, i.e., between engineering firms where they can build on the same drawing package. There is a firm called Hilltop Corporation in Japan with 3D printing capabilities which can seamlessly go from concept to prototype in less than five days. This is not meant to be an advertisement for this company and no fees were received. It is merely a reference for the reader. There may be many other companies.[4]

Certified Supplier Program

Certified suppliers generally have met the quality, production, and financial criteria necessary to support bypassing receiving and incoming inspection and can deliver directly to the floor using a breadman stock, Kanban warehouses, or lineside material process.

Risk Mitigation Plans

These plans are paramount in the event there is an unforeseen problem with a supplier's order. This is especially true at a strategic team, commodity team, or LTA level. The supplier should have this as part of their agreement. Another term for this is developing a failure modes and effects analysis (FMEA). This tool looks at all the things that could go wrong and the likelihood of it going wrong and the severity or impact if it does go wrong, and what corrective actions can be put in place in the event the unexpected happens.

Sole Source

Sole source suppliers always carry risks even if they are partnering suppliers. This is the case with natural disasters, such as the tsunami hitting Japan. True partnering suppliers will work to help out the supplier in trouble since it is in everyone's best interest to ensure the supply to the end customer. Buyers should still have backups for sole source suppliers in the event of some catastrophe. If there is enough volume, one could split the order 80%/20% and keep the second source viable. The other option is to have the backup capability in house.

Centers of Excellence Thinking

Centers of excellence have pros and cons. The concept known as centers of excellence is where one of multiple plants is selected to produce a family of parts for all the other plants. There are pros and cons to this approach but in general it is considered a batching approach, not a Lean approach. Just as centralizing anything creates problems that are masked by what are thought to be attractive economies of scale, we have seen this concept implemented in several companies, but in every case the cons have outweighed the benefits.

The pros are:

- Economies of scale
- Taking advantage of core competencies

The cons are:

- Lose control when you outsource even if it is to another division
- Centers of excellence are systemic of batch thinking
- Everything must be scheduled

Insourcing versus Outsourcing

There has always been a movement in industry to outsource as much as possible and chase the low labor rates as they move from country to country. The main benefit of outsourcing was to obtain the finished good at a low cost. With Lean thinking, we tend to go the opposite way. In manufacturing, we pull production back into the United States from China and Mexico where it is going to be distributed in the United States. In general, when companies outsource, they give up control of the item or service and are at the mercy of the supplier. If you have true partnering with your supplier, this can work, but where you don't, it can result in disastrous consequences. Many companies have seen what on paper looked like great ROIs vanish in overnight freight costs, constant expensive trips overseas to manage suppliers and expedite parts, high inventory costs, quality issues, loss of technology, or proprietary intellectual property along with major culture challenges. The lowest labor rate is not always the best solution and runs contrary to developing Lean suppliers who are local or within four hours of the company's location.

Chapter Questions

1. What is the strategic materials group concept?
2. What are the benefits of employing this type of approach?
3. What are the pros and cons of outsourcing?
4. What is an LTA?
5. What are flex fences? Are they important?
6. What are the pros and cons of commodity versus product line (value stream) buying?

There are pros for program or product buyers. The buyer gains expertise in the buying requirements for each program. The buyer is forced to learn about each commodity as they proceed, so they become cross trained. The buyer is held to a budget for the overall program and becomes an expert in the needs of the program, is many times then co-located with that program, and can make suggestions that can save the program money. This type of organization is more aligned with Lean or value stream thinking. The Lean organization is aligned with the customer and can react to customer suggestions or complaints much quicker. The cons to this approach are it takes longer for the buyers to become experts in the commodities and they do not always have the necessary background to obtain the best pricing. There can be missed opportunities to package parts up for pricing that could be spread across different programs and there can also have multiple buyers at a company calling the same supplier.

Notes

1. http://www.con-way.com/en/careers/operations-management-careers/supply_chain_management/. This is not meant to be an advertisement for this company and no fees were received. It is merely a reference for the reader. There are many other logistics companies.
2. E-mail correspondence with Technologies Solutions Group—Tom Jackson. For more information on ITCS and implementing passive or active RFID systems, please contact Technologies Solutions Group. This is not meant to be an advertisement for this company and no fees were received. It is merely a reference for the reader. There are many other logistics companies.
3. RF Controls, LLC, was formed in 2006 by Tom Ellinwood and Graham Bloy to commercialize and refine early-stage research and development work on a disruptive and highly innovative real-time, automated identification, location, and tracking system for commercial applications. Over 30 man-years of intensive product development effort resulted in an innovative smart antenna system, which will be applied to a range of wireless communications applications. Their initial focus has been on UHF RFID applications, including inventory monitoring and tracking, in both static and dynamic environments. This is not meant to be an advertisement for this company and no fees were received. It is merely a reference for the reader. There are other companies.
4. http://hilltop-corp.tumblr.com

Additional Readings

Henderson, B.A. and Larco, J. 1999. Lean Transformation. Richmond, VA: The Oaklea Press.

Iyer, A.V., Seshadri, S. and Vasher, R. 2009. Toyota Supply Chain Management. New York, NY: McGraw Hill.

Jennings, J. 2002. Less Is More. London: Penguin Group

Taylor, D.H. 2004. Lean Supply Chain (Practices & Cases). New York, NY: Productivity Press.

Taylor, D.H. and Brunt, D. 2001. Manufacturing Operations and Supply Chain Management. Boston, MA: Cengage Learning EMEA.

Wincel, J.P. 2004. Lean Supply Chain Management. New York, NY: Productivity Press.

Chapter 5

Importance of Creativity before Capital

The true sign of intelligence is not knowledge but imagination.[1]

Albert Einstein

Many people think it requires large amounts of capital to go Lean. This is far from the truth. Some of the most successful Lean solutions implemented on a production line require little or no capital (see Figure 5.1). It sounds ironic to hear some companies saying they implemented Lean and it cost them millions of dollars. The Lean team needs to be creative and stick to the basics of linking together the value-added operations and processes needed to complete a product. The team needs to avoid the common pitfalls associated with grandiose multitasking machines, fancy conveyors and material handling equipment, and other expensive complex solutions that can sometimes move you backwards on your road to Lean.

Creativity before Capital—Machines

Experienced engineers generally try to design machines that will do multiple operations with the thought that it will reduce operator labor, which often backfires for a number of reasons.

Cost of the Machine

Multitasking machines that attempt to eliminate large amounts of human labor generally require significant capital. The mechanisms and controls needed to simulate the functions and dexterity of a human worker become more and more expensive with each movement and task attempted to be replaced by the machinery. The combination of slides, grippers, manipulators, motors, and sensors requires complex design, assembly, wiring, programming, and debugging labor to make them fit for reliable production line performance. This labor is expensive since it requires highly experienced engineers and technicians to complete the design and implementation correctly. These types of machines generally cost a minimum of six figures to produce even when replacing only

DOI: 10.4324/9781003185796-5

Figure 5.1 Creative simple method of storing drawings at machine.

a few minutes of human labor. Many times, it becomes a project just to write the justification for purchasing the machine and to develop a return on investment (ROI) that is worth considering. Many justifications end up being based on assumptions that can't be verified until the machine is operational and other costs get missed. At Company X, robots were installed on a line; however, 1,300 of the part numbers could not be assembled by the robot and had to be moved to another line. Items like this don't get captured in the ROI justifications. Many careers have been cut short when these assumptions turned out to be incorrect. If the cost of the machine cannot be justified, even with some very "optimistic" assumptions, the people involved usually admit defeat and nothing is done to make the process Leaner.

Time to Implement

In general, custom machines automated to replace large amounts of operator labor take months to design and build. The Lean implementation is often put on hold while the machine is being produced, stopping any momentum created by the Lean implementation, which makes it very easy for the line to slip back to its old non-Lean ways. Quick, simple, and inexpensive solutions help maintain momentum and, in the long run, will make the implementation and positive results happen much quicker. The expensive and complex solution in many cases can actually push Lean backward instead of forward.

Automation

As we have shown earlier in this text, it is possible to achieve 20%–80% productivity improvements with virtually no capital expenditures. There may be some expenses for tools, to duplicate jigs or fixtures or small equipment items. We have found that for 20% of the cost one can semi-automate workstations or lines and get up to 80% of the improvement. To go to full automation, one receives the 20% balance of the improvement opportunity for 80% of the cost. We are not against automation as this at the end of the Lean Maturity Path, but be careful. Some companies which have gone to totally automated lines found they were so expensive to run and maintain they backed off to a semi-automated solution. This is particularly true in low to medium volume, high-mix model environments or environments with lots of variation.

The automation journey also can complicate Lean installations. Station balanced automated or paced lines generally need to run at the max volume level, requiring the line to be fully staffed all the time. This creates issues with staffing as these lines take priority over all other lines in the plant, so the output on the other lines may suffer. Cross-training becomes a major issue and both maintenance and downtime are higher. When the lines experience unplanned downtime, everyone is waiting and most companies don't do a good job of tracking the downtime and cost both in machine (robot) repairs, labor to repair it, maintenance response time. Dealing with the downtime and team members waiting is difficult because one never knows how long the line will be down so it is difficult to move the personnel unless maintenance knows immediately it will take a long time to get the line back up and running. All of this becomes a hidden cost.

Lesson Learned: There is a common misconception about paced lines and automated lines in general. Most companies will tell you for example that their line is running at 22 seconds. Our first question is, can the operators stop the line? In just about every case the answer is yes. So, in reality the lines have the ability to run at 22-second cycle times but seldom do!

Conveyors

What should conveyors do? The simple answer is: convey. However, most of the time they just store parts and junk. So many times, we visit companies and see conveyors everywhere. Conveyors are expensive, especially powered ones, and in some cases, they may be justified. When companies ask us for improvement ideas one of the first places we point to is the conveyors. We tell them they are storing, not conveying and they should be removed. Many times, we hear, "We just put those in." We ask, why? What are they doing? What are they saving you? Conveyors are an instant barrier and become monuments in many layouts and in most cases should be targeted for removal.

Right-Sized Equipment

As discussed before, it pays to have engineers who can design new equipment and make improvements to older equipment. Sometimes it is less expensive to go with three or four machines that do simple tasks than purchasing a large machine to do all of the tasks. These machines can then be outfitted with mistake proofing devices and designed to load and unload themselves. This leads to chaku-chaku (load-load) lines. We have seen companies use both strategies successfully; however, one is a much more expensive solution. Once again, we must also keep in mind the natural variation in the product or process and the percentages of volume and model mix.

Machines Can Carry Baggage (No Pun Intended)

Expensive automated machines can often force you to waste labor because of the way they run. When trying to implement machines in a production line with the goal of eliminating labor or with the desire to make the process faster, we find the things that the machine now forces you to do are not considered. For example, during a Lean Master Class on day 2, we had students to watch the packaging part of the line for 30 minutes. They found a machine which heat sealed a part in a plastic bag at the end of the line (see Figure 5.2).

The bagging machine would present the bag from a roll of bags to the assembler. The assembler would drop the completed unit into a bag. Once the assembler actuates the machine, the machine would heat seal the bag, tear the sealed bag from the roll, and drop the unit in the sealed bag into a bin under the machine (see Figure 5.3).

The class argued that the act of sealing, tearing, and dispensing of the next bag would be faster with the machine but after being forced to analyze and video the entire process, the class found it was costing us additional labor because it was driving us to batch. Because of the configuration of the machine, parts were stacked up in front of it forcing large batches through the entire packaging process. The packaging process included wrapping each unit with an instruction sheet and putting a rubber band around it to hold the instruction sheet, then bagging each unit followed by placing a label on each bag, and finally placing 10 units in a shipping box. After watching the video, the class found, like all batch operations, that this batch packaging process was creating a lot of wasted labor, handling, and motion at the end of our Lean assembly line. The class then suggested to minimize the batch to only one box full of units (10) at a time, but you still had to pick up each unit before every step and put it back down each time prior to the next step (remember we call these lot delays in the process flow analysis [PFA]).

Author's Note: At some companies, we have seen the requirement to package the 10 units at the end of the line, as in this example, referred to as "pitch." This term was discussed earlier in

Figure 5.2 Old counter bagger machine—eliminated with Kaizen during 5-day Lean Master Class.

Figure 5.3 Bin under counter bagger—not ergonomic and led to batching the labels.

the text; however, this is a misapplication of the use of the word "pitch." While pitch naturally refers to a batch of parts (box size for instance), it should never refer to a process which is totally "batched up."

The machine operation made it necessary to place a bin underneath to catch the bagged units. Not only did we have wasted labor associated with moving the bin of units and removing the units from the bin, but we also had a risk of damage to the units as they dropped into the bin. After watching the class, it was found the machine was prone to jamming and took significant time to load with a new roll of bags when the old roll was consumed.

Note: The company had even considering purchasing additional baggers and robots.

After covering more training materials, on day 4, the class then came up with a very creative and inexpensive solution that allowed for true single-piece flow through the packaging process. The solution was a custom-made single-piece manual bagger made up of spare parts we found in the plant tool room. The single-piece bagger included a simple holder for the roll of bags that were fed through a slot in the bagger. It also included a simple air nozzle to open each bag as it was pulled into the bagger (see Figure 5.4) and a simple manual bag sealer was then placed right after the bagger, and a label peeler attachment (see Figure 5.5) along with a foot pedal actuator (see Figure 5.6) was added to the existing label peeler to allow for single-piece flow through the rest of the process.

The new packaging operation consisted of putting the instruction sheet on the unit immediately after it was assembled, putting the rubber band around the instruction sheet, dropping the unit directly into the bag, ripping the bag from the roll, sealing the bag with the manual bag sealer, placing the label on the bag, and finally placing the bagged unit in the shipping box. All of these operations were done in true single-piece flow fashion eliminating all of the waste associated with the batch operation. The foot pedal and label peeler options added to the label printer several weeks later also allowed us to save the operator from having to wait for the label printer to print a batch of labels and manually pull each label from the backing. This creative solution developed by

Figure 5.4 After solution from 5-day Lean Master Class.

Figure 5.5 On demand one piece flow label printer which peels the label for you.

Figure 5.6   Foot pedal installed.

the front line team members allowed us to avoid spending over $15,000 for additional automated baggers and cost only a few hundred dollars for the label peeler and foot pedal. The labor for the packaging operation was decreased by over 40%.

Lean Creativity Solutions

Lean Is Ongoing Iterations of Improvement

After the team implemented the new packaging process, they continued to improve the process by eliminating the rubber band to hold the instruction sheet on the unit as it was determined to be adding no value to the customer. We believe the implementation of this creative solution also enabled the team to focus on eliminating all of the waste, which likely would have never happened with the automated bagging machine. In Shingo's book *Kaizen and the Art of Creative Thinking*, he outlines his view of Creative Thinking which he developed into a process flow model (see Figure 5.7). We all consciously or unconsciously utilize this scientific thinking mechanism when we begin to problem solve or innovate. Since each chapter is dedicated to parts of the model, we only mention it here as an additional resource for the reader to explore when working to develop classes and additional teachings on how to develop better and more creative ideas during the problem solving process.

Creativity before Capital to Create Flow

The idea of creativity before capital is to simply focus on making the best use of the labor in the assembly line by making sure it is used to add value to the product whenever possible and not spent idle watching a machine run. This connecting of the value-added steps is ultimately what

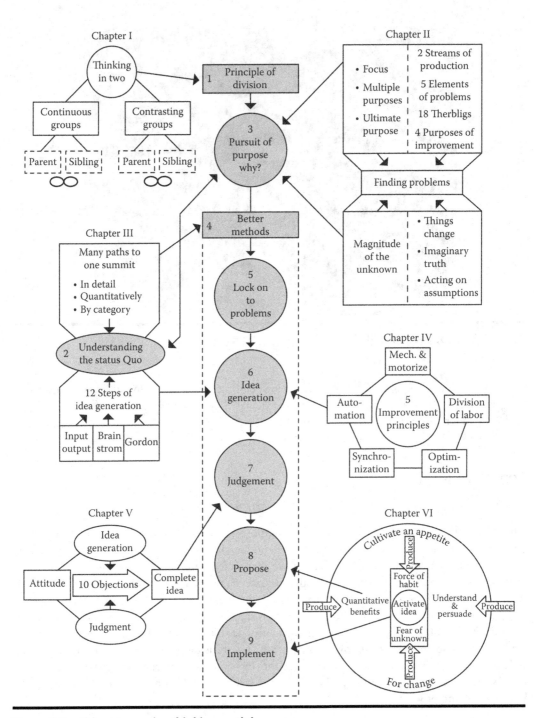

Figure 5.7 Shingo's creative thinking model.

allows you to create flow on the line. It usually ends up being much leaner to stick to basic tools and equipment, which are usually cheaper and perform short specific tasks.

If a complex multitasking machine is added to a Lean assembly line where operators flex up and down the line as needed, the longer cycle time of the machine can many times cause problems with flexing and bumping. The longer the cycle time of the machine, the better the chances the assemblers will get back to the machine with the next workpiece and have to wait for the machine to finish. Once this idle time is created for the first operator at this machine, it has a domino effect because the other operators either catch up to the idle operator or try to bump back to the idle operator. This can essentially cause the entire cell to go idle and makes it hard for the operators to return to their normal rhythm and running condition. Small-scale less expensive machines are better for flexible assembly lines to allow for proper flexing and handoffs. Most of the labor wasted on production lines is spent idle because the operator is working at a station they are tied to and can't help but have to wait for a machine to do its thing.

> For example, as the advanced manufacturing process engineer, we were once tasked with reducing labor on a station balanced assembly line. After watching the line run, we noticed a large amount of assembly labor was spent on the marking operation. The assembler would load the unit in the marking machine, actuate a clamping mechanism, and then start the marking process. They would sit idle while the marking machine ran its cycle. They would then remove the marked part. This operation was repeated in this batched sequence over and over until the entire work order was completed.

We came up with what we thought was the obvious solution to all this wasted labor, which was an automated marking station with a robot that would replace the assembler for loading and unloading parts on the marking machine (see Figure 5.8). The assembler would only be required to load all of the parts into a magazine the robot would pull from. This freed up the operator to go do something else. The automated marking machine cost over $100,000 and took about eight months to actually make it on to the assembly line. The expected amount of labor was saved and we took this as a huge victory.

Figure 5.8   Batching robot was eliminated.

After learning more about how to truly be Lean and discussing this with the team members on the line, we realized there was another solution which was nearly free and took less than a day to implement. This solution was to eliminate the robot and magazine and just put the marking machine on the assembly line with the addition of a simple control module that would allow the operator to load the part on the machine (which by the way was almost exactly the same amount of labor as loading the part in the magazine on the automated machine) and hit one button to clamp the part and start the marking machine. The operator would then move on to the next step of the assembly process with the unit that was already marked and waiting for them when they reached the machine (standard work in process [SWIP]). The machine would then mark the next unit before it was needed to keep the line continuously flowing. This was an example of focusing on the task that needs to be completed and approaching it in the most simplistic way to perform the task on a single piece at a time.

Another example is many times in light assembly operations an assembler will perform multiple operations on a small air press that is at the station they are assigned to. At this station, they will be adding parts to the assembly, adding locating and push tooling, and then actuating the press to perform the actual assembly. Subsequent press operations are done on this same press by switching tools and adding more component parts. To create the flow, you will have to add duplicates of the simple air press, as required, to break up the multiple operations once done on one press. Aside from creating better flow, this also builds more error proofing into the line because now each assembly step is done on a separate machine and only the bins of parts needed for that step are located at the press (see Figure 5.9).

Figure 5.9 Multiple presses replaced the robot so we could implement one piece flow.

You can generally save about the same amount of labor with inexpensive task-oriented machines than with a complicated automated machine for far less money (capital). Your money can be better spent on these simple task-oriented machines which allow for flow, good comfortable floor mats, and ergonomic height workbenches permitting the operators to move down the line (flow) adding value and bumping while the machines are running utilizing SWIP.

Lesson Learned: Lean is about becoming creative to eliminate offline monument machines and processes.

In one plant, the assembled products were sent outside of the assembly cells to a centralized spray wash system (see Figure 5.10). To enable continuous single-piece flow in the cell, a large quantity of standard WIP was needed to cover the time required to complete the wash operation and also the time required for the units to cool back to room temperature for functional testing. Many attempts were made to find a piece of wash equipment that could be put into the assembly cells to wash units right in-line. The goal was to eliminate the travel to and from the centralized washer as well as eliminate the large quantity of standard WIP. The large quantity of WIP created significant problems before and after the Lean line was installed because a failure due to a component problem or assembly issue could not be caught until after wash and cool at functional test. Many units could be affected by the problem, creating a large amount of scrap and rework. Small ultrasonic tanks were trialed in the cells and the travel was eliminated, but there was still a fairly large amount of WIP needed to cover the wash time and cool time. The tanks also caused safety issues because of the hot wash solution that could burn the operators and the solution in the tanks needed to be changed daily to properly clean the units. We found, in Internet searches, smaller spray wash systems designed to wash single units or small batches with short cycle times, which would work well in the cells but were quoted at over $35,000 each. Since the cost of these spray wash systems could

Figure 5.10   Batch washer required 45 minutes of WIP at the line in order to do one piece flow. Many times parts were delayed waiting for other batches to be cleaned and the machine had to be scheduled by production control.

not be justified by the amount of reduced labor time, scrap, and rework, the effort was nearly abandoned. Finally, the Lean team met with the front line team members and made one last attempt to brainstorm a solution with the plant's tooling group. The solution the group came up with was a low-cost custom single-piece flow spray wash machine. The machine had a chamber just large enough for the unit being washed, and it would inject a hot cleaning solution into the chamber followed by a long blast of compressed air to cool and dry the unit (see Figure 5.11). The new wash system has such a short wash cycle that after the air blast used to dry the unit, the unit is now cool enough to test immediately. This wash system also does not allow the operator to come in contact with the hot cleaning solution, which eliminates the safety issues with the ultrasonic machines. The cost of the materials to produce one of these wash systems was less than $5,000, and with the in-house labor to assemble and program the machine, the total cost was still less than $9,000.

Lesson Learned: Never give up trying to come up with a creative solution when an issue presents itself and having an internal resource for designing and building creative equipment solutions is priceless when implementing Lean in the manufacturing environment.

Figure 5.11   The advanced engineering group developed, in house, a one piece flow washer for 1/6th of the cost of developing it outside.

Capital Equipment

The capital equipment checklist given in Figure 5.12 contains points to consider when purchasing new capital equipment.

Creativity before Capital with Material Handling

Many products are inherently designed with subassemblies which are produced, off-line, before being assembled in the final unit. When implementing Lean single-piece flow, we always attempt to build the entire product from start to finish in the assembly cell including the subassemblies that used to be assembled outside the cell. It is common in order to maintain the product flow to

Business Improvement Group LLC
LEAN MANUFACTURING EQUIPMENT PURCHASE ASSESSMENT QUESTIONS

COST
- Is the equipment relatively low cost?
- Do the ROI and ROA justify the cost?
- Would last year's model satisfy your needs and cost less than this year's model?
- Could some other type of equipment be used that is less expensive?
- Is used equipment available?
- Do we currently have another machine or stand alone piece of equipment that can do all or a portion of the job? (i.e., stand alone drill press, gear machine, etc.)
- Would it make more sense to lease instead of purchase?
- Is it costly to upgrade to meet future needs?
- Will it be necessary to build stock ahead of time and is there a transition plan?

TPM READY
- Does the equipment require periodic calibration? How often?
- Is there easy access for periodic maintenance?
- Are schematic and equipment drawings provided?
- Are replacement parts ready available?
- What is the anticipated cost for maintaining the equipment?
- Do we have the skills necessary to perform periodic maintenance? If not, does the supplier provide training?
- Sensors for motors and cfm for MES systems
- PLCs for MES systems
- Have Supplier make TPM plan
- Have supplier identify and consign spare parts
- FMEA created for purchasing and installation and post installation process.

SET-UP
- Will the equipment support One Touch Exchange of Dies (OTED) or Single Minute Exchange of Dies (SMED)?
- Is equipment set up video available?
- Are parts within the equipment standardized so no special tools are required for set up?
- Can the machine be set up using a single tool?
- Is the equipment mobile?
- Can the equipment be programmed from a remote location?
- Does it have unlimited settings? If so, can it be modified to use only the required settings?
- Can Reagents or supplies be added vs. replaced to enable scheduled refills vs. running out in the middle of peak demand?

EQUIPMENT
- Is it automated or CNC controlled?
- Can one person operate it?
- Can it be operated standing up?
- Can it be used in-line? In a cleanroom environment?
- Is vibration an issue?
- Does it operate within allowable noise restrictions?
- What is the equipment's capability?
- Is it repeatable?
- What is its reliability in MTBF?
- Does it require frequent adjustments?
- Does it use standard jigs and fixturing?
- Is it compatible with existing equipment?
- Is it modular?
- Does it have an open architecture or is it proprietary?
- Will it be operating at approx. 50% capacity? (surge capacity support)

NOTE: Do not purchase with either 6 ft. or 12 ft. bar feeders.

INSTALLATION
- Does the equipment require any special installation?
- Will the equipment fit through existing openings?
- Do the existing facilities provide the power resources required to operate the equipment?
- Can the equipment be moved easily and safely?
- Does it require extensive work after being moved? (i.e., calibration, leveling, etc.)
- How can I install the equipment so it can be moved quickly if necessary to another location?
- Can I install it without a PIT or footer?
- Run rate tested and witnessed prior before tear down for shipment to your plant

CYCLE TIME
- Does the equipment support one piece flow?
- Can it be used in-line?
- Is the equipment cycle time capable of producing parts at less than 50% of the TAKT time for intended use? (Will allow for future growth and surges)

SAFETY
- Is special Personal Protection Equipment (PPE) required to operate the equipment?
- Are safe guards built in? (i.e., wire caging, splash guards, etc.)
- Does it require two hands to operate? Can it be safely modified to operate one-hand?
- Does supplier have safety manual if not can they develop it?
- Does it meet all

AUTONOMATION
- Can the equipment run without the operator having to stand and watch it?
- Can the equipment load and unload itself?
- Does it perform self-diagnostics?
- Does it warn when tools need replacement?
- Does it make sure the part it is working on was good before it started?
- Does it stop itself if nonconforming product is produced?
- Are the warnings audible or visible? (Andon)
- Are all the "bells and whistles" needed?

OTHER CONSIDERATIONS
- Will purchasing this equipment reduce a true bottleneck?
- Can existing equipment be modified to eliminate the need to purchase new equipment?
- Is it possible to eliminate the operation that the equipment is being purchased to perform?
- If the equipment is used, are repair records available?
- Does the supplier provide good product support?
- Have you seen the equipment in operation? If no, do you have feedback from someone who has?
- Can you visit a site where the equipment is being used?
- Are you aware of a new technology that will make the equipment obsolete? When?
- Is special training or skills required to operate the equipment?
- PPAP required? Customer Sign off req'd? Customer communication required?
- Is there a training plan developed?
- What is the quality sampling plan for the ramp up?

Business Improvement Group LLC
LEAN MANUFACTURING EQUIPMENT PURCHASE ASSESSMENT QUESTIONS

Why am I purchasing?
- Is it a replacement?
- Is it for HS&E?
- Does it generate additional revenue (capacity)
- Is it a cost savings?
- Is it less than 2 year paypack?

Figure 5.12 Capital equipment checklist.

Figure 5.13 Gravity is your friend. Simple creative way to move the part, which is a sub assembly, by skipping over a station.

have to build what used to be a subassembly (normally multiple subassemblies) somewhere on the new Lean line but not install the subassembly into the product until another point on the line. In this case, we try to sequence what used to be an offline subassembly in the processes on the line to minimize the amount of handling, carrying, picking up, and putting down the operators to do on the line. Many times, people come up with ideas that include the implementation of expensive conveyor belts or other motorized devices to move the subassemblies down the assembly line. While these may be effective, they are generally fairly expensive, hard to implement, and not very easy to change once they are placed on the line and something needs to be sequenced differently than planned. A creative and inexpensive solution to this problem is to use simple material slides, gravity fed rollers, or tubes to transfer a subassembly down the line to the place needed to be installed in the final assembly (see Figure 5.13).

In this case, a subassembly is produced on the line and then placed into the PVC slide tube to transfer it further down the line where it will be needed next. As the operator assembles another portion of the unit using the components in the bins in front of the slide tube, the subassembly slides through the tube and waits for the operator to get to it. The operator then picks the subassembly out of the tube to place it into the unit. Without this type of material transfer tube, the operator would either put the subassembly down or pick it up numerous times until it was needed for installation in the unit or the operator would have to travel back up the line to retrieve the subassembly. This type of slide or conveyor can also be used to easily feed components into an assembly line from outside the cell (see Figure 5.14).

Figure 5.14 This type of slide or conveyor can also be used to easily feed components into an assembly line from outside the cell.

Creativity before Capital in 5S

Creativity can be used to avoid spending large amounts of money when working 5S. A main 5S goal is to make things visual and very obvious when something is out of place. Inexpensive labeling, tool holders, and organization techniques can be used to achieve this goal without spending a lot of money (see Figure 5.15).

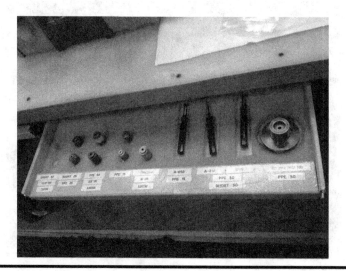

Figure 5.15 Creative solution for tools required for mixed models which are required at the same workstation.

Can You Implement Lean without Spending Millions of Dollars?

The answer is a resounding yes! Spending money for Lean provides no guarantee your Lean implementation will be successful. A successful Lean implementation will usually eliminate enough waste and save enough cost to justify large amounts of investment in capital but why spend it if you don't need to? Many times, a more creative solution to spending capital can be identified that will cost less and have a much quicker impact on your Lean efforts. What could you do with the money you save by being creative?—Grow your business? Improve your products? Improve your customer satisfaction? Or all of these? In Figure 5.16, a wooden template was fabricated in house to test the angle for presentation of the parts. The next step was to make a portable metal holder for the parts with the correct angle (Figure 5.17).

While it takes time to train people in creativity skills, there are usually many in organizations that already have this skill. Don't fall into the trap that many organizations do where they think spending a lot of money is required to be Lean. We have seen many companies that spend millions of dollars implementing Lean which are not much closer to being Lean than when they started.

> One of the greatest discoveries a person makes, one of their great surprises, is to find they can do what they were afraid they couldn't do.
>
> **Henry Ford**

When we begin a process improvement project, we always recommend the concept of creativity before capital. Money doesn't solve every problem. We can generally make many improvements for no investment or minor expense dollars; however, it has been our experience that most company layouts are in need of some type of major construction as part of a Lean project. The best time to design a new layout is when a new building is designed (greenfield); however, most companies miss this opportunity because either the company or the architect is not aware of Lean layout and workstation design principles. This oversight can cost companies millions in hidden costs.

Figure 5.16 Added wooden holder built in house to present materials in ergonomic position for the operators.

Figure 5.17   Wood template converted to metal holder.

It is recommended that a budget or dedicated funds for potential layout or equipment improvements be established and set aside up front each year, in the event they are required for Lean projects. If this is not done prior to the start of a project, the approval process may delay the project timeline, and if the funds for the improvement are not approved, it may impact the ability to achieve the outlined results. The optimization of the layout and workstation should be performed in conjunction with the frontline staff.

In Figure 5.18, a simple metal plate was used to store collets for turnovers and fastened to the top of the machine within easy reach for the setup person. In the past, these collets were all thrown in a drawer requiring quite a bit of time to search for the proper tooling. The drawer was also full of tooling that was never used. This tooling was removed and stored in a cabinet off-line. In Figure 5.19, a sink was required between operations. Previously, parts were batched up and then

Figure 5.18   Setup tools presented at point of use. (Courtesy of Ancon Gear.)

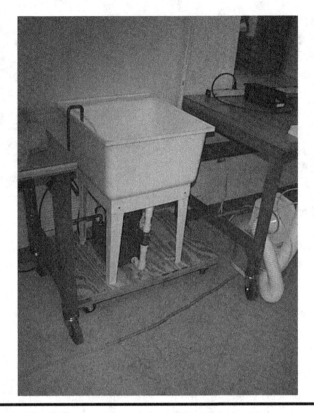

Figure 5.19   One piece flow wash sink put in line.

moved to a sink all the way across the room. The company designed and created a portable sink to be placed in between the stations (where it belonged based on the PFA conducted as part of the Lean implementation).

- In Figure 5.20, a simple wire rack was created with excess PVC piping.
- In Figure 5.21, a simple holder was fabricated to free up the operator's hands while performing the operation. In the past, the operator's hands were the fixture.
- In Figure 5.22, a portable smoke extractor was purchased for a stand-up soldering station.
- In Figure 5.23, small ovens were placed in-line at point of use (POU) versus batching parts to a large, centralized oven area.
- In Figure 5.24, a fixture was created to hold the part while an operation was being performed.
- In Figure 5.25, clocks were added for vibration cycle timing to make sure the operator returned in time to unload the parts.
- In Figure 5.26, a simple vacuum tool was created to place miniature parts inside the assembly. Prior to that, tweezers were used which resulted in a significant variation in cycle time.
- In Figure 5.27, a simple shutoff valve was created for the vacuum tool.
- In Figure 5.28, tools were placed at POU using a little Plexiglas fixture. Also, a wooden block was added to enable assembly at proper stand-up height.
- In Figure 5.29, tweezers were modified to pick up and place miniature balls into parts. Prior to this the operators used catalogue flat edge tweezers which constantly slipped off the round parts.
- In Figure 5.30, a stand-up cart on wheels was fabricated to move electric panels down the line.

Figure 5.20 Wire racks made from PVC pipes.

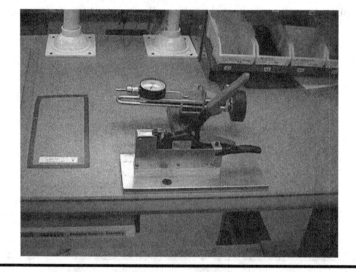

Figure 5.21 Fixtured hand tool to free up one hand and have tool location at point of use.

Figure 5.22 One piece flow solder exhaust.

Before   After

Figure 5.23   Replaced batch ovens on left with small ovens to do one piece flow.

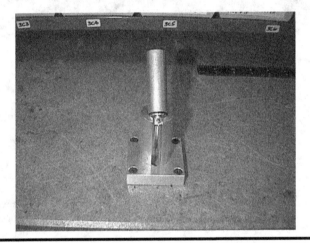

Figure 5.24   A fixture was created to hold the part while an operation was being performed.

Figure 5.25   Timers installed to notify operators when to change over the parts.

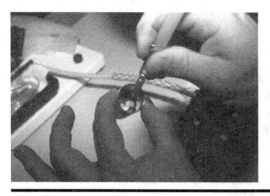
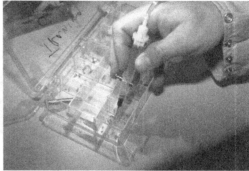

Figure 5.26   Vacuum tool.

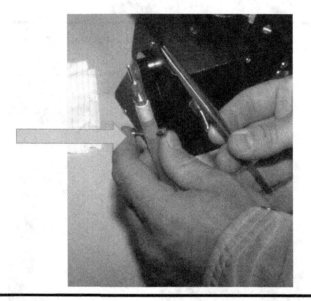

Figure 5.27   Simple shutoff valve.

Figure 5.28   Tools were placed at POU using a little Plexiglas fixture.

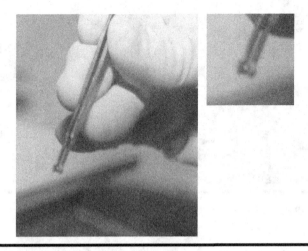

Figure 5.29 Tweezers were modified to pick up and place miniature balls.

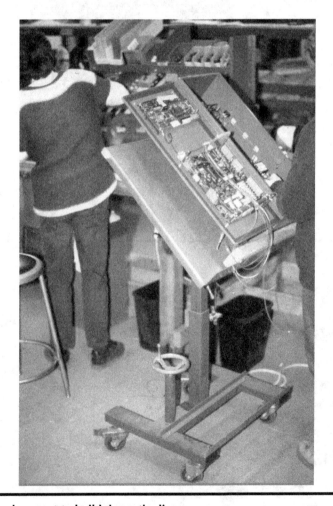

Figure 5.30 Stand up cart to build down the line.

Figure 5.31   Return for empty bins so that water spider could replenish.

■ In Figure 5.31, empty bin return was designed as part of the workstation, so materials can be replenished from behind.
■ In Figure 5.32, a wire rack was installed on the back of the workstation and fed through the front for the operator to use.

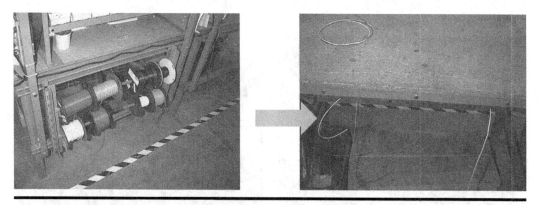

Figure 5.32   Wire reels mounted on back of workstation and fed through the front of the workstation to enable one piece flow. Eliminate all the 100 piece lots of separate wires which had to be pre-cut.

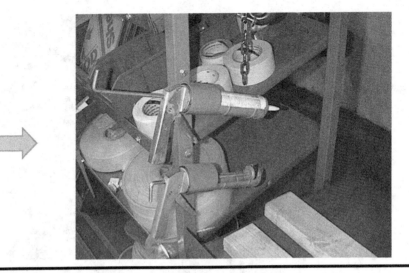

Figure 5.33   Tool placement at point of use.

- In Figure 5.33, two-bin caulking guns were stored on the side of the workstation.
- In Figure 5.34, tool holders were installed on the workstation at POU and in order of use.
- In Figure 5.35, a motor assembly station with parts in order of use and motors feeding in the center of the workstation where it was located based on the PFA was shown. Motors are sequenced by type and by order of job.

We could fill this book with examples of creative solutions developed by team members and, for the most part, fabricated in house. Leveraging the knowledge of the frontline staff will provide an overall better design and, in addition, help facilitate the adoption and the acceptance. One can develop a great process change or redesign, but if we do not continually work on the change and people side of the equation, the result may be zero.

Figure 5.34   Tool placement at point of use and labeled.

Figure 5.35   (a and b) Hand fabricated motor assembly station.

Chapter Questions

1. What additional expenses occur when adding a machine or robot?
2. What does the Lean principle of creativity before capital mean?
3. What principles of 5S should be considered during creativity before the capital process?
4. Can there be a direct correlation between machine expenditures and Lean line efficiencies?
5. How should the team approach evaluating the potential expenditure of a complex machine?
6. What creative material handling solutions can be used instead of complex material handling systems, such as conveyors?
7. What are the advantages of designing equipment in house?
8. What are the problems with centralized equipment like washers and ovens?
9. What should conveyors do?
10. How can gravity help you with creativity before capital thinking?

Exercise

Make one simple change in the classroom, office, or factory which improves a process.

Note

1. Read more at http://www.brainyquote.com/quotes/quotes/a/alberteins148802.html#0f1BEETsv UyK9Vtm.99

Additional Readings

Hawken, P., Lovins, A. and Lovins, L.H. 1999. Natural Capitalism: Creating the Next Industrial Revolution. Boston, MA: Back Bay Books.

Imai, M. 1986. Kaizen—The Key to Japan's Competitive Success. New York: McGraw-Hill.

Imai, M. 1997a. Gemba Kaizen. New York: McGraw-Hill.

Imai, M. 1997b. Kaizen. New York: McGraw-Hill.

Japan Human Relations Association/Kogyo 1989/1992. Kaizen—Teian 1—Developing Systems for Continuous Improvement through Employee Suggestions. Tokyo: Shimbun Publishing/Cambridge, MA: Productivity Press.

Japan Human Relations Association/Kogyo, 1992. N. Kaizen—Teian 2—Developing Systems for Continuous Improvement through Employee Suggestions. Tokyo: Shimbun Publishing/Cambridge, MA: Productivity Press.

Osborn, A.F. 1993. Applied Imagination. New York: Creative Education Press.

Robinson, A.G. and Schroeder, D.M. 2004. Ideas Are Free—Empowering Creative Work Environments. San Francisco, CA: Barrett Koehler Publishing.

Robinson, A.G. and Stern, S. 1997. Corporate Creativity—How Innovation and Improvement Actually Happen. San Francisco, CA: Berrett-Koehler.

Shingo, S. 2007. Kaizen and the Art of Creative Thinking. Vancouver, WA: PCS Press.

TBM 1994. Kaizen—Shop Floor Breakthrough. Durham, NC: TBM Consulting Group.

Tushman, M. 1997. Winning through Innovation. Boston, MA: Harvard University Press.

Yasuda, Y. 1990. 40 Years, 20 Million Ideas: Toyota Suggestion System. Cambridge, MA: Productivity Press.

Chapter 6

Engineering and Lean Solutions[1]

It is said that skill in design determines 70% of performance in quality, cost, and delivery (QCD).[2]

This chapter focuses on both aspects of engineering and Lean:

1. How to Design Lean into Products and Services?
2. How to Apply Lean Principles to the Engineering Process Itself?

How to Design Lean into Products and Services

Engineering, many times unknowingly, plays a vital role in Lean manufacturing and office transactional Lean processes. Engineering impacts all aspects of the design, not just the product design itself. For instance, engineering must consider the following when designing new products:

- Is it easy for the customer to service?
- Is the new design easy to use or operate?
- Is it easy to assemble and manufacture?
- Is it easy to service?
- Is it mistake proofed for design, service, and the customer?
- Is it easy to procure and supply for the length of the product life cycle, or are there end-of-life issues embedded in the design?
- Is it easy to market? Does it market itself?
- Is it easy for total productive maintenance (TPM)?
- Is it smart? Does it diagnose and or solve its own problems?

Design for Lean: The 3P Process

There are various names for designing Lean processes. The most familiar is the 3P process. The three Ps stands for product, preparation, and process. This process focuses on designing the

DOI: 10.4324/9781003185796-6

product or service (and must be cross-functional) to ensure it can start out Lean versus having to be leaned out later. It encompasses various tools:

1. Design Fishbones and process mapping
2. DFMA—design for manufacturing and assembly
3. FMEA—failure modes effects analysis
4. Transitioning the product to production
5. Target costing principles

Note Regarding Transactional Processes

The same design process can be performed on a transactional process. Instead of parts, we may be using paper, e-mails, authorization, and approval forms (with distances noted), etc.

Note: Lean principles and tools such as design for Lean (DFL) apply to transactional processes and information systems.

1. Design Fishbone: This process involves literally taking each part that goes into an assembly and laying the part out on the floor in the order it is assembled. Generally, this process starts with disassembling a prototype unit (but can be a production unit if further down the design path). The unit is reassembled and then disassembled again. When the exercise is complete, it takes the form of a fishbone on the floor resulting in a very enlightening process (see Figure 6.1).

    If performed correctly, the fishbone process yields the following results:

    Every assembly and disassembly step is questioned.

    The usage of each part is questioned. Could it be designed out, simplified, or combined with another part?
    – Can the operator assemble it wrong? How can it be mistake proofed?
    – How will it go together on the shop floor? What are the cycle times for each step?
    – What tools are required to assemble versus disassemble?
    – How do we reduce the number of tools to assemble?
    – Are there subassemblies? Does it make more sense to build it as separate subassemblies or from the ground up?
    – Subassemblies will reduce throughput time if they are built in parallel. While the benefit is gained only on the first unit built, it can be a big benefit for high mix environments.
    – Are adjustment and tweaking required?
    – Are we tied to a test set?

    The result should be a finalized shop floor process with standard work or standard operations routine sheet, work instructions, cycle times, and part production capacity sheet. The team can also perform an FMEA and measurement systems evaluation as part of the process.

2. DFL Manufacturing and Assembly: DFMA[®3] influences the effect a product design can have on the manufacturing enterprise and more importantly Lean manufacturing implementations. The product design also has a major impact on the cost and production performance throughout the product life cycle, which often becomes lost after the product is launched on the manufacturing floor. Attention to DFL is just as important as leaning out the production system; because removal of waste at the design stage is even more important as it can greatly minimize the amount of Lean effort needed to maximize value-added operations

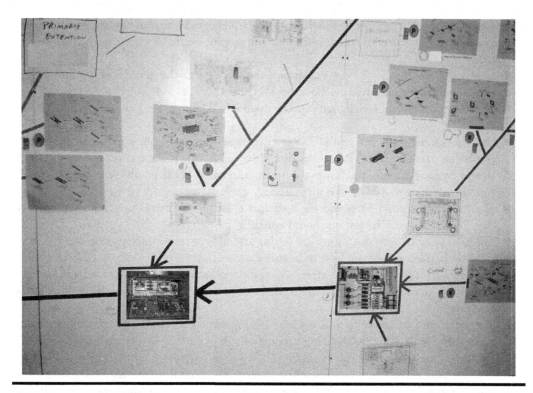

Figure 6.1 Design fishbone.

after the fact. In a 1987 Quality Digest article entitled Process Improvement the authors, Ronald Moen and Thomas Nolan, state: "The leverage for improvement during these phases is many times greater than improvements made downstream during manufacturing."

Lesson Learned: The best way to eliminate waste is to design it out!

Lean methodology's number one principle is to create a culture of removing waste in the process and fill the void with true value-added functions. What would make us believe that Lean would not have a place in our business? Or in our design process? Our experience has found many opportunities to apply Lean not only to design but to the process of designing as well.

Poor Engineering Design Symptoms

We have experienced many lines with symptoms of poor engineering designs. These symptoms manifest themselves in operations in the following:

■ There is no go/no go test. Operators must interpret results (guessing equals variation) or take time to review data and make decisions. In some cases, we have seen test result screens that appear for only 5–10 seconds and then disappear. This forces the operator to stand there and watch the screen until the results appear. If they miss it or don't see it clearly, they must go through a multitude of steps to get the screen back.

■ Operators must print out the data. Why doesn't it print out by itself or keep a log that can be emailed or texted to the customer?

- Operators must stand and wait while testing is conducted to read the results of the test. Placing an andon after the result is read by the machine would be a better way to accomplish this.
- Operators must push a button to advance the software to the next phase of the test. The machine should cycle based on the test result.
- The test or equipment is designed to retest upon initial failure. The part should pass the first time!
- Operators must read the results. The test set passes the parts, but a graph on the display shows the parts are bad. Test results should be consistent. If the test set says it is good, it should be good! Otherwise, just make the interpretation of the graph the criteria (in which case the machine should do this for you).
- The test set fails good parts and the operators must rework them even though they know they are good parts. The test set should not fail good parts.
- The parts must be constantly tweaked during assembly or tuned during assembly. With rare exceptions, parts should not have to be tuned or tweaked.
- The parts are built by trial and error, which means that they may have to be torn down at some stage and rebuilt. The design should be robust enough that it can be built right the first time.
- The parts must be tested to add a selected component (out of a range of components) to make them work properly. The design should be robust enough that it can be built right the first time.
- The first part must be subjected to a first article test, which it may or may not pass prior to producing the part. This is generally due to shimming or some tolerance stack up or flatness issue on one of the parts. The design should be robust enough that it can be built right the first time.
- The line has a rework area due to all the rework generated off the line. The design should be robust enough that it can be built right the first time!

Lessons learned for engineers from a fellow engineer:

1. Ensure drawings are made for the operators building the products versus made by engineers for engineers.
2. Ensure drawings for the shop provide explicit notes and requirements for the first part inspection and eliminate interpretation. The other measurements on the drawing have no value and confuse operators and quality personnel.
3. Design panels are made for the ease of manufacture… not for ease of drafting.
4. Dedicate engineers for each product line to eliminate the following excuses:
    a. Well, the other plants don't have that problem when they build it.
    b. We're too busy working on new products to support the existing ones.
    c. We don't have time to support new and existing products; how can we support obsolete products.
    d. Quality is relative only to those who build it.
    e. The product is built by us (engineers); therefore, an assembly can build it.
    f. Finally…. When one plant does something well, communicate it to other plants as other plants are doing things differently (and smarter) in some cases.
5. The engineer designing the equipment should see the problems firsthand rather than complain. Let them come out and drill a gazillion holes! There are still draft people

that have never been on the shop floor. The design team members should attend a minimum one-week training class before they design anything on the floor to provide them with an appreciation and an understanding of the constraints faced in a manufacturing environment.

6. The plant is the part of the company that truly earns the money, thus committing to staffing to ensure quality, cost, and delivery (QCD) metrics are achieved.

Developing Complex Lean Lines

Countless mistakes are being made by operations managers, who have experienced past successes with Lean methodology implementation and, without forethought, employ a team to apply traditional Lean approaches to a troubled production system (like the ones with the problems referenced earlier) where cost is excessive and/or delivery promises are not achieved. Batching covers up all those problems and Lean principles must be applied to uncover issues and to ensure customer QCD commitments are achieved.

Unfortunately, it takes skills, expertise, and a willingness to compromise some of the Lean principles to balance complex lines with poorly designed products. After their efforts to launch the new Lean line, they realize that they do not have the expertise to implement or sustain the Lean methodologies and revert to batching. Sometimes even after regrouping and throwing a second effort or another group of external consultants at it, they still find it impossible to run or sustain so they revert to the old processes.

While we have been successful applying Lean to these types of processes for years, processes with high variation and rework are the most difficult lines. These lines contain fundamentally flawed product designs that are the root cause of the variation and rework. As soon as we apply Lean to these types of lines, the retests and rework become very visible and must be addressed. At this point, there is no question the problems are traceable back to the design. In some very rare cases, we have paradoxically set up one-piece flow rework lines.

The ideal solution would be to review and redesign the product, but in many cases, the company is unwilling to commit the resources or funds necessary for revising equipment, sourcing new parts, or requalification of the product. They feel that the level of rework is tolerable as it is already factored into cost, the output, and scheduling and thus becomes boiled frog-type waste. A common cause of this type of Lean failure, engineering design, usually becomes invisible once a product is launched into production. The reason is once the nonrecurring design activity is completed and released to production, the complexity becomes accepted and absorbed into the routine of manufacturing operations.

While it is often not accepted or many times even considered, engineering, in the end, ultimately owns the recurring cost and inefficiency, but this is normally not part of the engineering objective nor is engineering held accountable and it is rarely measured by finance. It is not unusual, during a Lean implementation, to have the engineers come out of their offices down to the line (some may have to remember where the shop floor is located) and make them build what they have designed for a day or week or more to develop a compelling need for them to make changes to the design.

Again, a DFMA analysis is much easier to sell when the design is controlled by the company versus being controlled by the customer. Where designs are controlled by the customer, it is even more paramount to make sure a DFMA analysis and FMEA are conducted prior to submitting the designs to the customer for qualification testing and approval. We seldom see engineering held accountable to supply the standard work package with key points and reasons for key points, cycle times, and standard work-in-process calculations as part of their deliverables during the transition to production phase to manufacturing.

P(C)DCA

During the planning phase (engineering phase), the Control function as Shingo states, should be added prior to the Do or transition to the production phase. The Control function should guarantee the design is stable, include the corresponding process capability, and ensure it can be built right the first time. A control plan should be developed jointly with production and released with the drawing package.

A point to remember is no amount of Lean after the fact can fix a design that is deficient and inefficient to manufacture. The fact that a part can be assembled doesn't mean that it is a stable, repeatable, or an efficient design. The part must be able to be produced right the first time. Too often, production must pay for the sins of a bad design or lazy design engineer. Whenever production involves the engineers, the first thing the engineers do is blame the production people. In the end, if the engineer mistake proofs the build process, then the production team members can't build it wrong. However, most engineers do not see this as part of their responsibility and, in many cases, are under so much pressure to release the design that they don't have time to understand what it will take to build the product.

Prior to launching a new Lean program on an existing product line with a poor engineering design, it is best to first perform a design for assembly (DFA) analysis. Why do this before the Lean activity begins? The chances of sustainability are much more improved on a line where retests and rework are eliminated, and the line can be stabilized. This is the main reason why the practice of concurrent engineering is employed into the design activity and should begin as early in the design cycle as possible or when the earliest engineering effort is initiated ... at the paper napkin stage.

Lesson Learned: The purpose of the manufacturing enterprise is to generate a profit. Manufacturing profitability is ultimately dependent on the engineering design and manufacturing equipment available.

Design for Manufacturability Example: These Results Were Achieved While Analyzing an Assembly Video

It's not uncommon during the product design cycle of a product to find the attributes of manufacturability are usually the last thing on the designer's mind. Yes, there may be one or two design features that were addressed for the benefit of manufacturing, but more often the assembly efficiency is overlooked and is seldom measured or even part of the engineering deliverables package. Engineers must also be cognizant of the equipment available in manufacturing. Another great manufacturability analysis tool is the video camera.

At a company in South Baltimore, we found they used to "craft assemble" their blender for injection-molded plastics, then take it apart, paint it, and then put it all back together (see Figure 6.2). During a DFMA exercise (design for manufacturability and assembly analysis), using an assembly video, the engineer was surprised to learn that the fabrication department was doing an operation in two steps. The engineer stated he had designed it to be a one-step operation. The fabrication manager explained that their equipment did not possess the capability to do all the ops in one step and thus it had to run across two machines. During this review, it was amazing that once the engineer saw the equipment and how the parts were

Baseline metrics (1/1998)		Metrics (5/1998)		Metrics (3/1999)		
Operators	3	1	−66%	1	−66%	Includes:
Units per day (includes OT)	.33	1	+200%	2.67	+700%	Water spider
WIP (pieces)	14	2	−86%	1	−70%	Team leader
Hours/unit	92	8	−91%	2.9	−97%	
WIP dollars	$95k	$13k	−86%	$13k	−86%	*Note*: Reduced total
Floor space (ft^2)	900	600	−33%	400	−44%	labor time (DFMA)
Throughput time (working days)	5	2	−60%	1	−80%	by 85% !
Cycle time (est. batch minute)	1440	450	−69%	180	−88%	

Lean product
team results

97% Increase in productivity

Figure 6.2   Results of a DFMA workshop—reduced total labor time by 85%.

produced, he started "red-lining" (correcting) drawings on the spot. The result was a significant reduction in throughput time and increase in first pass yield along with an instant jump in profitability.

When we begin to design something, we are usually guided by one of two scenarios:

1. We are out to develop an improved design that already exists whether it's someone else's product or currently one of our own.
2. We are tasked with creating something entirely new and nonexistent now.

The first scenario where we are setting out to make a better product is usually easier to initiate. The first step is to benchmark the product. As designers, most of us face this situation more often, and it is much easier to improve something than to start from scratch.

The second scenario is more daunting but also more enjoyable as the possibilities abound. It will be us pulling out the set of Lincoln Logs, Tinker Toys, and the Erector Set.[4] The benefit to this is that we are now in the position to set the benchmark and we'll also have future opportunities for subsequent product improvements of our own benchmark.

Either way, it's all about the money. We tend to forget what the manufacturing business is. Whether we are selling our time and experience to the enterprise that hired us or if we are the pioneer, we simply need to pay the rent, and manufacturing is the function of converting raw materials into something others find value in. We may not consider ourselves a capitalist, but is it possible we would work for free for very long?

When we say all about the money, we are really looking at the total cost of the design throughout the entire product life cycle. Our motivation should be how to take all waste possible out of the product design.

Design Roots

Designing products and manufacturing them for sale are the basis of the global economy or, in more local terms, the degree in which we all support ourselves. As an example, let's design a product that costs $1 to manufacture and sell it for $10. In addition, let's make it so simple that we can make many of them in a day's work and make it reliable enough so that our customers really sense the value and become repeat customers.

This process has been going on since the beginning of history. We gathered sticks, rocks, and mud and created something of value to trade. We made a tool to trade for a piece of meat to feed the family. If it is a successful venture and if the customer senses the value, they will come back for more and bring their friends. This business process has not changed over the years and is the foundation of our free-market economy.

Definition

We have discussed design for manufacturability (DFM) in very simple terms. Let's explore the science and basic principles. DFM is the practice of creating elegantly simple designs that exceed the customer's expectation of value and provide for a profitable and successful product that is efficient to manufacture with the caveat it all happens before the design is released to production.

We Need a Crystal Ball!

We do that by eliminating production waste before launching into production. Got a crystal ball? Since there is such a high demand for crystal balls to peer into the future and see what's coming, one would think that they should be readily available. Some clever persons would be living large now if they invented it. The lack of the crystal ball explains why many companies fail miserably in business. Luckily, there are tools and techniques that mimic the crystal ball, which we will share with you.

Create a Design Plan

Very few successes in business opportunities happen without creating a plan. Without a good plan for success, the option is simply luck. Luck and high risk are easily found in the same sentence. Planning for a successful product is well worth the time. First, we need to identify what success looks like. We want the product to be well liked, efficient, producible, and profitable. Visualizing a successful operation usually doesn't include visualizing the waste. It's for this reason that product designers are generally oblivious to it, and waste sneaks into the product design like rats boarding a ship in port. The waste becomes evident when the design is released into production, however, even then, the product design may not be recognized as the root cause.

Time to Break Out the Lean Tools

Ridding the product manufacturing process of waste before it is released usually will take some serious forethought, experience, and lessons learned. An analysis tool such as DFMA is designed to help remove this waste. DFMA is an analysis technique and a calculating tool embedded in a convenient software program. The design is loaded with specific data into the input fields, and then the software will calculate the manufacturing efficiency based on those inputs. It will provide quantitative results in dollars, time, and percentages. The program will analyze our benchmark design and then direct our attention on where to focus to improve the manufacturability of the product. The tool and process will enable improvement using what-if scenarios creating a secondary analysis, based on the benchmark, and the calculations. Results of both the baseline and the benchmark will be placed side by side clearly showing the value of making the changes.

The technique is very effective and performing several iterations of these analyses on the same design can drive design elegance in terms of manufacturing efficiency. It is common to experience 50% reductions in the bill of material (BOM) part count, touch labor, and overall cost with an increase in quality and functional reliability. It is much cheaper to improve the design at this stage than to redesign it at some point after release.

There will always be waste to Lean out in production. It's inherent in the business, and the law of entropy dictates waste will occur in the process and design, however, it is important to remember that waste designed into the product cannot be effectively or sustainably Leaned out. A design change will eliminate the waste and the more waste eliminated before the design is released for production, the more likely the vision of success, both yours and the company's, will be realized and rewarded.

Waste Removal during Design

Lean is about the removal of waste that gets in the way and impedes the flow of material, ultimately leading to late deliveries and both time and money needlessly spent. Engineers need to be aware of the seven (eight) wastes. This knowledge can be used during the product development process to minimize the need for Lean on the other side.[5] Early in the product development phase, it helps to review the designs proactively with a focus to remove as much waste as possible from the value stream.

Engineering Velocity

The original seven forms of waste as developed by Taiichi Ohno, and subsequently defined by Dr. Shingo[6] were identified as the use of any material or resource beyond what the customer requires and is willing to pay for. Once we familiarize ourselves with how these wastes can dilute efficiency in manufacturing, we can apply the knowledge to product design and work toward waste elimination before it has a chance to occur. Materials that require specialized processing or part features not necessary to the function of the product generally are not in the customer's interest.

The words Lean enterprise and material velocity are frequently used in the same sentence. The goal is to ensure materials are converted via processing as efficiently as possible into the final product including delivery to the customer. This velocity focuses on bringing in raw material (as required) and getting it out as a finished product. Once the money is invested, the stored materials are not valuable to the enterprise until they are made into products and converted into cash.

Homework: Take a moment to see if you can identify and write down the eight wastes described earlier in the book.

DFMA Supports Lean

Although we can get more "bang for the buck" using the DFMA program in new product development, it can be equally effective for designing product improvement projects. It bears repeating that case studies show users will typically realize cost reduction and savings of approximately 50%

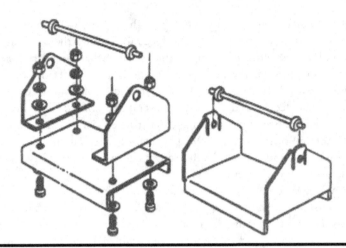

Figure 6.3 DFMA improvement—is a separate part required in relation to the other parts already assembled?

from the original design. This is significant, dramatic, and well worth the time and investment to utilize DFMA.

Engaging DFMA in the concurrent engineering team allows a focus on minimizing the design complexity and costs while maximizing value for the customer. DFMA will help minimize the following:

■ Part count
■ Material cost
■ The amount of time the materials are in the process
■ Defects and rework

When the assembly of our product is designed with the least amount of parts needed, yet maintaining product integrity, the customer will realize the value in reduced initial cost as well as a more reliable product. Like how reducing steps in a process eliminates the opportunities for defects, reducing parts in design, results in fewer opportunities for parts to wear out or break down since there are fewer parts (complexity has been eliminated). The DFMA process generally results in better product integrity and reliability.

The three DFMA question[7]:

1. Does the part move, in relation to other parts already assembled, in such a way that the movement cannot be obtained by elastic properties or final deformation of the material?
2. Is it necessary that the part must be of another material or must be isolated from other materials already assembled?
3. Is a separate part required in relation to the other parts already assembled, because otherwise, the assembly of remaining parts becomes impossible? (see Figure 6.3)

What Is a Part Worth and What Are the Design Impacts to Assembly?

The total number of parts in an assembly directly correlates to the time and cost of the product. The following equation is listed in a book called *Product Design for Manufacture and Assembly*.[8]

The equation is

$$E_{ma} = \left(N_{min} \, \text{Å} - T_a \right) \div T_{ma}$$

where

E_{ma} is the assembly efficiency

N_{min} is the number of parts

T_a is the theoretical time to assemble each part (in a perfect world)

T_{ma} is the actual assembly time

I have heard engineers state "Well, it's only one more part" or "It's cheaper to add four screws to it." Every design decision has the potential to add additional costs, which many times may be hidden. For instance, each part included in the design generally:

- Requires a drawing. Drawings take time and often must be revised
- Must be added to the BOM
- Must be added to material requirement planning (MRP)
- Requires labor to purchase it, receive it, and inspect it
- Space to store it and then more labor to pick it, assemble it, ship it, and pay for it
- It may have to be fabricated or may require an outside process
- It may get rejected and would require a site visit to the supplier
- It may quickly become obsolete
- It may be the sole source
- It adds process steps/time
- Potential for correction

All these steps add time and cost to the product that makes us less competitive. Based on the following[9]:

- The assembly diagrams
- Cost breakdown
- BOM
- Assembly drawing(s)

we can ask these questions:

- Is the part or the process necessary?
- Can the part or process be simplified?
- Can the part be replaced by a standard component or be replaced by a commercial part?
- Can the part be made from a different material?
- Is the movement of the parts necessary? Is adjustment required?
- Will integration or combination of parts give problems?
- Which functions does the part have? Are all these functions necessary?
- Can we modify the assembly to make the functions of the part simpler?
- Can we eliminate unnecessary machining or tight tolerances on the specific part?

Where to Begin

Let's explore how to begin a product design project. First, we want a team who will be contributors to the value. These members should be a cross-functional team representing the main functional areas and typically include the following:

- Mechanical designers
- Electrical designers
- Manufacturing engineers
- Supply chain management
- Quality assurance
- Production—this group is critical for a manufacturing firm
- Suppliers—if parts and materials will be procured, it's important to involve potential suppliers as much as possible
- Customers

This team will select the project with the big hairy audacious goal[10] and make it a stretch goal. An example would be a 50%-part count reduction from our baseline. Would this goal make anyone nervous? There should be no fear of failure to achieve the goal, and the team and company must be willing to assume the risk. Case studies are shown in Table 6.1 that reinforce the value of DFMA.

Lesson Learned: Formal professional training in the use of DFMA prior to the design team initiating a design project will accelerate the confidence and skill levels of design engineers leading to a successful outcome. Once the team agrees on the goal and the use of the DFMA process, the

Table 6.1 DFMA Case Studies

Brown and Sharpe—CMM
  84% Reduction in assy time
  67% Reduction in different
    parts
  74% Reduction in total
    number of parts
  77% Reduction in total
    number of operations
  71% Reduction in metal
    fabrication time
  45% Reduction in weight
	Motorola—vehicular adaptor
	  Assembly time cut from
	    2742 seconds to 36
	    seconds
	  Assembly count cut from
	    217 to 47
	  Fasteners cut from 72 to 0
		NCR—2670 Point of sales
		  terminal
		  65% Fewer suppliers
		  75% Less assy time
		  100% Reduction in assy
		    tools
		  85% Fewer parts
		  Mfg cost reduction of 44%
		    (millions of dollars)
		  Estimated removal of a single
		    screw is $12,500 over life of
		    product

Digital equipment—computer mouse
  – Benchmarked competition on assembly times, parts counts, labor costs, total cost of the
    product, and consulted with hourly personnel that assembled the mouse
    + 592 seconds of assembly reduced to 277 seconds
    + Screws reduced from seven to zero
    + Adjustments were eliminated (the old design had eight)
    + Reduced operations from 83 to 54
    + Product design cycle (including hard tooling) reduced to 18 weeks		

Source: From G. Boothroyd and P. Dewhurst, *Product Design and Manufacture for Assembly,* Marcel Dekker, Inc., New York, 1994.

computer-aided design work will soon follow with minimal design rework, and a product that has higher margins, higher quality, high customer satisfaction, and likely lower schedule delays.

DFMA Simulation

The next step in the process is creating or modifying the product BOM. Whether it's from a benchmark design or a new conception, we'll need this baseline to begin improving. This list is loaded into the DFA module that will apply all the program-driven attributes to each individual piece part to include size, cost, part handling, and insertion qualities. And once the baseline design is filled in, the product is analyzed for cost, ease of assembly, and assembly efficiency (the DFA index) after the baseline design is filled in. The program will produce an initial report, analyzing the results in different ways which provides different views that are useful to the design team. There is a report called Suggestions for Redesign, which shows the areas of production inefficiencies (areas for improvement). It depicts, if they were corrected, what amount of improvement will be gained as well as a percentage of improvement. At this initial stage, the team will find this most useful as these become the improvement targets.

Implementing DFMA Principles

General guidelines to consider are as follows:

- Don't tie operators or customers to machines
- Semiautomate where possible
- Provide easy-to-use fixturing for operators
- Design in mistake proofing
- Eliminate, simplify, and combine wherever possible

Eliminate

After the improvement report is generated, we must go back to the drawing board. Remember, our goal is to reduce the part count by 50% of that initial or original benchmark.

A place to start is fasteners. As a rule, fasteners are a waste of time on the assembly floor. Most probably, they are some types of threaded fasteners. This means there needs to be a threaded mate for it to go into, that is, a nut, insert, standoff, or worst case a tapped hole. A threaded fastener requires both acquisition of and handling the part and a tool to install it. There are likely washers and locking devices to accompany them, thus designers should design a different method of part attachment and retention. Brackets are another big waste of time and material. In most cases, a feature can be added to the piece parts of the assembly to take the place of the bracket(s). Delete the need for the bracket, and we'll also eliminate the need for the fasteners (or whatever the thought was for attaching them). If left in, the brackets will produce waste out on the other side thus the designers must ensure the design does not include brackets, if possible. The overall goal is to standardize on tools and parts across product lines and minimize tools and parts across all product lines.

Combine

The designers should seek to design an assembly with unitized parts. Design two or more parts as a single piece noting this is a common method for creating a minimally elegant design.

Simplify

Designers also need to focus on the ease of part handling or how easy the parts are to insert into the assembly. These attributes of manufacturability are hidden gems within a product design. With labor cost being such a minor portion of the cost mix, we might think "why bother?" But the greater the part count, the more important these become. Attention paid to these attributes may only account for seconds of manufacturing time, but if the parts are easier to manipulate and put into their place in the product assembly, the simpler the design is to put together. As we move further down the Lean path our goal is to flatten the BOM. Since we combine the sub-assemblies into the Lean line versus making and stocking in the past, this greatly simplifies the work of the planner because they now only must print out and release one work order at the top BOM level.

Parts Handling

With the ease of handling, we look at what the assembler must perform to pick the parts up and move the parts to the assembly. Is the part so small that the human fingers have difficulty picking it up without the use of a tool (i.e., tweezers) to grasp it with? Try to design that situation out:

- Are there springs that tangle and nest together? If springs are necessary, there are methods available in spring design to prevent this (good case for vendor involvement in the design cycle). Are there parts that resemble "spaghetti" when staged in a parts bin? This all adds time and complexity to the assembly process.
- If the part is too heavy to be lifted comfortably during a typical 8-hour shift, does it require two hands to lift, does it require a means of picking it up (i.e., a lift assist) and safely moving it to the assembly?
- Part insertion is forever overlooked in the product design. Part insertion issues include parts that jam, that are difficult to insert, that require holding down and aligning, that must be released, and that need to be dropped in properly, that is, sticky, oily, dirty, or greasy parts. Design elegance includes effortless assembly processes, such as a chamfer lead on a part that is placed into a hole gets the job done quicker.
- Is the part affixed later and requires fasteners to secure it?
- Does the part require the use of two hands, gloves, and magnifying glass?
- Does it require the use of mechanical assistance?
- Is it fragile?
- Are there storage considerations, fatigue considerations, or safety considerations?
- Review the thickness and size. Is it very small, slippery, sharp, and flexible?
- Is it cold or hot?
- What is its symmetry—alpha axis or beta axis?
- Does it require design locators for stacked assemblies (mistake proofing)?
- Does it require drilling?
- Is vision obscured while the part is being placed into the assembly?
- Is part insertion met with a resistance that will require a tool to complete it such as pressing or swaging? Attention to part insertion increases the material velocity.
- We should limit the use of tools as much as possible as well. Tools can be disruptive and require maintenance so try to design products to be assembled without the need for them

as much as possible. The best tool in the world is free ... gravity! Design for a single axis of insertion and from the top-down. Down utilizing gravity holds things together during the assembly process.

■ If there are multiple axes of insertion, the assembly must be turned around, and it creates more complexity in assembly and tends to lead to more tools required to get the job done. Placing the parts in from one direction will speed up the flow and can eliminate ergonomic issues.

Robust Processes

It is important that engineers design processes that are robust. Robustness is a difficult concept, and unlike other measures of efficiency, there is no simple equation for robustness. "Mathematicians consider a model to be robust if it is true under assumptions different from those used in building the model."[11] For a process or system to be robust, it should be stable, repeatable, and able to regulate itself. In some cases, even though designers have developed what they feel are robust systems, sometimes unusual or unexpected situations can affect them. Highly optimized tolerance was the term coined by Carlson and Doyle[12] in 1999 to describe this. To determine or measure the robustness of a process or system, we need measures that are reliable and accurate, and we need to agree on a common definition of what is robust. In simple terms, operations are looking for processes that can be standardized and generate the same consistent work product that successfully tests over and over with no trial-and-error processing, tweaking, or adjusting. Scott Rosenberg writes in his book *Dreaming in Code*[13] "At the end of the day most computer programmers entrust their meeting notes to notebooks not bytes; foolscap in their eyes is more foolproof."

Homework: Review your product portfolio and manufacturing data. Are your products robust?

Mistake Proofing

Mistake proofing should be considered throughout the design process:

■ Simple inspection methods and mistake proofing should be designed in.
■ Every operation should be designed in such a way that we never pass on a bad part (i.e., built-in quality at the source or process level). The goal should be to eliminate the need for final inspection.
■ Always make sure the parts can be installed only one way versus anyway.

The use of DFMA will automatically address ease of handling and insertion when a DFA analysis is performed in the product design cycle.

Reviewing an Assembly Using DFMA

Using DFMA to run a DFA analysis involves using a baseline or benchmark assembly. If a new design is being created without having an existing design model to follow, a first pass at the creation is what will be used. In the following simple example, the pneumatic piston assembly shown in Figure 6.4, it's a relatively small assembly that operates by air pressure to raise or lower the piston subassembly. This assembly, as designed, is already quite simple, contains only eight individual piece parts, and goes together in about 1 minute.

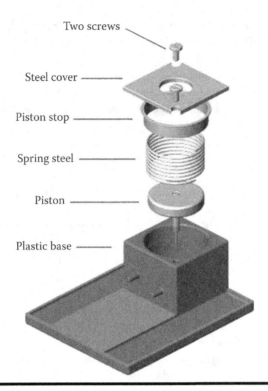

Figure 6.4 Pneumatic piston assembly.

As we break down the assembly into its elemental pieces, we begin to see the degrees of difficulty within the assembly process. The waste that this small assembly design is displaying becomes evident when we start processing it back into a completed product. The piston has a small cylindrical shaft that does not enter the hole in the bottom of the base until the piston disk enters the bore in the base. This represents an insertion difficulty, possibly taking multiple tries to get it right. The two screws require a tool (screwdriver) to install the cover, and the cover must be held down against the force of the spring to do it. The spring itself will exhibit handling difficulties because the loose springs entangle, and when one is grabbed out of a parts bin, 25 come with it. The cover requires an orientation to align the slots to the threaded holes. All these minor difficulties contribute to the manufacturing inefficiency designed into this product.

The processing required to fabricate and prepare the components for assembly contains waste as well. The steel parts must be finished in some manner to prevent corrosion. The piston subassembly requires pressing the shaft into the piston disk, allowing for unnecessary movement of materials, and likely stocking the subassembly that probably necessitates the administrative tasks and material planning that would not be required if the piston subassembly was made from a single part.

First, we need to determine the functional value of each part within the design. This becomes the theoretical minimum number of components required to make the design basically function. These will be the parts that cannot go away because of the functional requirements of the product design. We will have to answer questions relating to material, movement, and assembly access. If any one of the three questions is answered yes, then the part is a subset of the theoretical minimum. This could be a grouping or an individual component.

Using the DFMA program, we will measure each part, determine its purpose and necessity for the design to function, assess the configuration and physical attributes, and enter those characteristics into the respective fields within the input screen of the program. Once each individual piece part is addressed, the program will supply various reports grading the efficiency of the design. At this stage, most of the effort used in making a DFA analysis has been performed. From this point forward, we will use what we have input to create what-if scenarios to improve the manufacturability of the product. One of the useful reports the DFMA program provides is the Suggestions for Redesign. The report identifies where most of the time and inefficiencies are based on their attributes previously input.

The next step is to redesign the part(s). To recall the theoretical minimum parts, we have the base as it's basis part, the spring that must be steel for this design, the piston because it must move relative to the adjacent parts of the assembly, and the piston stop as it needs to be removable to assemble the piston into the block as well as limit the piston movement. The rest is disposable. The analysis shows the two cover screws bring the most touch labor to the assembly of this product. Can we eliminate them? Yes, if the piston stop piece can be self-retaining. With this example, the cover can be combined with the piston stop and be made from plastic. It can now be designed to snap into the base and retain itself, thus we have eliminated three parts and are down to five parts where there were once eight.

Going further, let's review the two-piece piston subassembly. Currently, the piston disk and the shaft are separate machined metallic details pressed together to form the subassembly. They can be combined into a single component. As an added manufacturability attribute, the piston and base are redesigned so the shaft enters the hole in the bottom of the base before the piston enters the bore allowing alignment before it drops fully into place increasing the manufacturing efficiency. Combining these parts, as was accomplished with the cover and piston stop, is also known as unitizing. Doing this has the total part count down to just four pieces. This product assembly now consists of only the original theoretical minimum list. The newly redesigned assembly is shown in Figure 6.5. The part count is 50% of what the original design contained. The results from the DFA analysis are illustrated in Table 6.2.

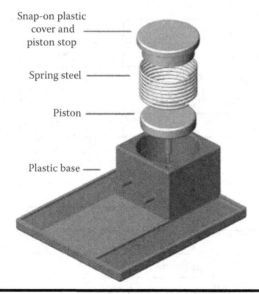

Snap-on plastic cover and piston stop

Spring steel

Piston

Plastic base

Figure 6.5   After DFMA—part count is 50% of what the original design contained.

Table 6.2 DFMA Analysis Totals Comparison Report

		Piston Original	Piston Redesign
Per Product Data			
Entries (including repeats)		10	5
Number of different entries		9	5
Total assembly labor time, minute		1.01	0.35
Weight, oz		2.12	1.98
Per Product Costs			
Labor costs, $		0.44	0.15
Other operation costs, $		0.00	0.00
Mfg. piece part costs, $		2.57	1.67
Total cost without tooling, $		3.01	1.82
Assy tool or fixture costs, $		0.02	0.02
Mfg. tooling costs, $		0.25	0.41
Total costs, $		**3.28**	**2.25**
Production Data			
Product life volume		100,000	100,000
Overall plant efficiency, %		85.00	85.00
Labor rate, $/hour		22.35	22.35
Production Life Costs			
Labor costs, $		44,477	15,444
Other operation costs, $		0	0
Mfg. piece part costs, $		257,000	167,000
Total cost without tooling, $		301,476	182,443
Assy tool or fixture costs, $		1,600	1,600
Mfg. tooling costs, $		25,154	41,068
Total costs, $		**328,230**	**225,111**
DFA Index			
Theoretical minimum number of items		4	4
DFA index		19.3	55.7
Custom Fields			
Unique count	Supplier name	4	4

Source: Courtesy of Boothroyd Dewhurst, Inc.

DFA Results

If we think of the DFA index as a manufacturing efficiency score, by redesigning this simple piston assembly, the efficiency has nearly tripled. The amount of manufacturing waste eliminated prior to design release is tremendous. Review the seven wastes and what they represent, then take a moment and recap what was done here.

- The part count was reduced by 50%.
- Material cost was reduced by 35%.
- Total assembly time was reduced by 65%.
- Total cost reduction/avoidance is 31%.

The two major benefits of taking the time to perform this redesign exercise are cutting the number of materials (parts) in half and being able to now produce nearly three times more assemblies in any given time. Remember, the main goal of Lean methodology is to increase the material velocity. In this example, a large part of this goal has been accomplished before the design has been released for production.

Not all DFMA projects will be this successful, however, there are plenty of case studies that exceed these figures. Another point to remember is these types of results shown here are typical so why would anyone not see the time spent as worth the effort? Think of the amount of money that would be lost when the design is released if it's not done.

Beyond Time and Dollars: The Hidden Benefits

The motivating factors for using a DFA and DFM in the early stages of the product design are to cut the cost to produce (CTP) and to reduce the complexity of assembly and fabrication. As we begin to use these methodologies, we soon realize that the product manufacturing efficiency improves dramatically (see Figure 6.6). Cost and time are the common denominators; thus most in the engineering and manufacturing community embrace DFM methods in product design.

There are instances when we will run a design analysis only to arrive at the new CTP as being lackluster or not significant enough to be motivated to initiate improvement(s). The engineering team will need to conduct a "deep dive" to justify an improvement if this occurs. The key ingredient to discuss improvement with management is cost as it is quantifiable and easy to calculate. In addition to cost, there is a reduced amount of time to assemble or produce a finished product. When an opportunity to reduce the part count is encountered, the manufacturing efficiency will naturally increase, thus a cost reduction is expected. But what if cost improvement doesn't happen? We experience only a 5% improvement in cost … or even less. What the heck? We've cut the part count by 50%, and there's only a 1% improvement in cost. While not that common, it sometimes can happen if we redesign our fabricated components to reduce the part count to increase the assembly efficiency. Depending on the motivation, it may be worth a cost increase to be able to improve the material velocity. If improvements have facilitated being able to produce two, or three times as many finished products in a day, would that be worth forgoing a large cost reduction? The use of DFMA will allow us to get a quantifiable set of data to allow this type of justification.

There are instances when a small cost reduction appears which requires the engineering team to look beyond the cost factor in justifying an improved efficiency. Efficiency can be measured, but it is an attribute, and attributes are typically not easy (if not impossible) to measure. If we do

Product design/Mfg. opportunity

Supplier was welding on
the inside where the
power supply fits in,
forcing the operator to
spend several minutes
filing the holes of the
power supply to
put in the nuts and bolts.

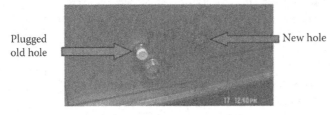

Plugged
old hole

New hole

Connection had to be plugged and moved because it was in
the wrong place on the drawing. — REWORK

Figure 6.6   Improvements made with DFMA.

find ourselves following an efficiency metric, like most of us, it's not likely we are following the whole picture.

There are many "hidden" benefits to DFM that won't be thought of during product development. As mentioned before, it's natural to focus on the cost of materials and labor during the design phase. In addition to the labor cost and the cost of parts and materials, lay another element of focus which is overhead or burden. Unless we have a process-intense design or one that contains a high number of secondary operations (such as soldering, adjustments, etc.), the inventory of our materials is most of our CTP. Typically, labor represents a mere 4%–6% of the CTP. Materials typically represent between 70% and 75% of the CTP (see Table 6.2). Burden and overhead, or the support costs, is the balance which is typically 20%–25% of the total.

Inventory is typically the boon of the large company operation metrics. We want to know how much we are buying, how much we maintain in stock, and how long it takes to process it through the enterprise to analyze the return on investment. Many manufacturing companies simply do not know how long they retain the purchased materials in their possession before being sold as finished goods (i.e., inventory turns).

The driver of the inventory metric is the design of the product. The design drives the inventory procurement, maintenance, and processing flow; thus, design improvements are required to fix any failure of a successful material inventory metric. Again… no amount of Lean assembly changes can fix a design that is inefficient to produce. In Figure 6.7, the chart represents an industry-typical cost distribution for the manufacture of products. Obviously, there is no standard mix, however, most manufacturers are within these values though many in the industry are surprised when they see this representation graphically. So why is labor such a small component of the overall scheme?

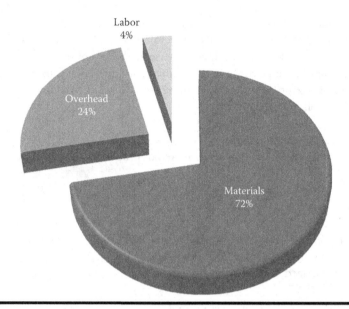

Figure 6.7 The chart represents an industry-typical cost distribution for the manufacture of products.

Why would we drive the axiom of making the product easier to put together if the labor is such a small piece of the pie? Hold that thought.

Materials generally represent the largest piece of the pie; thus, product designers often remain focused on piece part cost. While that is a necessary control to have on the product development, focusing on that alone will limit the innovation and creativity that can drive successful manufacturability attributes. The pie chart in Figure 6.7 is like a balloon. Squeeze one end and the other end grows bigger. Reduce the material cost and the labor and overhead increase. Likewise, drive an efficient-to-assemble design and the labor will decrease. When labor content drops, so will the overhead.

Overhead is often a piece that is hard to control. Many manufacturing firms simply resign themselves to that element of cost and simply accept that "it is what it is." No matter how it's looked at, overhead is waste, though it is the element that is needed to support the material and supply chain, and the labor that is needed to process the materials into the products we sell. Overhead is non-value added, whereas material and labor are value added. Overhead will reduce using DFMA, as it reduces when we reduce product part count and the level of effort it takes to process them.

Using DFMA as a tool to gauge, the design will guide us toward a product with fewer parts and a more efficient production line. DFMA gathers all the attributes of manufacturability and quantifies them into data that can be calculated into usable metrics. We can utilize the metrics to compare different design scenarios and ensure intelligent choices and decisions will be made.

Overhead has a large share of hidden manufacturing costs. In a manufacturing firm, overhead mainly supports the material supply chain and manufacturing processing, which has a direct effect on the profit margin. DFM helps to focus the analysis in areas that provide the opportunity to reduce overhead associated with supply chain and manufacturing processing. The inventory metrics most companies maintain become significantly affected by DFM. The metrics gauge inventory value, the rate at which the inventory turns, and how often the materials are consumed and replenished. A part count reduction within a design will reduce the overall inventory dollars and accelerate the material velocity through the value stream, increasing the inventory turns. Higher inventory turns results in a cash flow increase as the inventory won't be sitting on a shelf doing nothing but awaiting to be consumed. The inventory turns of a company is rarely a concern of the designer during the product development but should be! Part count reductions will have a positive effect on the following support areas:

- Utilities and facility maintenance
- Supply chain management including material procurement, handling, inspection, and storage
- Sustaining technical support
- Quality assurance functions
- Finance and accounting
- Sales and marketing—ability to provide shorter lead times to customers
- Second effort activities such as repair and reworking product defects will decrease
- Reduction in the need for tooling or fixtures

Reviewing an Assembly Using DFMA

Using DFMA to run a DFA analysis involves using a baseline or benchmark assembly. If we are creating a new design without having an existing design model to follow, a first pass at the creation is used. In the following simple example, the pneumatic piston assembly shown in Figure 6.4 is a relatively small assembly that operates by air pressure to raise or lower the piston subassembly. This assembly, as designed, is already quite simple, contains only eight individual piece parts and assembles in about 1 minute.

As the assembly is broken into its elemental pieces, we begin to visualize the degrees of difficulty within the assembly process. The waste that this small assembly design displays becomes evident when we start processing it back into a completed product. The piston has a small cylindrical shaft that does not enter the hole in the bottom of the base until the piston disk enters the bore in the base. This represents an insertion difficulty, possibly taking multiple tries to assemble it correctly. The two screws require a tool (screwdriver) to install the cover, and the cover must be held down against the force of the spring to do it. The spring will exhibit handling difficulties when the loose springs entangle, and when an operator removes one from the parts bin, 25 come with it. The cover requires an orientation to align the slots to the threaded holes. All these minor difficulties contribute to the manufacturing inefficiency designed into this product.

The processing required to fabricate and prepare the components for assembly contains waste as well. The steel parts must be finished in a manner to prevent corrosion. The piston subassembly requires pressing the shaft into the piston disk, allowing for unnecessary movement of materials, and likely stocking the subassembly that probably necessitates the administrative tasks, and material planning that would not be required if the piston subassembly was made from a single part.

The functional value of each part within the design needs to be determined. This becomes the theoretical minimum number of components required to make the design basically function. These will be the parts that cannot be removed because of the functional requirements of the product design. Questions relating to material, movement, and assembly access need to be addressed. If any one of the three questions is answered yes, then the part becomes one of the theoretical minimums. This could be a grouping or an individual component.

Using the DFMA program, we measure each part, determine its purpose and necessity for the design to function, assess the configuration and physical attributes, and enter those characteristics into the respective fields within the input screen of the program. Once each individual piece part is addressed, the program will supply various reports grading the efficiency of the design. What's next? We are going to redesign it! To recall the theoretical minimum parts, we have the base because it's the basis part, the spring because it must be steel for this design, the piston because it must move relative to the adjacent parts of the assembly, and the piston stop because it needs to be removable to assemble the piston into the block as well as limit the piston movement. The rest is disposable. So then looking at what the analysis results produced, the two cover screws bring the most touch labor to the assembly of this product. Can they be eliminated?

Yes, if the piston stop piece can be self-retaining. With this example, the cover can be combined with the piston stop and be made from plastic. It can now be designed to snap into the base and retain itself. And in doing, we eliminated three parts, and we are down to five parts where there were eight. Going further, let's look at the two-piece piston subassembly. Currently, the piston disk and the shaft are separate machined metallic details pressed together to form the subassembly. They can be combined into a single component. As an added manufacturability attribute, the piston and base are redesigned so the shaft enters the hole in the bottom of the base before the piston enters the bore allowing alignment before it drops fully into place increasing the manufacturing efficiency. Combining these parts, like the cover and piston stop, is also known as unitizing. Doing this has the total part count down to just four pieces now. See Figure 6.8. This product assembly now consists of only the original theoretical minimum list. The newly redesigned assembly is shown in Table 6.1. The part count is 50% of what the original design contained. The results from the DFA analysis are illustrated in Table 6.2.

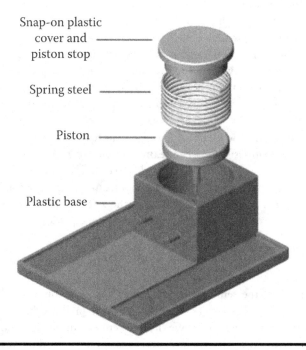

Snap-on plastic cover and piston stop

Spring steel

Piston

Plastic base

Figure 6.8   Total count down to just four pieces.

DFA Results

If the DFA index is thought of as a manufacturing efficiency score, by redesigning this simple piston assembly, the efficiency has nearly tripled. The amount of manufacturing waste eliminated prior to design release is tremendous. Look back at the seven wastes and what they represent, then take a moment and recap what was done here:

- The part count was reduced by 50%.
- Material cost was reduced by 35%.
- Total assembly time was reduced by 65%.
- Total cost reduction/avoidance is 31%.

The two major benefits of taking the time to perform this redesign exercise is cutting the number of materials (parts) in half and being able to now produce nearly three times more assemblies at any given time. Remember, the main goal of Lean methodology is to increase the material velocity. In this example, a large part of this goal has been accomplished before the design has been released for production.

Not all DFMA projects will be this successful, however, there are plenty of case studies that exceed these figures. Another point to remember is these types of results shown here are typical so why would anyone not see the time spent as worth the effort? Think of the amount of money that will be lost when the design is released, and it's not performed:

1. Transitioning Product to Production:
   Engineering should stay with the design from concept to the end of production. This is a challenge for most organizations, but the analogy that works well here is like one we use on the shop floor for welders:
   a. A welder that must clean their own welds will do it faster than the welder that has someone else to clean up their welds. This creates ownership and accountability.
   b. In the same spirit of continuous improvement, engineers who own their designs from inception to completion will find many opportunities to help the shop floor kaizen once the design is transitioned to production. This ongoing learning experience will help overcome mistakes and will create improvement opportunities for future designs.
2. Target Costing Principles:
   It is important to engage the financial management team in the process so they can understand the value and help assist the Lean teams and managers in quantifying the results. This will aid in the adoption of a Lean culture and conversion to a Lean accounting–based structure. When pricing services in the Lean value stream, we employ something called target costing. Once aligned in value streams, we use the voice of the customer to understand the value created by each value stream. This takes us to the equation

$$\text{"Selling price} - \text{cost} = \text{profit."}[14]$$

The customer sets the selling price. We work out how much can be charged for each product or service, and then work out the cost level in the value stream by subtracting required profit from the target price. We then target Lean implementations or events to drive reductions in cost (by eliminating waste) and reposition the product or service into the right place financially. If we can calculate the customer value into real numbers, the customer value-added proposition, then we have the customer value driving the Lean change. This is a difficult concept for most companies. Looking at the earlier equation let us manipulate it and solve for profit. Therefore, profit = selling price − cost, we know the customer sets the selling price based on what the customer is willing to pay (a fixed number). We can realize increased profit by reducing/driving down costs by eliminating waste by applying Lean principles.

Lesson Learned: Lean and Lean accounting principles drastically change the way we view traditional financial methodologies. Once Lean is organized around value streams, it enables a totally new paradigm to emerge, but will result in major changes to the overall organization.

The objective of a target costing program is to:

■ Lower costs of new products so required profit levels may be obtained
■ Motivate all employees to achieve the desired profit levels during development
■ Target costing should be a company-wide effort and part of the strategic plan. The formula we utilize is

$$\text{Target cost} = \text{target sales price} - \text{target operating profit}$$

Target costing should follow the following process steps[15]:

■ Life cycle planning
■ Profit planning (medium and long term)
■ Marketing survey
■ Product development (concept)
■ Development plan
■ Determine the target selling price
■ Determine target cost for product
■ Determine plant capital investment required
■ Categorize target costs into product and department (functional) elements
■ Categorize target costs into parts elements
■ Calculate specific parts costs
    − Direct material + manufacturing + processing + development non-recurring engineering (NRE)[16]
    − Create a transition to production plan
■ Measure performance to plan
■ Costs subject to target costing:
    − Material costs
    − Transportation costs
    − Coating, lubricants, and adhesive costs
    − Purchased parts cost
    − Direct labor costs
    − Variable allocated overhead costs
    − Depreciation of new equipment required
    − NRE—prototyping costs
    − New training costs

Costs not subject to target costing:

– Indirect fixed mfg. costs

Other engineering formulas to consider as part of the target costing effort:

■ Drawing efficiency = actual drawing time ÷ standard drawing time
■ Cost per drawing = total design expenses ÷ no. of drawings
■ Design charges = total design expenditures ÷ total design hours
■ Outside contractor expense ratio = outside contractor expense ÷ total design expenses
■ Subcontracting expense per drawing = outside contractor expense ÷ number of drawing pages
■ Value added per drawing
■ Overtime ration = overtime worked ÷ total labor hours
■ Design change rates = number of pages of design drawings with design changes ÷ total number of pages of drawings
■ Design change loss rate = total losses caused by design ÷ total losses caused by a company
■ Design loss rate = total losses caused by design ÷ total sales volume

How to Apply Lean Principles to the Engineering Process Itself

One of the most difficult areas to apply Lean in any company is in the engineering department itself. This is not because it is difficult to apply Lean thinking principles to engineering, it is because of the typical resistance to change we encounter. Degree of difficulty = 4.

Lean Implementation Degree of Difficulty Scale

Our degree of difficulty scale for implementing Lean is listed in the following text. This scale is based on the resistance to change as the main criterion[17] (ranking is lowest to highest):

1. Assemblers (shop floor), office staff
2. Assembly, machining, and administrative supervisors
3. Engineers—designing for Lean
4. Company board of directors
5. Finance, sales, and marketing, engineering departments
6. Machinists
7. Doctors
8. Scientists
9. Executive union leadership and senior-level managers
10. CEOs

Resistance to Change

Most engineers feel Lean is only a shop floor initiative. They reason, they are not lowly shop floor people, so it doesn't really apply to them. They already "know it all anyway." Anyone can put something together but designing takes years of education. If manufacturing can't assemble it, then something is wrong with them not us. It is surprising even today the egos and high opinions and self-esteem engineers carry about them. The only groups more resistant than engineers tend to be doctors and then scientists. Many today still believe Lean applies to only manufacturing on the floor. The following are reasons behind normal engineering resistance levels to Lean:

■ The NIH syndrome (not invented here)
  – If they didn't invent it … they want nothing to do with it.
■ The ugly baby syndrome
  – Some people love their ideas so much that they refuse to see the problems with it. They are immediately in a paradigm and cannot be objective.
■ Low assembly costs versus entire cost base
  – Low cost becomes the entire driver versus looking at the total cost of the design. The total cost would include not just the price of the part but what it takes to receive it, inspect it, stock it, install it, tools required, machines required, etc.
■ Low volume
  – The feeling here is that the volume is too low to justify putting much time into the design.
■ We are unique
  – Lean doesn't apply to us.
■ We have been doing it this way for the last 34 years
  – Why change now? It would ruffle too many feathers! Or it might rub people the wrong way.
■ This is the same as value analysis
  – The feeling here is that value analysis or value engineering is only needed after a design has been completed. Many engineers see this exercise as a waste of time as generally no changes really come out of all the effort, they put into it.
■ It leads to products difficult to service
  – Many feel because Lean makes it easier for the operators to assemble it makes everything else more difficult.
■ Design rules are better
  – The feeling here is that it is better to follow tried and true design rules or what they were taught in school versus venturing out into the application of new principles.

We know some of us think Lean won't work for our operation. Maybe a high mix exists or there is a job shop–type environment. Maybe we have experienced generic Lean training, participated in point kaizen events, tried to 5S the workplace, realign the material flow, or develop visual controls, and it still has not moved the needle enough for the time and expense we put into it. Maybe we think Lean applies only to the shop floor, not engineering.

Lesson Learned: At Company X, when training participants in Lean, we learned to mix in the engineers with other personnel. The worst mistake we ever made was to conduct a Lean seminar for just engineering. The engineers had this "superiority complex" during the entire seminar. When we did assembly exercises, they felt none of it applied to them. I am sure some of the blame must go to the trainer; however, they fought us the entire time. Part of the training was a DFMA exercise. We brought a new design into the training class that was ready to be launched in a couple of months. We had the engineers set up a Lean line for the parts. We then had the most experienced operator from the floor come in to assemble the unit. Since the operator had worked with us on a Lean line already, she had no problem sharing all the improvements required in the new design. We then made the engineers build the unit. The first argument we heard was "you can build this; I don't see the problem." We told the engineer they didn't have to build every day for 8 hours a day with the convoluted methods they designed.

A slight few of the engineers were humbled by this exercise, and one engineer told me it was the best class he ever attended. The rest of the engineers were of course very defensive and refused to make the necessary changes to the design because of course they thought they knew more than their shop floor team members as to how to build and assemble the units. So does all this resistance mean that Lean won't work for an enterprise? Author Jamie Flinchbaugh[18] writes:

> What is the hardest field in which to apply Lean?
>
> It doesn't seem to matter what field you're in, they all think theirs is the hardest and they can back it up with evidence. One of the most frequent questions I get is "Who else in my industry is doing Lean?" because no one wants to be first, and no one wants to be last.

Boeing Utilizing Innovation Teams to Increase 737 Production

The Wall Street Journal reports how Boeing is looking into employee ideas and innovation teams to find ways to raise 737 production rates. So far, there are 1,300 teams throughout the company's commercial plane division.[19] Bloomberg News (2/7, Ray) reports, "Boeing Co. and General Electric Co. completed configuration plans for new engines on the 737 MAX, the upgraded version of the world's most widely flown plane, an important step toward eventual production," a GE executive said. David Joyce said, "We're going to take full advantage of the integration we do with Boeing and with Spirit to make sure the overall engine-airplane combination is incredibly efficient from an integrated propulsion system and the engine is really optimized for this airplane." Boeing is now right-sizing and building much of their equipment in house.

Where to Start: Overall Engineering Effectiveness Scale for a Project

Calculate the overall engineering effectiveness (OEE) for a day or for a particular project. For instance, if you are a design engineer, how much of your time is spent physically or mentally working on a new design? The components of OEE are like that of a machine: available time, operating rate, and quality of work.

1. Available Time:

   Items that impact available time are things just like on the floor that impact machines. To calculate your available time per day, start with the length of your workday. For example, we start with the time you are paid. If it is for an 8-hour day, then we start with 480 minutes. Next subtract all breaks (coffee, lunch, socializing, etc.), and the time left is your available time to work on a project supporting a customer. As an example, the company offers 30 minutes of breaks per day. For this example, your available time is 450 minutes per day to work. The maximum amount of time left is 450 minutes for the day. The next step is to determine the percent of time working on direct value-added customer activities. For this example, assume you spend 85% of your time working on what you are supposed to be working on which is customer value-added design activities. Next, we determine your operating rate.

2. Operating Rate:

What is your level of concentration? How efficient are you? Are you searching for everything? Are you working on 10 projects at once? Do you have a headache? Are you feeling well? Let's assume you are working at 95% efficiency. The next step is to review your overall quality levels.

3. Quality:

   a. How much of what you do is normally done right the first time?

   b. How many reviews does it have to go through? Internal, customer, qualification testing?

   c. What is your first time through percentage? How many of what you do makes it through the whole process without a problem (defect)?

   d. How often do you have to rework it?

   e. Let's assume 80% of what you do is done right the first time (no rework!)

To determine the OEE, multiply these number percentages together to obtain the OEE, thus, $0.85 * 0.95 * 0.80 = 64.6\%$ efficient, and this assumes you return from breaks on time.

Homework: Calculate your OEE.

Low-Hanging Fruit

The best place to start is by collecting data. Collecting data will quantify the benefit obtainable by reducing the low-hanging fruit. Some low-hanging fruit examples are as follows:

Meetings

How much time is spent in meetings, preparing for the meetings, making presentations, etc.? An analogy we use is that in hospitals, we find nurses and doctors usually spend less than 30% of their time with the patients. We have found similar scenarios with engineers. Only about 30% of their time is spent related to their passion, which is design. The balance of time is wasted in a variety of ways.

- Are you attending too many meetings?
- What percent of your time is spent at meetings?

Homework: Track how many hours are spent attending meetings; note how many meetings ran too long, did not have an agenda, you didn't need to be there, percent of your time spent, which was value added.

Planned Downtime

For the engineer, planned downtime is any recurring scheduled meeting, that is, monthly design review, daily engineering team huddle, weekly material review board (MRB) meeting. Note: Any true project design–related meeting can be considered value added if the end customer is receiving value from your time at the meeting. Otherwise, it is non-value added and should be subtracted from your OEE available time. For instance, MRB meetings are non-value added and should be eliminated. Clearly, the customer doesn't want to pay for you to attend a meeting that could result in them having to issue a waiver, deviation, or some relaxation of the specification! We have successfully eliminated formal MRB meetings at every plant we have tried.

Unplanned Downtime

For our engineer, any "spur of the moment" meetings or unplanned calls to action where you must stop what you are doing to go fix some urgent or nonurgent situation. These can be generated by a boss, subordinate, another department, manufacturing floor issue, etc. Note: These all get subtracted from your OEE available time.

Phone Calls

Track your time spent per day on phone calls. How many minutes or hours per day are spent on the phone? Was the call value added? Were you the right person for the call? Were all the right people required on the call?

Value-Added Criteria for Engineer (Must Meet All Three)

1. Is the customer willing to pay for it?
2. Did it physically change the thing (information) you are working on?
3. Was it done right the first time?

The conceptual phase for the engineer is considered value added.

Searching—3 Seconds Rule

Whether you are looking for files on a computer, paper in a cabinet, pen in a drawer, etc., it is considered wasted time. Your space should be organized so that you can find anything in 3 seconds or less!

How to Start Leaning the Engineering Design Process: A Transactional Process

Note: The following information is quoted from or directly influenced by a book called *Design Team Revolution*,[20] which should be read by every engineering student.

What Is the Design Process?

The design process can be defined as the process of creating drawings or submitting information (which we call specifications) to processing by people (or machines) that possess technical knowledge:

■ The product of the design process is the drawings themselves.
■ The users of the drawings are the workers on the floor and subcontractor factories.

■ The workers in the design process are the designers. However, designers are different from general equipment operators in that they have high levels of specific technical knowledge, a sense of design, and abundant skill.

Perhaps the most essential design equipment, however, is the human mind. In factories, the primary materials are tangible objects. In design, however, the primary materials are intangible information:

■ About user needs and parts required for assembly
■ Technologies, technical information
■ Information about competitors

The difference between the factory process and the design process is even more pronounced if one considers that in the factory process, the result is a tangible product suitable for marketing to consumers. When the design process is defined in this way, then knowledge of design itself is a technology possessed only by the individual. However, knowledge of how to shorten lead times and reduce headcounts is a technology that can be shared—a common knowledge. Consequently, the rules for improving the design process do not vary from one design department to another.

Seven Wastes of Design

In the book *Design Team Revolution*,[20] the authors discuss the seven wastes for engineering, which are as follows:

■ Attending too many meetings and conferences
■ Questioning unclear requirements and specifications
■ Altering designs to correct defects
■ Retrieving or searching for drawings and materials
■ Permitting designers to set their own schedules
■ Preparing new drawings
■ Designing new estimate drawings and reference drawings

Other Engineering Wastes

1. Design rework:
   a. Requirement changes
   b. Design errors
   c. Inconsistent factory or support process
   d. Inadequate program plan
2. Lack of design reuse
3. Poor factory yields due to design (low sigma):
   a. Lost material (material that had to be scrapped or inspected/sorted due to not meeting engineering specs)
   b. Lost labor (repair, rework, manual, or operators interjected into the in-process or final test cycle to press a key, decide—these should be go/no go)
   c. Engineering support required due to poor designs

4. Overdesign—exceeds customer requirements:
   a. Expensive parts designed into the product
   b. Excessive test designed into the product
   c. Excessive software costs
   d. Design too complex
5. Wasted labor due to inadequate staffing both cross-functional and functional

Batching versus Sequential Engineering Design Processes

The design process takes a long time sometimes even for simple products. In a way, it's like sports. You think about how much value-added time can be found in baseball, football, soccer, or the game of golf. In soccer, only one person has the ball at a time; everyone else is idle. In baseball, the pitcher and catcher are busy, but other than the batter and occasional runner, everyone else is mostly idle. In football, most of the time is spent in huddles, waiting for commercial breaks to end or in time-outs. In golf, we have a four-piece batch. We must wait while four people individually hit the ball in sequence before the group can move forward. In fact, over 90% of golf is waiting or transporting.

This is analogous to making one product or part at a time in a batch of four pieces. Delays result from poor scheduling, slow golfers, or a golfer that spends a lot of time searching for a lost ball. Then there are those that must practice six swings before finally hitting the ball.

In the engineering design process, we run into similar problems as those that hold up the golfer. When we apply our Lean analysis tools of following the product and then the operator, we find similar results. Most of the time, either the design itself is in storage or the engineer is waiting. Delays are caused by the following:

Salespeople

Lack of technical training—they make wrong assumptions, errors of fact, or make judgment calls without checking with engineering or manufacturing. They neglect the specifications or sign up to specs they don't know if they can meet.

Poor Design Process

There are many delays and approval cycles within and outside the organization. As with batching in production, engineers work on the easiest drawings first.

Rework

There are too many projects at the same time, which are allowed to set their own schedules and spend a lot of time reworking designs.

Lack of 5S

They spend time searching for drawings, tools, and materials.

To correct some of these delays, we need to train sales in the specifications and make sure that they don't try to sell a product before it is designed or commit to specifications that can't be met.

What We Find in the Engineering Process

- Batching—When you batch in the design process, you fall victim to the same evils as when you batch in any process, which means we work on the easiest drawings first.
- Too many projects are delegated to too few people at the same time.
- Many times, we permit designers to set their own schedules. For some designers, this may work out well, but for most, you may never see the design completed.
- Engineers spend their valuable expensive time searching for drawings and other materials to do their job. In some cases, it may be searching through e-mail or through mountains of directories to get to the file they need. Like manufacturing, engineers too need the right tools and materials at their station when required.
- We find too much time spent reworking designs. Rework is time-consuming, frustrating, and non-value added.
- And for some of you, you may find that you are spending too much time in too many meetings, most of which you did not need to be there and were a waste of your time.
- Salespeople generally have a lack of technical training, neglect to obtain critical specifications, or take special orders to specs they can't possibly meet. Cross-functionality creates a better understanding of needs from all areas.
- We also find poor design processes in general. We find delays in handoffs from engineer to engineer or to outside parties.
- We find delays are also incurred during the approval cycles.

Use the BASICS® Model to Begin Cutting Design Process Lead Times by Half

We follow the BASICS® process just like in manufacturing or for any transactional process. Every engineering process has a product or thing going through the process. For instance, ECR is following the engineering change request form. After we do the process flow analysis (PFA), we then video the operators and engineers, working on the process or things going through the process. It is amazing to see all the waste that occurs. The improvement procedure can be broken down into the following BASICS® steps:

1. Baseline—understand the current conditions
2. Assess—make the waste visible
   a. Conduct a PFA or wall map exercise
   b. Film each engineer during the process and analyze the videos with the engineers
3. Suggest solutions based on the videos. Map out an assembly line–type process for the information production line. Envision the linear flow of design information
4. Implement—create a pilot line. Physically line up the desks along the design routes of each type of design
5. Check—do continual follow-up studies to repeat the process
6. Sustain (Act)—build in goals designed to continuously improve the flow of design information. Update the standard work processes

Baselining the Process: Study the Current Design Lead Time

The design lead time is the total time spent in actual design work (actual time [AT]) plus the time when the designs are not in process (storage time [ST]). The ratio of AT to ST is probably one to nine. By merely cutting the design ST by half, you can cut the design lead time also by half.

Value Stream Map the Process

The best place to start in engineering is with a high-level value stream map (VSM). This VSM will allow the team (and manager) to visualize the overall process. It is not an easy map to construct as we are mapping information flow against information flow. To do this successfully, one must start with the thing you are going to follow through the process. Out of this, VSM will pop several potential projects. Each project will probably end up with its own VSM.

VSM the entire process—from ordering and establishing specifications to working on design and shipping the drawings. These maps can become quite complex. The point of creating such charts is to make clear at a glance those parts of the process not understood. Another purpose is to visually show the entire system, make it more transparent, and highlight wherever there are process delays.

Conduct a PFA on the Process and Draw a Point-to-Point Diagram

- Follow each step, starting with the request for drawing or specification, until the design is completed. Then get a layout of the office or building and draw a point-to-point diagram of how the request travels from point-to-point numbering each one. This is difficult as the request will morph into different pieces of information as it travels throughout the process.
- Film each engineer or staff person through each step of the process and prepare a spaghetti diagram.
- Review the videos with the supervisor, engineer, and someone who knows nothing about the process. This person will be able to ask all the "stupid" questions and question every step. Look for waste and hidden waste, that is, waste that hides behind other waste. Look for duplication and problems the engineer normally runs into. Try to surface every issue and opportunity that presents itself:
    - Why is a particular employee so often absent?
    - What is the cause of so many business trips?
    - Why do employees spend so much time conferring with each other?
    - What percentage of design activities is beneficial?
    - The answer is usually less than 25% because the remaining time is usually spent in "office routines."
    - Why must fabrication drawings be made one at a time?
    - Why do retrieving documents take so much time?
- Then draw a spaghetti diagram that traces the routes walked by workers as they go through the design process. You will be surprised by all the waste discovered in the videos as well as seeing how much distance and the paths that are traveled by everyone connected to the process.

Ten Rules for Improving the Design Process[20]

1. **Prepare in advance whatever can be prepared in advance.**

    The first rule for improving the design process is to prepare in advance whatever can be prepared in advance. The most conspicuous problem in the preparation phase is starting to work on the design before the specifications are set. When this happens, the work degenerates into "it's-probably-like-this" design and "imagine" design. Under normal conditions, there is already a lot of waste inherent in the design process. It is therefore especially important to eliminate the factors that create a need to begin the design process prematurely before specifications are set.

Managers in charge of design often think of their designers as "design machines," so when new projects are on the block, the managers work hard to decide "which designer should be assigned (saddled) with them." Managers don't often consider how to improve the efficiency of design work or how to find new ways to produce the drawings or to promote the flow of information.

Level load the design work. There should be a smooth scheduling of the design process. Normally, peaks and valleys of design load are cruelly extreme, and a lot of overtime must be put in because of tight schedules. Smoothing out the process can allay the need for this excessive overtime. Smooth production scheduling in the design process is based on value-adding activities or sales. Beware of scope creep. Any changes requested in house or by the customer should go through some type of formal budgeting process and reviewed prior to adding to the design scope of work.

2. **Restrict the choices of specifications by compiling recommended specifications into a specification decision book. Don't allow the customer to demand specialty items on a haphazard basis.**

   Marketing representatives, whose job it is to get work for the company, may confuse the customer by claiming the company can do this or that even when it comes to minute details. Often, they end up promising what amounts to highly specialized projects, thereby causing design changes and jeopardizing quality levels, delivery deadlines, and profits.

   Instead, have the marketing representatives use a specification decision book, one that includes an option system by which designs and products can be delivered inexpensively and on time. The marketers can then sell themselves to the customers to the degree they can say, "Leave the specifications of the main unit, before options, to me."

   In making a specification decision book that discourages troublesome demands, include illustrated technical materials and catalogs that can be easily understood. In addition, make sure the salespeople possess not only technical education and service capabilities but also technical service backgrounds. Salespeople should also attend study tours of customers' factories and participate in setting the product specifications.

3. **Begin work on designs only after classifying their content as full change (FC) or running change (RC) and classifying customer prospects as hot (H), warm (W), or cold (C).**

   The third rule may seem to be an extension of the first. It involves analyzing the degree of difficulty of the tasks involved in the design project. To begin, marketing divides the customer prospects into three categories: hot (H), warm (W), or cold (C). It then gives this information to the design department, which creates drawings for use in making estimates. To prevent the design from wasting time on estimate drawings, which takes nearly as long as making entirely new drawings, the company should come up with an estimate request form. Design can then provide the estimated drawings in accordance with the prospect's category (H, W, or C). First, however, the company should be aware of the costs involved in making estimated drawings. The following list shows the time (in days) required to perform each of several tasks in the design process. The number assigned to each task relates to an arbitrary baseline value of 1.0, which is assigned to the task of working with familiar standard designs:

   – 2.5 Preparation of new drawings required for estimates and drawing new designs for authorization or approval

- 1.7 Working on new designs, but without cost estimates
- 1.4 Experienced designers working with designs with which the company has no experience
- 1.0 Working with familiar standard designs
- 0.8 Using composite designs for part of the drawing process
- 0.5 Using standard-use designs and composite designs
- 0.1 Recycling old designs

Generally, by employing standard-use designs, you can significantly reduce design times. For example, employing standard-use designs can reduce the time required to produce a size A4 drawing from about 2 days to 1 day. When you compare this with the time required to create drawings for new designs (including those needed for estimates), the importance of informing the design department of the strength of the customer prospects becomes obvious.

4. **The key to cutting design lead times by half is performing**

    Utilize the BASICS® model and then plan–do–check–act to continually improve your design lead times. Map out your design cycles for existing, new, and modified parts. Then look at each step to see what you can eliminate, rearrange, simplify, or combine.

5. **Make design production lines and create methods that cause design information to flow into the creation of drawings:**

    a. Use commonsense to eliminate waste in the design process. There is more waste in some companies than in others. For example, some companies waste time deciphering illegible drawings and producing defective products based on incorrect designs. Because the factory bears the brunt of these problems, these forms of waste would become more obvious if people from design met with people from the factory floor. Begin by eliminating those forms of waste easiest to remove.

    b. The first form of waste, rework, is caused when design work starts before user needs are fully understood. The roots of this trouble usually lie in the marketing process. The marketing representative, anxious to close a deal, agrees to certain specifications without consulting the designers.

    c. The second type of waste is reworking drawings in response to design changes requested by the factory, subcontractors, or purchasing department. The causes of this type of waste are the same as for the first type of waste.

    d. The third waste is idleness that stems from missing drawings. The drawings should be turned over to the factory in the amounts needed and at the time when they are needed. Often, however, because designers tend to work on the easiest designs first, the factory is deluged with drawings it doesn't need. Therefore, time is wasted in the factories because the drawings the factory does need aren't forthcoming. This phenomenon is often seen when the design department forgets its true obligation and instead concentrates on how efficient the design department itself can be. In such cases, the design department should reexamine its objective.

    e. The fourth waste is idleness caused by delays in specification decisions. This type of waste is like the first type and is caused by poor performance in the predesign steps.

    f. The fifth waste is repeated submission of drawings for an estimate. Although the customer-first mentality is desirable, care must be taken because it can cause the design department to lose sight of true priorities. Remember the third rule: Begin work on designs only after classifying their content as FC or RC and classifying customer prospects as H, W, or C. Other forms of waste, such as waste caused by design "office work" and waste caused by unnecessary motion, are obvious and thus need not be discussed. Search for waste from three angles, from the perspectives of preparation, process delays, and the design processes themselves. The following sorts of waste are associated with preparation because they can be minimized by improvements to the preparation phase:

    I. Design changes caused by the weak determination of specifications

    II. Excessively long design lead times

    III. Creation of entirely new drawings

    IV. Frequent repetition of the same design

    V. Factory idleness due to missing drawings

    VI. Repetition of strength calculations for each design

    VII. Repeated examination and correction of designs

g. Arrange the desks so that tasks may be divided and work may flow in a manner like that of a factory production line. Arrange the desks and the instruments in a straight line or in a U-shaped line. Eliminate cubicles between engineers in general, especially those working on the same projects. We have also added purchasing, project managers, and other value stream members to the team and co-located them in the same area.

6. **Make new designs, but don't prepare new drawings.**

    For example, you can do the following:

  – Use a standard catalog; prevent order forms from entering the design process.

  – Provide standard options assembled into products in the factory; prevent design request forms from entering the design process.

  – Prevent RCs (changes in which a small part is added to the product) from entering the design process; create a system whereby RCs are handled in the factory prototype line. Parts should be placed on a Kanban system and should be drawn directly from parts stores.[2]

  – Standardize parts and modular units.

  – Establish standard-use drawings and encourage their application.

  – Compiled design (or composite design) refers to the practice of lifting those portions from existing drawings that illustrate product components that have worked well in the past and then incorporating these excerpts into new drawings. Any repetitive elements in design work should be incorporated into the compiled designs.

  – Distribute standard-parts drawings and standard-use drawings, standardizing designs. Ideally, no encoding is done until the newly compiled drawings are completed. This is because drawings of individual components or parts are not by themselves sufficient to transmit design information.

7. **Work first on the drawings that require the longest design lead times and the products that have the longest manufacturing lead times.**

    The seventh rule for improving the design process is to work first on those drawings that require the longest lead times and those products that have the longest manufacturing lead times. This rule is extremely important in preventing factory idle time caused by missing drawings. Make separate standard schedules for FCs, modified changes, and RCs, and then create a design control board, following the philosophy of visual control (see Figure 6.9).

    Create withdrawal Kanbans for completed drawings and position them between the factory and the design department. The aim is to provide drawings to the factory at the time the factory needs them, in the order in which they are needed, and in the amount, they are needed. The design scheduling plan serves as a gauge for the process and should be advanced by the design control board. However, adjustments in drawing completion schedules should

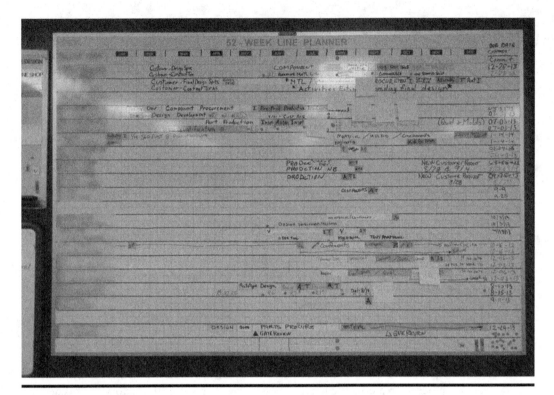

Figure 6.9   Visual design control board.

be controlled by the withdrawal Kanbans for completed drawings. Once you understand the fundamental philosophies, it is easy to apply Kanbans to the design process.

Locate the withdrawal Kanbans near or on the design control board. The design section manager divides the withdrawal Kanbans among the designers and directs the completion of designs according to the design control board. If a designer is unable to meet the deadline listed on a design directive Kanban, he or she reports to the section manager and makes the necessary arrangements.

8. **For those designs whose lead times need to be shortened immediately, implement parallel design systems.**

   Pareto analysis helps identify major causes or factors by creating a bar graph that ranks the causes from most frequent to least frequent (reading left to right). A scale on the right vertical axis measures the cumulative effect of each cause.

   Parallel Design and Sequential Design

   Sequential design is a system in which a single designer oversees various designs and takes each of them through the entire design process. This system effectively prevents designers from becoming idle: however, it leads to delays in the projects themselves. The situation can be likened to one in golf, in which one person is making a shot and the other team members must stand by, idle. Because each shot takes, on average, only about 10 seconds (including the time it takes to address the ball), this sequential process presents no problems. In design, however, entire sets of designs are brought to a standstill when designs are done in batches. Thus, eliminating the storages caused by sequential processing is important to shortening lead times. You can get immediate results by taking a sequential design previously handled by a single designer and distributing the work in a parallel design manner between four designers. When a parallel design is successful, making design production lines is not that difficult—and not much different from making a production line in a manufacturing organization.

Method of Shortening Throughput Times

Throughput time can be defined as the time it takes to produce designs. It is generally calculated through the use of the following formula. Assume for now that the net time for design is equal to the actual design processing time.

$$\text{Throughput time} = \text{processing time} + \text{storage time}$$

Here, processing time includes the total time required for each process, plus the time required for the inspection of drawings as well as the time required for transportation. ST is the sum of the time that drawings are delayed. Drawings can be delayed when an engineer is batching them or they are batched for the same step between engineers (lot delay) or when all the drawings are waiting for the next step (between processes). To be more precise, we must include the time that drawing lots await transportation and that drawings await inspection. Drawings are delayed within the process when for some reason work is interrupted or we are waiting for information to complete the drawing.

Create Ways to Eliminate Storage Delays in Design

The lot delay can be eliminated through a move to one-piece or one-drawing flow. If for some reason you can't flow the drawings through like an assembly line then cut the batch size to the smallest quantity possible. Where you cannot do one-piece flow you can use Kanbans to link the processes together.

Aggressively Eliminate the Causes of Delays

In manufacturing tangible goods, the most important thing you can do to assure quality control is to eliminate the storage that conceals the root causes of defects. This applies to the engineering design cycle as well. Generally, both causes and corrective actions are associated with storage. Determine which causes create the greatest delays in your department and then focus all your energies on eliminating those causes one by one.

Create a Smooth Flow of Processes

9. **Incorporate the inspection of drawings into the design production line.**

Historically, such inspections have not been carried out properly. In all companies, there are boxes for each design marked Reviewed By, and in each box, there is a reviewer's signature. However, no company really examines or reviews the designs—the designs are merely rubber-stamped as they are completed. This is because design departments know that it takes more time to thoroughly examine designs than it takes to make the designs in the first place.

Although all companies regard the inspection process as necessary, they believe it is too much work to inspect the designs. Besides, the general feeling is that all designers are experienced in their profession and therefore produce designs probably flawless anyway. However, recently, there has been an increase in the number of wide-variety small-lot designs, and the total number of design projects has increased. In addition, the number of inexperienced designers (with less than three years' experience) has increased. The result of these trends is that in the worst design departments, 86% of the designs require changes, and in the best design departments, 24% of the designs must be modified.

Making a design line and (even though it is an onerous task) inspecting each design in-line are essential to improving the design process. Some useful hints on improving the inspection process follow:

- Use cut-and-paste (compiled) design, employing designs from products that worked well.
- Promote standardization of parts, eliminating the need to make new drawings.
- Mold the design process into a production line and create a system of division of labor. Because the work is being segmented, overlap can be designed into the work transfers, thus creating an automatic 100% inspection system. Special attention should be paid to tie-ins and connections.
- Inspect the board and lay out the vertical and horizontal drawings for 100% inspection.
- Have two designers working together through the entire process. It becomes a total collaboration where when one works the other checks the work.
- Have the designer working at the next process give the stamp of approval.
- Have the designers used a public self-training chart?
- Run training programs for newly hired designers.

10. **Rather than starting with the standardization of design, first tackle the standardization of parts.**
    - Success in standardizing designs is difficult to obtain. Although some department managers succeed in imposing strict adherence to standardization, many design department managers find it difficult to ensure that the standardization is performed thoroughly. For example, few companies are even thorough in their use of standard bolts, nuts, and screws:
    - Prepare in advance whatever can be prepared in advance.
    - Restrict the choices of specifications by compiling recommended specifications into a specification decision book. Don't allow the customer to demand specialty items on a haphazard basis.
    - Begin work on designs only after classifying their content as FC or RC and classifying customer prospects as hot (H), warm (W), or cold (C).
    - The key to cutting design lead times in half is performing a Pareto analysis on the process delays and focusing on the lead times associated with the major causes of delays.
    - Make design production lines and create a method that causes design information to flow into the creation of drawings.
    - Make new designs, but don't prepare new drawings.
    - Work first on the drawings that require the longest design lead times and the products that have the longest manufacturing lead times.
    - For those designs whose lead times need to be shortened immediately, implement parallel design systems.
    - Incorporate the inspection of drawings into the design production line.
    - Rather than starting with the standardization of design, first tackle the standardization of parts.

Importance of Design and +QDIP Delivery Lead Times

It is said that skill in design determines 70% of manufacturing performance. Quality is the one -metric currently emphasized in design management. However, if design is defined as the technology of integrating available technological knowledge into drawings according to given specifications, then the constraining conditions of delivery deadlines should take precedence over all other concerns. Delivery deadlines are often ignored when the focus is on quality or cost. Yet the overriding factor is that designs be completed within the agreed-upon delivery deadlines, even when unforeseen changes introduce unknown factors along the way.

Safety, quality, delivery, inventory, and productivity (+QDIP) boards can be implemented in engineering just like on the shop floor. Each letter takes on a different significance. For example, quality may be the accuracy of the BOM submitted to manufacturing. Delivery may be the timeliness of engineering responses to manufacturing, sales, customer service, etc.

Tool Boards Exercise—Which Tools Don't Belong?

These are tools on an actual tool board used for assembling sheet metal-based products. It is missing the air-powered impact gun in the top right-hand corner. If the product was truly engineered and designed correctly, which tools do you think we would/should really need? Don't forget to consider the crowbar, measuring tape, and air hose located on the bottom (See Figure 6.10).

Answer

If you said that the following should not belong, you would be correct:

- Wrenches—hand wrenches are poor ergonomically. Preference would be to use some type of socket driver.
- Hammers—we should never need a hammer if the design is good.

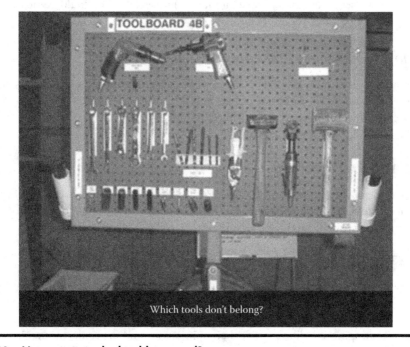

Which tools don't belong?

Figure 6.10   How many tools should we need?

Figure 6.11   Excess tools pictured on the right after 5S Sort.

- Drill bits—with drill bits present, one would infer that a hole must be drilled or it is in the wrong place or not the right size. The proper hole should have been punched into the sheet metal prior to assembly. If we don't need drill bits, then we don't need the drill!
- Measuring tape—should not need if everything is designed correctly.
- Crowbar—we should never need it on the assembly line.
- Drift pins (on right in PVC pipe holder)—we should not need the pins to align the holes if everything lines up correctly.
- Sockets—why do we need so many? Can't we standardize on one bolt size?

In summary we need the airline, impact gun, and one socket. One could argue that we might need one wrench to hold the nut on the other side.

How Many Tools Does It Take to Put Together a Unit?

Which are the right tools? The picture on the left side of Figure 6.11 is the base workstation. After 5S'ing all the stations (see the right side of Figure 6.11) we had all these tools left over. We discovered there were many tools there that were never used.

Change and Engineers

The real key to Lean is creating a culture where it is easy to implement ideas. One of the barriers one runs into is ideas that require engineering support. Between Dr. Shingo and Mr. Ohno, they came up with three types of Engineers[21]. In the words of Dr. Shingo[22]:

Three Types of Engineers Who Hold Up Improvement

I often explain that in Japan there are three types of engineers who get in the way of improvement:

1. Table Engineers—like to voice their opinions around the conference table. Their arguments are based on theory. They like to enthusiastically debate around the

conference table but never go onto the shop floor and dirty their hands by doing anything themselves. The loudest engineer wins the debate and has his or her plans implemented. However, things never turn out very well.

2. Catalog Engineers—like to collect catalogs for new equipment and propose the machines that look best to them. They are proud when new equipment is purchased and put into use. They have no problem buying more equipment or more features than what is really needed. Their ideas are never their own. Likewise, the machines they buy are inevitably equipped with extraneous functions designed to meet the demands of a wide range of companies. Ordinarily, suitable equipment can be constructed in-house at one-third to one-fifth the cost of these market machines because the outside vendor breaks down the sales price into three equal parts:

    a. Idea fees and design costs
    b. Actual manufacturing costs
    c. Profit and the cost of rework risk, etc.

    Manufacturing the same equipment in-house would entail only actual manufacturing costs. In addition, the people who designed and built it would be on hand to make rapid repairs should any problems arise. In-house construction need not involve producing every equipment part in one's own factory. Significant cost reductions can be obtained simply by having subcontractors build parts and by doing as much of the assembly work as possible. Ohno stated "Years ago I made myself unpopular by suggesting people in Toyota's production engineering department were 'catalogue engineers.' You can't, I told them, just look at catalogues and tell us that this machine looks good or we could double or triple productivity with that machine. We need machines that you guys have developed yourselves."[23]

3. NYET Engineers—This is the third and most dangerous type of engineer. This type stems from the days when Andrei Gromyko, then Soviet Ambassador to the United Nations, was nicknamed "Mr. Nyet" because he resoundingly vetoed all Western proposals. These engineers are the first to say No it's impossible or No it's too difficult without giving any real thought. Answering all proposals with a 'nyet' no doubt precludes any improvement at all. No improvement can take place unless we keep an open mind and a positive attitude. And most important of all is a readiness to try any possible improvement. Understanding the basic techniques of how improvement should be carried out lies at the heart of production management improvement.

Change and Engineers: Factory Work Is beneath Them

In a paper written by Charles W. Protzman Sr. entitled A Survey of 70 Japanese Companies in 1949 during the WWII GHQ Occupation of Japan, he states as follows:

These sites lacked both practical engineering concepts as related to manufacture and fundamental management concepts and practices for effective control of the business. I discovered the theoretical and research phases of engineering were emphasized and that for prestige, an engineer must go into the laboratory or research fields. To work in the factory on manufacturing, production or inspection problems was beneath the dignity of the engineer. He was not generally responsible for production planning, manufacturing techniques or costs. The management weaknesses were evident in loose supervision, lack of knowledge of costs, absence of control techniques, failure to recognize the inter-relationships of various company functions and in many instances, one man domination.

Obviously quality control in even its most elementary form was impossible under these conditions. Beyond this, the company was in dire financial straits (inventory, cash flow etc.) due, to a considerable extent, to their failure to do a good job of internal management and control. But until the management could be convinced that action must be taken and find ways of taking the initiative, we could not work toward our objectives of improving quality or getting the company on a sound economic footing.

Conditions were further aggravated by the attrition of skilled supervisor and management personnel due to the new career planning approach and dropping of sound economic production concepts due to the lack of competition. Defined basic policies were often lacking or were changed to fit the expediency of the moment; organization structure was frequently haphazard, top-heavy, and lacked coordination. Authority matching responsibility was not delegated downward to the point of action; jobs were undefined. Few lower supervisors knew what their job encompassed and fewer yet had any training or managerial background. Even the higher executives were frequently in a fog as to what they should be doing or how to do it. Management tools in the form of integrated methods, organization control, instructions, operational techniques, personnel policies, material controls, worker efficiency measurement, etc. Were almost completely lacking.

Accounting and cost structures and methods were antiquated and inadequate from the standpoint of usability for operation and control. As a result, both productive and non-productive costs were excessive. Factory managers had no yardstick for adequate measurement of operations or overhead. Neither profit nor loss could be related to the specific functions, products, or operations, which were responsible for the conditions. Hence no effective corrective action was taken. There was a lack of real management leadership. Management did not tap the resources of ideas available in lower levels in the absence of two-way communications, in the frustration and lack of cooperation, enthusiasm and morale at lower supervisory and worker levels.

In most cases there was a real desire on the part of these lower levels to contribute and that it would take very little encouragement to generate a high degree of enthusiastic support and cooperation in programs of improvement. What was needed was a feeling on the part of all the employees they were contributing beyond the mechanical performance of the job to the well-being of the company.

Charles W. Protzman Sr.
Civic Communications Section

We once made the mistake of handing this survey out to a meeting of plant managers and asking them if any of these points applied to their plants. Each one wanted to know whose plant was cited in this because they were afraid it was theirs. Upon telling them that this was written about companies in Japan in 1949, they were all very upset we had "fooled them" into thinking this was one of their plants. Judging from the response and subsequent visits to their plants, we found most of these applied.

Lesson Learned: People tend to get upset over things that hit very close to home.

Homework: Do any of these points apply to your plants today? If so, be honest and list them out and discuss with your senior staff. Lean is about turning everyone in the company into an industrial engineer. A good Lean line starts with the engineering design!

Change and Toyota Engineers

In 1998, Toyota was able to reduce the Corolla by $1,500 compared with the 1997 model. In the USA Today article below see Figure 6.12 they state, "the 1997 Toyota Camry goes on sale cheaper than the 1996." On the same page was another article entitled "Ford Backs Down from Higher Priced Strategy." Remember our cost equations? Which one is Toyota using versus Ford? Toyota treats administrative processes, for example, an engineering change order, the same way as it would any floor delay. They urge people to simplify the process and learn from their failures and successes as they assume risks to improve.

Here is an example of engineering improvements from Toyota:

■ Lean principles apply to other parts of the auto business, not just manufacturing. Product development is another area that Toyota has targeted in recent years. Toyota has a learning culture, and they can develop a car in 18 months or less. In 1997, they redesigned the Camry, which was bigger than the 1996 and priced lower. They made it roomier inside and modified the old chassis versus redesigning a new one. They also used fewer parts in the front bumper, which was able to withstand a 5-mph impact versus 2.5. Then the next year, they redesigned the engine in the 1998 Corolla with 25% fewer than the 1997, made it 10% lighter, and more fuel-efficient. On top of this, Toyota reduced the price. Toyota eliminated several brackets by molding them into the engine block and simplified it by combining several electronic sensors.

■ The way Toyota does that is by applying the principles of the Toyota production system to the engineering and product development. But Toyota has begun developing similar models simultaneously, so the engineering tasks overlap. This enables the suspension team, say, to work on several different versions at once. Toyota urges engineers to look around at other projects to simplify the development process.[24]

Engineering Software Development

There is a company called Menlo Innovations located in Ann Arbor Michigan, which is pioneering new techniques in the field of software programming. Once you start to study what Rich Sheridan, CEO and Chief Storyteller and Games Goebel, co-founder have created, we believe you will discover a new paradigm shift. This shift will not just affect the software industry but may impact everyone's thoughts on how a traditional office environment should function. Mr. Sheridan was kind enough to supply the following synopsis of Menlo's journey and philosophy below.

Figure 6.12 Which equation are you using? Cost + Profit = Selling Price; Selling Price – Cost = Profit. (CCS manual, 1949.)

Author's Note: Once again this story validates our recurring theme of Lean being a 50/50 combination of people and task.

Menlo Innovations History and Context

James Goebel's and Rich Sheridan's journey to developing a Lean-spirited organization began in 1999 when Rich was a VP of R&D for what had been a tired, struggling public company called Interface Systems, Inc. in Ann Arbor, Michigan. Rich hired James as a consultant to help with a major transformation of the software development processes and approaches used by the R&D team he was leading. Rich recounts the story here:

> Interface was struggling building the right products in a fast-moving internet-speed software market. The software that Interfaces Systems did build seldom worked at all, and when it finally did, it was delivered late with much gnashing of teeth throughout the organization. The products were difficult to use, to configure, to support, to maintain and to deliver. We seldom met the clients' actual needs.

Over the next two years, James and I led the transformation of the product development team at Interface Systems and revolutionized the way product requirements were gathered, and software was designed and developed. This led to the acquisition of Interface Systems by a California company in September of 2000.

By April of 2001, the Internet bubble had burst, and our California parent company decided to shutter every remote office they had including our Ann Arbor, Michigan office. Even though we had created one of the most high-performing teams we had ever had the chance to lead, we were both now out of work. They could take away everything from us (job, title, salary, stock options) but one thing. They couldn't take away what we had learned in those two years.

James and I co-founded Menlo Innovations in 2001 and brought our learnings into a new company focused on the "business value of joy" with a mission "to end human suffering in the world as it relates to technology." We were not students of Lean per se, but as we studied Lean, we found that we had employed many of Lean's most fundamental principles. This article in Fortune captures the essence of our Lean journey. We were particularly proud when Jeff Liker, author of The Toyota Way and related books, had this to say:

> But arguably the most novel element at Menlo is one that put southern Michigan's auto industry on the map decades ago. Just as Kichiro Toyoda standardized the manufacturing and quality control processes for car production, Menlo has created its own standardized process for making software. Thousands of companies have attempted to duplicate Toyota Motor Corp.'s success when it comes to quality and culture, but Menlo is one of the few that captures the core principles, says Jeffrey Liker, an engineering professor at the University of Michigan and author of The Toyota Way. The concept of Lean production was introduced in the 1980s and that was considered as big a revolution as moving from craft production to mass production," says Liker, who has studied Menlo's operations. Any piece you see in Menlo you'll see somewhere else. What you won't find [elsewhere] is all the pieces working together....

The Tangible Elements of the Menlo Way

The book, *Joy, Inc.: How We Built a Workplace People Love* outlines the very tangible elements of the process, practices, and philosophies of Menlo's radical approach to software design and development. Here are some of the highlights:

- One big, open, flexible, and visual high-human-energy workspace, where everyone, including the cofounders, sit out in the open room. Earbuds are banned. Menlo's counts of the serendipity of team members overhearing the ideas of others to fuel their creativity.
- Paired project work: all project roles are paired. Two people, one computer, side by side every minute of every day working on the same task at the same time. These pairs are assigned and switched every 5 working days. The result is a learning organization, a scalable team (up and down), and the ability to have a humanly sustainable pace of 40-hour work weeks and never weekends. Strongest rule: no single line of production code can be written without two programmers at the keyboard together.
- Rigorously followed automated unit testing practice, where tests are written for every public method before the production code is written, then the tests are automated and run several times per day. This results in an "emergency-free" culture. The last time the team recalls a software emergency is 2004.
- An unusual interview practice for adding new talent that is entirely experiential: no questions are asked. It first screens for culture fit and then for skills.
- Visual management tools where all project planning and project management are done with paper rather than software. We choose paper as we have found these tools work better for humans.
- Simple rituals like a daily standup for the entire team, each day at 10 am, called by an alarm in a dartboard, and controlled by a plastic Viking helmet used as a "talking stick." Menlo likes the two-horned Viking helmet for one simple reason: they work in pairs, so they report out in pairs and having a two-handled token just makes sense!
- Short cycles: all work at Menlo is done in a 5-day cycle of planning, execution, and is completed with a Show & Tell check in with our clients where the client shows us the work our team did in the previous 5 days while the team who did the work watches the client's reaction to the work.
- A process so well understood by all team members that the team regularly leads tours (one to three tours per business day) for over 3,000 people a year who come from all over the planet just to watch and see the Menlo process in action.

Maintaining Energy

Leigh Buchanan of Inc. Magazine called Menlo "the most joyful company in America." Our spirit and energy are maintained over the long haul for one simple reason: our team has a shared belief in our approach. They want Menlo to survive to see another day as they get to regularly get to experience our definition of joy:

> Joy is defined as seeing the work of our hearts, hands and minds delivered to the world and delighting the people it is intended to serve. We have people regularly thank us for that work saying they LOVE the software we have created because we made their lives better.

The fact that the focus of our culture, our process, and our team is external to our organization, taps into a fundamental element of the human spirit: we all want to work something bigger than ourselves. We believe teams are ultimately motivated most by serving others. Our team is reminded of this often. It makes the hard work worthwhile and meaningful.

Summary of Engineering Considerations

Test Lean Suggestions

- Digital readouts
- Problem diagnostics and messages to operators
- Simple to test—go/no go, no knobs
- Build tests and mistake proofing into fixtures
- Use of templates and lighting (from underneath) to highlight errors
- Early error detection
- Test as you go (100% if possible)
- Don't tie operators to machines
  - Use macros in software
  - Build-in andon lights and sounds for problems and test completions

When an operator encounters a test failure, they should be able to fix it on the spot. Escalation protocols must be in place if operators are not able to correct in real time.

Production—Preparation—Process (3Ps)

- Lean products out during the engineering stage
- Opportunities to address are materials, manufacturing labor, software, setups, test, supplier materials and labor, lead times, standard options, mistake proofing, serviceability, and maintenance
- Reduce time to market
- All jobs should be released to the floor Leaned out with additional kaizen targets

Product Design/Product Flow

- Group technology matrices.
- Keep it simple! Don't add complicated features.
- Standardizing on suppliers and parts.
- Isolate special requirements (such as noise) at their source.
- Design out electrostatic discharge issues.
- Tolerances—What is really required—stacking tolerances.
- Multifunction parts—can parts be used for dual purposes (i.e., serving additional functions like a housing or cover providing structural integrity)?
- Design to the product cell and families.
- Production tooling (turret punch, lathe, or milling center—families of parts).
- Don't build aerospace quality into commercial applications (unless no additional cost).
- Don't design in lots of variabilities (25 control knobs vs. 3—welding).

- Design products and parts for future—obsolescence curve? New product generations—product strategy/vision—that is, Sony Walkman (future innovations—spinoffs) upgrade path?
- Interconnected parts (matrix, nesting/shear plans). Shear after parts is punched. Minimize bends and bends fixturing.
- Final packaging of product.
- Can it be done online? Protect product—reusable? What does the customer want, and how long to get it up and running?

Materials

- Reduce part count.
- Total part costing.
- Modular assembly/subassemblies.
- Eliminate discrete fasteners—use self-fasteners.
- Use standard commercial off the shelf (COTS) parts.
- Eliminate cables.
- Parts handling and storage requirements.
- Don't get sole sourced by a supplier (AMP, Harris).
- Don't design in special plating and finishes. Are prefinished parts available?
- Eliminate honing, grinding, shaving, and reaming (all rework).
- Type of material chosen—metal, plastic, or composite material—can a metal piece be molded into a plastic part (eliminate Helicoil insertion, etc.).
- Use simple shapes (machining).
- Machine only where needed and clean up only where needed.
- Customers.
- Ease of use—hardware and software.
- Standardizing on software approaches and user feels across product lines.
- Can options be attached (modularity)?
- Canfield service sell upgrades to customers in the field?
- Don't create 4,000 options or varieties of a product. Make parts interchangeable for specials.
- Minimize customer customization.
- Upfront by getting with customers.
- Have option packages to make decisions easier and products more profitable.
- Don't tailor connection panels (cut out one hole and add placement variations through subplate attachments).
- Joining—adhesives, fasteners, welding.
- Use quick cure adhesives.
- Eliminate fasteners.
- Can welding be semiautomated.

Target Floor Cell for New Product

- If new equipment is required, bring the shop floor into the decision process.
- Video new design during prototype phase.
- Use DFMA techniques.
- Develop a job standardization package prior to release to the floor.

- Work on the floor yourself with a new design and help train the cell team on assembling product design.
- Be open minded. There is always a better way.
- Standardize, standardize, standardize.
- Interface with customers to determine what they really need, not what we think they need.

TPM

- Consider field service and customer repairs
- Ease of service
- Availability of spare parts
- Modular fixes
- Real error messages
- Cycle time to repair unit
- Diagnostics—process maps
- Cold boots
- Auto save information
- Suggested maintenance plans
    - Operator
    - Customer maintenance personnel
    - Factory/field service personnel

Chapter Questions

1. What is a table engineer? Are they beneficial to a Lean enterprise?
2. What is DFL 3P?
3. Explain how the Lean engineering process is applied to transactional processes.
4. What are three considerations engineers should strive for increased and efficient TPM?
5. What is DFA, and how should the engineering team approach DFA?
6. What is a design fishbone, and how would engineers use one?
7. List and describe three wastes in the design process.
8. How should test be integrated into the design and manufacturing processes?
9. What standards should be used by engineering to help ensure the products and processes support the Lean enterprise?
10. What is the difference between DFA and DFM?
11. How do we streamline engineering processes?
12. What roles do engineers play with Lean?
13. What did you learn from this chapter?

Discussion Questions

1. Why do so many engineers think Lean does not apply to them?
2. Why is it so difficult for DFMA techniques to get traction in organizations?

Exercise

Pick an assembly and see if you can figure out ways to reduce the number of parts.

Notes

1. The late Dave Vranson was an advanced manufacturing engineer, ITT Aerospace Controls.
2. Keisuke Arai and Kenichi Sekine, *Design Team Revolution: How to Cut Lead Times in Half and Double Your Productivity*, Productivity Press, April 1, 1994. Used with permission.
3. DFMA is a software program product of Boothroyd Dewhurst, Wakefield, RI (www.dfma.com).
4. Toy construction sets created by Lincoln Logs, John L. Wright; TinkerToys, Charles H. Pajeau and Robert Pettit; and Erector Set, A. C. Gilbert.
5. For the purposes of this writing, *The Other Side* will refer to the crossing back and forth between manufacturing and engineering.
6. Dr. Shigeo Shingo—Japanese industrial engineer known as one of the world's leading experts on manufacturing practices and the Toyota Production System.
7. Furnished by Cees Knegt, Process Engineer, February 2012.
8. Boothroyd, Dewhurst, Knight, Marcel Dekker, Inc., *Product Design for Manufacture and Assembly*, ©1994.
9. Furnished by Cees Knegt, Process Engineer, February 2012.
10. Jim Collins, *Good to Great*, New York, Harper Business Press, ©2000.
11. The Santa Fe Institute website defines robustness in 18 or so different, sometimes contradictory, ways.
12. Carlson and Doyle—www.ccsr.uiuc.edu/.../Frey%20UIUC%20Seminar%20v5.pptShare, Highly Optimized Tolerance. Carlson and Doyle (2000) coined the term intended to reflect systems designed for high performance in an uncertain environment; Dan Frey, Associate Professor of Mechanical Engineering and Engineering Systems, MIT.
13. Scott Rosenberg, *Dreaming in Code: Two Dozen Programmers, Three Years, 4732 Bugs, and One Quest for Transcendent Software*, Three Rivers Press, February 26, 2008.
14. CCS Training Manual, Charles Protzman, Sr., and Homer Sarasohn, 1948–1949 (prepared by Nick Fisher and Suzanne Lavery of ValueMetrics, Australia).
15. TPS, Monden. TPS Shingo, Kanban Japan Management Association.
16. NRE refers to the costs associated with one-time tooling or setup charges by a supplier.
17. This list is based on over 20 years of experience in implementing Lean and is totally subjective and unscientific. Obviously, this is a very broad generalization, and not everyone in these groups is resistant to Lean at these magnitudes.
18. Jamie Flinchbaugh is the coauthor of *The Hitchhiker's Guide to Lean: Lessons from the Road* and cofounder of the Lean Learning Center.
19. Boeing, GE Complete 737 MAX Engine Configuration Plans, 2/7 Subscription Publication, https://www.wsj.com/articles/SB10001424052970203436904577155204034907744
20. Kenichi Sekine Keisuke Arai, *Design Team Revolution*, Productivity Press, ©1994.
21. Shingo, *Non-Stock Production*, Productivity Press, 1988, pp. 192 and 193; Shingo, *The Sayings of Shigeo Shingo*, Productivity Press, ©1987, pp. 110–111; Ohno, *Workplace Management*, ©1982, p. 136; *The Shingo Production Management System*, Productivity Press, pp. 46, 47.
22. *The Shingo Production Management System*, Productivity Press, pp. 46, 47.
23. Ohno, *Workplace Management*, ©1982, p. 136.
24. Source reference: How Toyota defies gravity its secret is its legendary production system. Though competitors have been trying to copy it for years, nobody makes it work as well as Toyota. Alex Taylor III reporter, 1997.

Additional Readings

Anderson, D.M. 1990. Design for Manufacturability. Lafayette, CA: CIM Press.

Bakerjian, R. 1976. Tool and Manufacturing Engineers Handbook. New York: McGraw-Hill Book Co.

Beauregard, M. 2000. Experimenting for Breakthrough Improvement. Tolland, CT: Resource Engineering.

Boothroyd, G. and Dewhurst, P. 1994. Product Design and Manufacture for Assembly. New York: Marcel Dekker, Inc.

Kennedy, M.N. 2003. Product Development for the Lean Enterprise. Richmond, VA: Oakley Press.

Kuhn, T. 1996. The Structure of Scientific Revolutions, 3rd edn. Chicago, IL: University of Chicago Press.

Mascitelli, R. 2002. The Lean Design Guidebook: Everything Your Product Development Team Needs to Slash Manufacturing, Costs. Northridge, CA: Productivity Press.

Morgan, J.M. and Liker, J.K. 2006. The Toyota Product Development System. New York: Productivity Press.

Osborn, A. 1993. Applied Imagination. Buffalo, NY: Creative Education Press.

Pisano, G.P. 1997. The Development Factory—Lessons from Pharmaceuticals. Boston, MA: Harvard Business School Press.

Sekine, K. and Arai, K. 1994. Design Team Revolution. Portland, OR: Productivity Press.

Smith, P.G. and Reinertsen, D.G. 1998. Developing Products in Half the Time. Stamford, CT: Thomson Publishing Inc.

Wheelwright, S.C. 1992. Revolutionizing Product Development. New York: Free Press Simon Schuster.

Appendix A - Study Guide

Chapter 1 Questions and Answers

1. What is the number one rule of layouts (you do not want to see)?
   No isolated islands.
2. Why are there problems with isolated islands?
   Isolated islands create bottlenecks and limit communication between operators.
3. What is a block diagram? Why is it important?
   Once the initial analysis is completed, we construct a block diagram. The block diagram takes the output from the (to be) PFA and (to be) workflow analysis (WFA) and combines them into one flow. We develop this tool with the operator and supervisors present. The block diagram sets the stage for the workstation design and layout.
4. Should you plan rework into a line?
   No, the team should work to ensure no rework is in the line; however, if you absolutely must have a rework area, make sure it is highly visible and someone is assigned as the owner and held accountable.
5. What do you normally find when you first go to bring up a line?
   We often find major installation issues.
6. Why is it important to have a flip chart out on the line when you first start to implement?
   Have a flip chart and markers ready on the floor (or office) to capture any problems or ideas that are found. The Lean Practitioner should work with the team leader to assign actions and due dates to work on the problems or implement the ideas.
7. What does fit up mean? Why is it important?
   Fit up means identifying all the utilities necessary for maintenance to implement when setting up the new area or line. It also means consulting with HS&E on any safety or ergonomic issues. It's important to address the facilities piece as it could impact the layout and where you plan to move equipment or furniture etc. due to existing monuments or electrical closets etc.
8. Who should review the layout before it is approved?
   Health, safety, and environment (HS&E) and facilities should review before approval.
9. Should we have walls in our layout?
   No walls should be in the layout.
10. What is important when doing workstation design?
    Everyone should be involved in workstation design. It is critical that the frontline staff is fully engaged in the redesigning of their workstations, as it reinforces their acceptance.
11. What is a plan for every tool? Where should the tools be located? Are shadow boards the best way to present tools to the operators?

The plan for every tool is similar to the plan for every part (PFEP). The plan describes the tools used and important information to consider about the tool. Each tool should be identified (where possible) as to its location so if it is found anywhere in the factory, one knows exactly where it belongs.

12. Are toolboxes good or bad? Why? Are there alternatives?

Most toolboxes are unorganized and a mess; even organized toolboxes are wasteful as operators are always searching for a tool. Place the tool at the location the operator needs the tool.

13. What should we do with fixtures designed for batching?

Batching fixtures need to be modified to support one-piece flow, which is an example of mistake proofing. Once the fixture is modified to support one-piece flow, the operator can only do one piece at a time on the fixture.

14. Should we have personal tools in a machine shop? Why?

No personal tools as each person has to have a toolbox that ties up space. No one will lend tools and if a tool is needed, it is often locked up.

15. What are four of the guidelines to layouts?

No isolated island. No drawers, doors, walls, or partitions. Flexibility. Staff on inside and replenishment on outside of line.

16. Why is flexibility important in a layout?

What you are building today may change tomorrow. Future changes will be more efficient (and faster).

17. Should everything be on wheels if possible? What is the value?

Yes, each workstation should be on wheels where possible with air lines, lights, and other utilities designed to be as flexible as possible.

18. What is hanedashi?

A hanedashi device is used for automatic removal of a workpiece from one operation or process that provides proper state and orientation for the next operation or process and is critical for a chaku-chaku line.

19. What is the problem with the T-shaped layout?

When you have people on both sides of a table or conveyor line, the ability to replenish materials without interrupting the operator is lost.

20. What is a point-to-point diagram?

The point-to-point diagram follows the major products through the master layout.

21. Is it worth the cost to install flexible utilities? Why?

Yes. Flexible utilities, even though a bit more costly up front, can make future changes very cost effective.

22. Discuss the use of a chair as related to a Lean line.

In general, chairs should be removed from the line as they add inefficiencies and restrict movement.

23. What is a water spider and the value to Lean lines?

Water spiders can be the material handlers and can perform duties on the line. They help ensure the operators can perform their duties without delays.

Chapter 2 Questions and Answers

1. What is a cross-training matrix?

The cross-training matrix shows the staff who trained for what process and how many team members are needed to be trained for the process.

2. What is a PPCS?

   The PPCS is the part production capacity sheet.

3. Are robots always useful to increase efficiency? Why or why not?

   No, robots are not always useful to increase efficiency. Sometimes, people are better than robots. Robots have their place as they are good for repetitive tasks, dangerous tasks, and for total automation. Robots are not useful for Lean if the robots batch up parts and should do one-piece flow just like people.

4. Is standard work used for assembly lines only?

   No. Standard work can be used for more than assembly lines.

5. What does it mean to wet and dry up the line?

   We call the first cycle, where we have to wait for the SWIP, wetting the line and when a machine or line is empty and has zero SWIP, we call it dry.

6. SWIP is used only on the manufacturing floor. Is this statement true or false?

   False. SWIP can be used in other applications outside of manufacturing such as in a hospital.

7. What is SWIP?

   Standard work in process (SWIP).

8. Discuss how to use Little's law. What is its relationship to standard SWIP?

   We can approximate the calculation of SWIP in the process using Little's law which is

$$\text{Throughput time} \div \text{cycle time} = \text{SWIP}$$

9. What is the difference between cycle time and TT?

   Cycle time (CT) is how often a part is completed by a specific process and takt time (TT) is the customer demand calculation to determine how often a part must be completed by a specific process to match customer demand.

10. What is a work standard?

    Work standards are typically for tasks that are not repeatable but follow a sequence of steps or troubleshooting. It could be a checklist.

11. What is the difference between operator standard work and supervisor standard work?

    Operator standard work is the standard work for an operator. Supervisor standard work is a higher level than the operator standard work and should be posted in the cell or at each station in the cell. It can take the form of a standard work sheet or standard operations routine sheet. It is a guide for the supervisor or anyone else who is observing or auditing the work performed in the cell that defines the order and timing for each major step.

12. What did Shingo mean by network of operations?

    The PPCS sheet combines the product and operator or as Dr. Shingo called it, the network of operations.

Chapter 3 Questions and Answers

1. What is the difference between VMI and consigned inventory?

   Vendor Managed Inventory (VMI) is a material strategy that supports Lean. The firm contracts with a supplier and the supplier procures the material, delivers it to the firm, and places the material on the lean lines. The supplier ensures the VMI parts are constantly available including inventory control. Consigned material is owned by the supplier until used; however, the actions performed by a VMI supplier (i.e., placing material at the line) are performed by the firm.

2. What are some advantages of recyclable containers? How are they green?

   Recycled containers eliminate all the packaging allows for the containers to be used multiple times. The recycled containers are green as there is less packaging and less disposal of shipping containers.

3. What impact do material requirements planning (MRP) systems have on initial Lean implementations?

   MRP and enterprise resource planning (ERP) systems can interfere with Kanban implementations and could cause lean line to run short of material and/or cause excess inventory.

4. What does POU mean?

   The term POU (point of use) means exactly what it says. In a POU system, the parts or tools are exactly where they are needed when they are needed.

5. What is a class A system?

   Class "A" performance in a business resource management program is based on meeting 50 measurement criteria that are composed of operational and behavioral measurements. Behavioral metrics deal with doing the right things, while performance measurements assess doing things right. If you are not a class A MRP or ERP user, you will always incur parts shortages.

6. What does it mean to have true partnering with suppliers?

   The goal of true partnering is to move suppliers from the typical antagonistic environment to one where the supplier becomes a true partner or an extension of your facility. The goal to develop and nurture a partnering supply base, which means the supplier literally becomes an extension of your company similar to any internal manufacturing or transactional area. Picture a fast-food company in a college or gas station. True partnering is managed differently than non-partnering suppliers. For instance, they don't need report cards as they are receiving constant feedback from their customers. They share the same systems and update their customers immediately if any problems surface. True partnering is getting your suppliers involved early in the design phase to suggest cost-saving ideas for materials used, labor required, setup time reduction, and standardized tooling requirements.

7. What is a PFEP? Why is it useful?

   PFEP is an acronym for plan for every part. The basic idea is to literally plan each part in terms of usage, locations, replenishment quantities, container sizes, and supplier information, and in many companies, we add how the part is planned if it is in MRP. The vision for the PFEP is to create a pull system from the customer through the entire supply chain.

8. Where should supplies be placed?

   In general, suppliers should be located at the point of use (POU). In redesigning a work area or administrative process, ensure the right supplies and equipment are located at the right place at the right time to perform the activity.

9. What is a breadman system?

   Breadman is a term normally applied to parts consigned or vendor managed and centralized in one or several locations within the plant and taken to the lines by operators, supervisors, or material handlers.

10. Why is looking at peak demand important for Kanban sizing?

    Peak demand is very important to consider especially the build requirements are not level loaded. Our experience is it is better to err on the side of too much inventory in the beginning and then to wean yourself off it rather than trying to cut the turns so low that you run out of material. If the Kanban runs out, the "I told you so's" will surface and the effort may fail. Until you eliminate the peaks, you must consider them in the demand and Kanban sizing.

11. What is ABC analysis? Why is it used?

    ABC is a classification system to define classifications of parts, typically by volume or by cost. It is used to ensure that the proper resources are applied in managing the material. For example, the number of resources to manage a very high value printed circuit card assembly (an A part) should be higher than a basic washer (a C part).

12. Is there a correlation between the amount of inventory in the plant and where they are on the Lean Maturity Path?

    In general, yes, there is a correlation between inventory and Lean Maturity Path. An organization that is mature on the Lean Maturity Path will have high inventory turns with very low idle inventory. We have found that the size of the stockroom many times will indicate where a company is in terms of their Lean Maturity Path. An organization that does not have a stockroom or does not perform kitting will be very mature on the Path.

Chapter 4 Questions and Answers

1. What is the strategic materials group concept?

   The strategic materials group is responsible and accountable for managing the partnered suppliers. The strategic group is responsible to send the suppliers one-, three-, and six-month forecasts of upcoming requirements and negotiate flex fences to cover surges or decreases in demand.

2. What are the benefits of employing this type of approach?

   This approach reduces and localizes the supply base. It is much easier to manage a small number of high-quality and value-oriented suppliers than a large number of mediocre suppliers. The closer the supplier facilities are to the plants, the easier it is to set up milk runs that facilitate lean lines.

3. What are the pros and cons of outsourcing?

   The main benefit of outsourcing was to obtain the finished good at a low cost. With Lean thinking, we tend to go the opposite way. In general, when companies outsource, they give up control of the item or service and are at the mercy of the supplier. There are multiple cons of outsourcing such as overnight freight costs, constant expensive trips overseas to manage suppliers and expedite parts, high inventory costs, quality issues, loss of technology or proprietary intellectual property along with major culture challenges.

4. What is an LTA? What are some of the components of an LTA?

   An LTA is a long-term agreement with a supplier. LTAs are annual or multiple-year contracts with suppliers. The goal is to lock in the best pricing with a long-term quantity and quality commitment but only take material as it is needed. LTA may have any of the following components:
   - Can range from a year to five years
   - A fixed price is the norm
   - Some escalation factor built in, that is, price of precious metals pegged to an index
   - Continuous improvement requirements
   - Lean assessment components
   - Rebate if certain thresholds are met
   - Options for pricing for additional years
   - Flex fences
   - Shipping terms

5. What are flex fences? Are they important?

Flex fences is a concept that provides flexibility to an LTA. Flex fences examine the overall horizon of the agreement and build in risk mitigation plans in the event the projected volume was to increase by 10%–30% or reduce by 10%–30%. A company may pay the supplier to keep extra raw materials on hand to increase the delivery volume by 30% over a specified period of time.

6. What are the pros and cons of commodity versus product line (value stream) buying?

There are multiple pros for using commodity buying. When buying commodities, the buyer gains a certain amount of expertise within the industry main sources, brokers, delivery expectations, and amount of negotiation possible. Another advantage is that only one representative of the company contacts each supplier. There are also cons for commodity buying. For example, if a buyer is behind in placing requisitions, the buyer can negatively affect every program in production. When incurring a problem, the manufacturing floor doesn't know who to call, so they escalate the problem to manufacturing or operations management who calls the materials manager, who then communicates the problem to the proper buyer. In addition, the buyer never learns about the overall programs or product lines for which they are buying.

There are pros for program or product buyers. The buyer gains expertise in the buying requirements for each program. The buyer is forced to learn about each commodity as they proceed, so they become cross-trained. The buyer is held to a budget for the overall program and becomes an expert in the needs of the program, is many times then co-located with that program, and can make suggestions that can save the program money. This type of organization is more aligned with Lean or value stream thinking. The Lean organization is aligned with the customer and can react to customer suggestions or complaints much quicker. The cans to this approach are it takes longer for the buyers to become experts in the commodities and they do not always have the necessary background to obtain the best pricing. There can be missed opportunities to package parts up for pricing that could be spread across different programs and there can also be multiple buyers at a company calling the same supplier.

Chapter 5 Questions and Answers

1. What additional expenses occur when adding a machine or robot?

The cost of spare parts is often omitted and the time to bring the robot online. Also, there are often parts the robot cannot build without extensive modifications that are time consuming.

2. What does the Lean principle of creativity before capital mean?

The Lean team needs to be creative and stick to the basics of linking together the value-added operations and processes needed to complete a product. The team needs to avoid the common pitfalls associated with machines, conveyors, and material handling equipment that often move you backwards on your road to Lean.

3. What principles of 5S should be considered during creativity before the capital process?

A main 5S goal is to make things visual and very obvious when something is out of place. Inexpensive labeling, tool holders, and organization techniques can be used to achieve this goal without spending a lot of money.

4. Can there be a direct correlation between machine expenditures and Lean line efficiencies?

In general no. Spending large sums of money on capital does not directly correlate to lean line efficiencies and in fact adding large expensive machines could stall lean line progress.

5. How should the team approach evaluating the potential expenditure of a complex machine?
   The team needs to ensure all the creative approaches that are generally low cost are considered before evaluating the need for a machine. Procuring a large and expensive machine should be the very last consideration.

6. What creative material handling solutions can be used instead of complex material handling systems, such as conveyors?
   Sequence what used to be an offline subassembly in the processes on the line to minimize the amount of handling. A creative and inexpensive solution is to use simple material slides, gravity fed rollers, or tubes to transfer a subassembly down the line to the place needed to be installed in the final assembly.

7. What are the advantages of designing equipment in house?
   The in-house team knows the overall product and can quickly assess the situation and make refinements for continuous improvement. There is no need to involve purchasing or engineering to write a specification to support requesting a quote.

8. What are the problems with centralized equipment like washers and ovens?
   There is often much waste to move and travel through the factory to a central asset, such as an oven or washer. The better approach is to place a right used oven or washer in the line.

9. What should conveyors do?
   Very simply conveyors should convey (or move) material or products and should not be used as a storage location.

10. How can gravity help you with creativity before capital thinking?
    Gravity is essentially free and can be leveraged. One example which is a creative and inexpensive solution is to use simple gravity fed rollers to transfer a subassembly down the line to the place needed to be installed in the final assembly.

Chapter 6 Questions and Answers

1. What is a table engineer? Are they beneficial to a Lean enterprise?
   Table Engineers are not valuable to the lean journey and voice their opinions around the conference table. Their arguments are based on theory and they like to enthusiastically debate around the conference table but never go onto the shop floor.

2. What is DFL 3P?
   DFL stands for Design for Lean. There are various names for designing Lean processes. The most familiar is the 3P process. The 3 Ps stands for product, preparation, and process.

3. Explain how the Lean engineering process is applied to transactional processes.
   The Lean engineering design process can be performed on a transactional process. Instead of parts, we may be using paper, e-mails, authorization, and approval forms (with distances noted), etc.

4. What are three considerations engineers should strive for increased and efficient TPM?
   Any of the following considerations engineers should strive for increased and efficient TPM:
   − Ease of service
   − Availability of spare parts
   − Modular fixes
   − Real error messages
   − Cycle time to repair unit

5. What is DFA, and how should the engineering team approach DFA?

   Prior to launching a new Lean program on an existing product line, it is best to first perform a design for assembly (DFA) analysis. The chances of sustainability are much more improved on a line where retests and rework are eliminated, and the line can be stabilized. The practice of concurrent engineering should be employed into the design activity and should begin as early in the design cycle as possible or when the earliest engineering effort is initiated.

6. What is a design fishbone, and how would engineers use one?

   This process involves literally taking each part that goes into an assembly and laying the part out on the floor in the order it is assembled. Generally, this process starts with disassembling a prototype unit. The unit is reassembled and then disassembled again. This process helps engineers to understand the design and assembly flow.

7. List and describe three wastes in the design process.

   - Attending too many meetings and conferences-spending time in meeting and not directly working on the design
   - Altering designs to correct defects-making design changes that often have masked an original design error or deficiency
   - Retrieving or searching for drawings and materials-spending time (waste) searching for design drawings or reference materials

8. How should test be integrated into the design and manufacturing processes?

   There is no go/no go test to avoid operators having to interpret results.

   Placing an andon after the test result is read by the machine would be a better way to accomplish testing.

9. What standards should be used by engineering to help ensure the products and processes support the Lean enterprise?

   Robust process and mistake proofing are critical to help ensure products and processes support Lean.

10. What is the difference between DFA and DFM?

    DFA is design for assembly where DFM is design for manufacturing.

11. How do we streamline engineering processes?

    The BASICS® model should be applied to the engineering process.

12. What roles do engineers play with Lean?

    Engineers must design Lean into products and services and should be involved in applying lean principles to the engineering process

13. What did you learn from this chapter?

Appendix B - Acronyms

5Ws	when, where, what, who, why
5W2Hs	when, where, what, who, why, how, how much
5 whys	asking why five times in a row in order to get to the root cause
AGV	automatic guided vehicle
AI	artificial intelligence
AP	accounts payable
ASL	approved supplier list
AT	actual time
AT&T	American Telephone and Telegraph
BASICS®	lean implementation model for converting batch to flow: baseline, analyze (assess), suggest solutions, implement, check, and sustain
BFT	business fundamental table
BIG	Business Improvement Group LLC based in Towson, MD
BOM	bill of material
BPD	business process development
BRIEF	Baseline Risk Identification of Ergonomic Factors
BVA	business value added
C	Cold
CAD	computer-aided design
CAP	change acceleration process
CEO	chief executive officer
CM	centimeters
COGS	cost of goods sold
CQI	continuous quality improvement
CTP	cost to produce
CTQ	critical to quality
CV	coefficient of variation
CWQC	company-wide quality control
CYA	cover your ass
DBH	day by hour
DFA	design for assembly
DFM	design for manufacturing
DFMA˙	Design for Manufacturing and Assembly
DIRFT	do it right the first time
DL	direct labor
DMAIC	design, measure, analyze, improve, control

DMEDI	design, measure, explore, develop, implement
DOE	design of experiments
DPMO	defects per million opportunities
EBIT	earnings before interest and taxes
EBITDA	earnings before interest taxes depreciation, and amortization
ECR	engineering change request
ED	emergency department (emergency room)
EDD	earliest due date
EDI	electronic data interchange
EHS	environmental, health, and safety
ERP	enterprise resource (requirements) planning
ERSC	eliminate, rearrange, simplify, or combine
EHS	Environmental Health and Safety
ETDBW	easy to do business with
EV	earned value
EVA	economic value added
FC	full change
FG	finished goods
FIFO	first in, first out, replaced by EDD, earliest due date
FISH	first in still here
FMEA	failure modes and effects analysis
FPY	first pass yield
FT	feet
FTT	first time through (thru)
FWA	full work analysis
GE	General Electric
GM	general manager
GMS	global manufacturing system
GPI	global process improvement
H	hot
H	hour or hours
HBS	Harvard Business School
HEPA	high-efficiency particle absorption
HPWT	high-performance work teams
HR	human resources
HS&E	health safety and environmental
ICE	SMED formula, identify, convert, eliminate
i.e.	that is
IL	indirect labor
IN	inches
INFO	information
INSP	inspection
ISO	International Organization for Standardization
IS	information systems
IT	information technology (computing/networking)
IT	idle time
ITCS	intelligent tracking control system

JB	job breakdown
JEI	job easiness index
JI	job instruction
JIC	just in case
JIT	just in time
JM	job methodology
JUSE	Japanese Union of Scientists and Engineers
KPI	key process indicators
KPO	Kaizen Promotion Office
KSA	knowledge, skill, or ability
LB	pound or pounds
LBDS	lean business delivery system
LCL	lower control limit
LEI	Lean Enterprise Institute
LIFO	last in, first out
LMAO	laughed my butt off
LMP	lean maturity path
LP	lean practitioner
LP1	lean practitioner level 1
LP 2–5	lean practitioner level 2 through level 5
LRB	lean review board
Max	maximum
MBD	month by day
MBTI	Myers-Briggs Type Inventory—personality styles
MH	man hours
Min	minute or minutes
Min	minimum
MM	materials manager
MPS	master production schedule
MRB	material review board
MSA	measurement systems analysis
MSD	musculoskeletal disorder
MSE	manufacturing support equipment
MSE	measurement system evaluation
MT	meter
MTD	month to date
MVA	market value added
NIH	not invented here
NOPAT	net operating profit after taxes
NOW	not our way
NRE	Nonrecurring engineering
NTED	no touch exchange of dies
NVA	non-value added
NVN	non-value added but necessary
OCED	one cycle exchange of die
OE	order entry
OEE	overall equipment effectiveness

OEE	overall engineering effectiveness scale
OPBSF	one-piece balanced synchronized flow
OPER	operator
OPF	one-piece flow
OPI	office of process improvement
OPS	operations
OR	operating room
ORG	organization
OSED	one-shot exchange of dies
OTD	on-time delivery
OTED	one-touch exchange of dies
OTP	on-time performance
PC	production control
PCDCA	plan–control–do–check–act
PDCA	plan–do–check–act
PDSA	plan–do–study–act
PEST	political, economic, social, and technological
PFA	process flow analysis (following the product)
PFEP	plan for every part
PI	process improvement
PI	performance improvement
PIT	process improvement team
P/N	part number
PM	preventative maintenance
PO	purchase order
POU	point of use
POUB	point of use billing
PPCS	part production capacity sheet
PPF	product process flow, synonymous with PFA
PPM	parts per million
PPV	purchase price variance
Prep	preparation
PSI	pounds per square inch
PWI	perceived weirdness indicator scale (1–10) developed by Charlie Protzman
QC	quality control
QCD	quality, cost, and deliver
+QDIP	safety, quality, delivery, inventory, productivity
QTY	quantity
RC	running change
RCCA	root cause corrective action
RCCM	root cause counter measure
Rchange	resistance to change
REQ	requisition depending on the context
Reqmt	requirements
RF	radio frequency
RFQ	request for quote
RFID	radio-frequency identification

RM	raw materials
ROA	return on assets
ROI	return on investment
RONA	return on net assets
RR	railroad
RTC	resistance to change
RW	required work
S	second or seconds
SASL	signal acquisition source locator
SIPOC	suppliers–inputs–process–outputs–customer
SJS	standard job sheet
SMART	specific, measurable, attainable (achievable), realistic (relevant), timely
SMED	single-minute exchange of dies
SMG	strategic materials group
SOP	standard operating procedure
SORS	standard operation routine sheet, same as SWCS
SPACER	safety, purpose, agenda, code of conduct, expectations, roles
SPC	statistical process control
SPEC	specification
SQC	statistical quality control
ST	storage time
STRAP	strategic plan
SWCS	standard work combination sheet, same as SORS
SWIP	standard work in process
SWOT	strengths, weaknesses, opportunities, threats
TBP	Toyota Business Practice
TCWQC	total company-wide quality control
TH	throughput time
TIPS	transport, inspect, process, store
TL	team leader
TLA	three letter acronym
TLT	total labor time
TM	team member
TOC	theory of constraints
TPM	total productive maintenance
TPS	Toyota production system
TQ	total quality
TQM	total quality management
TT	takt time
UAI	use as is
UCL	upper control limit
UHF	ultrahigh frequency
USW	United Steelworkers
VA	value added
VMI	vendor-managed inventory
VOC	voice of the customer
VOP	Value of the Person

VS	value stream
VSL	value stream leader
VSM	value stream map
W	warm
WACC	weighted average cost of capital
WADITW	we've always done it that way
WE	Western Electric
WFA	Workflow analysis, following the operator
WIIFM	what's in it for me
WIP	work in process
WMSD	work-related musculoskeletal disorder
WOW	ways of working
YTD	year to date

Appendix C - Glossary

5 whys: Method of evaluating a problem or question by asking *why* five times. The purpose is to get to the root cause of the problem and not to address the symptoms. By asking why and answering each time, the root cause becomes more evident.

5 Ws: Asking why something happened—when, where, what, why, or who did the task.

5W2H: Same as the five Ws but adding how and how much.

5Ss: Method of creating a self-sustaining culture that perpetuates a neat, clean, and efficient workplace:

- **Shine:** Keep things clean. Floors swept, machines and furniture clean, all areas neat and tidy.
- **Sort:** Clearly distinguish between what is needed and kept and what is unneeded and thrown out.
- **Standardize:** Maintain and improve the first three *Ss* in addition to personal orderliness and neatness. Minimums and maximums can be added here.
- **Store:** Organize the way that necessary things are kept, making it easier for anyone to find, use, and return them to their proper location.
- **Sustain:** Achieve the discipline or habit of properly maintaining the correct procedures.

Absorption costing: Inventory valuation technique where variable costs and a portion of fixed costs are assigned to a unit of production (or sometimes labor or square footage). The fixed costs are usually allocated based on labor hours, machine hours, or material costs.

Activity-based costing: Developed in the late 1980s by Robert Kaplan and Robin Cooper of Harvard Business School. Activity-based costing is primarily concerned with the cost of indirect activities within a company and their relationships to the manufacture of specific products. The basic technique of activity-based costing is to analyze the indirect costs within an organization and to discover the activities that cause those costs.

Affinity diagram: One of the seven management tools to assist general planning. It organizes disparate language information by placing it on cards and grouping the cards which go together in a creative way. Header cards are used to summarize each group of cards. It organizes information and data.

Allocation: A material requirement planning (MRP) term where a work order has been released to the stockroom; however, the parts have not been picked for production. The system allocates (assigns) those parts to the work order; thus, they are no longer available for new work orders.

Andon: Andon means management by sight—visual management. Japanese translation means light. A flashing light or display in an area to communicate a given condition. An andon can be an electronic board or signal light. A visual indicator can be accompanied by a unique sound as well.

Assembly: A group of parts, raw material, subassemblies, or a combination of both, put together by labor to construct a finished product. An assembly could be an end item (finished good) or a higher level assembly determined by the levels in the bill of material.

Backflush: MRP term used to deduct all component parts from an assembly or subassembly by exploding the bill of material by the number of items produced. Backflushing can occur when the work order is generated or when the unit is shipped.

Backlog: All customer orders received but not yet shipped.

Balance on hand (BOH): The inventory levels between component parts.

Balancing operations: This is the equal distribution of labor time among the number of workers on the line. If there are four workers and 4 minutes of labor time in one unit then each worker should have 1 minute of work.

Batch manufacturing: A production strategy commonly employed in job shops and other instances where there is discrete manufacturing of a nonrepetitive nature. In batch manufacturing, order lots are maintained throughout the production process to minimize changeovers and achieve economies of scale. In batch manufacturing environments, resources are usually departmentalized by specialty and very seldom dedicated to any particular product family.

Benchmarking: Method of establishing internal expectations for excellence based upon direct comparison to the very best at what they do. Benchmarking is not necessarily a comparison with a direct competitor.

Bill of material: A list of all components and manufactured parts that comprise a finished product. The list may have different levels denoting various subassemblies required to build the final product.

Bin: A storage container used to hold parts. Bins range in various sizes from small to very large containers and can be made of plastic, wood, metal, cardboard, etc.

Bin location file: An electronic listing of storage locations for each bin. Generally, locations are designated to the work area, rack, and shelf, and location on the shelf, that is, 1—A—2 defines assembly area 1, rack A, and shelf 2 position on the shelf.

Blanket order: An order generally issued for a year or longer for a particular part number or group of specific part numbers. The blanket order defines the price, terms, and conditions for the supplier, thus allowing an authorized representative of the purchasing team to issue a release against the blanket order to the supplier.

Blanket order release: An authorization to ship from the customer to the supplier a specified quantity from the blanket order.

Block diagram: A diagram where the processes are represented in order of assembly by blocks denoting the process name, cycle time, utilities required, standard work in process (SWIP), etc.

Bottleneck: Generally referred to as the slowest person or machine. However, only machines can be true bottlenecks as we can always add labor. A true bottleneck runs 24 hours a day and still cannot keep up with customer demand.

Breadman: Centralized floor stock systems where the suppliers normally own and manage the material until it is used.

Budget: A plan that represents an estimate of future costs against the expected revenue or allocated funds to spend.

Buffer: Any material in storage waiting further processing.

Buffer stock: Inventory kept to cover yield losses due to poor quality.

Capacity: The total available possible output of a system within current constraints. The capability of a worker or machine within a specified time period.

Carrying costs: The cost to carry inventory, which is usually determined by the cost of capital and cost of maintaining the space (warehouse) and utilities, taxes, insurance, etc.

Catch ball: Communications back, forth, up, down, and horizontally across the organization, which must travel from person to person several times to be clearly understood and reach agreement (consensus). This process is referred to as *catch ball*.

Cause and effect diagram: A problem-solving statistical tool that indicates causes and effects and how they interrelate.

CEDAC: Anachronism for cause and effect diagram with the addition of cards. Problem-solving technique developed by Ryuji Fukuda. A method for defining the effect of a problem and a target effect statement. Through the development of a CEDAC diagram, facts and improvements will be identified that allow action.

Cellular layout: Generally denotes a family of product produced in a layout, which has the machines and workstations in order of assembly. Does not necessarily imply the parts that are produced in one-piece flow.

Chaku-Chaku: Japanese term for *load-load*. Refers to a production line that has been raised to a level of efficiency that requires simply the loading of parts by the operator without any effort required for unloading or transporting material.

Checkpoint: Control item with a means that requires immediate judgment and handling. It must be checked on a daily basis.

CNC: Acronym for computerized machining—stands for computer numerical control.

Consigned inventory: Normally finished goods stored at a customer site but still owned by the supplier.

Constraint: Anything that prevents a process from achieving a higher level of output or performance. Constraints can be physical like material or machines or transactional like policies or procedures.

Continuous flow production: Production in which products flow continuously without interruption.

Continuous improvement (kaizen): A philosophy by which individuals within an organization seek ways to always do things better, usually based on an understanding and control of variation. A pledge to, every day, do or make something better than it was before.

Contribution margin: Equal to sales revenue less variable costs leaving how much remains to be put toward fixed costs.

Control chart: A problem-solving statistical tool that indicates whether the system is in, or out, of control and whether the problem is a result of special causes or common system problems.

Control item: A control item is an item selected as a subject of control for maintenance of a desired condition. It is a yardstick that measures or judges the setting of a target level, the content of the work, the process, and the result of each stage of breakthrough and improvement in control during management activity.

Control point: Control item with a target. A control point is used to analyze data and take action accordingly.

Cost cutting: Eliminating costs in the traditional way, that is, reducing expenses, laying people off, requiring people to supply their own pens, making salary workers work much more overtime, etc.

Cost of capital: The cost of maintaining a dollar of capital invested for a certain period. Normally over a year.

Cost reduction: Reducing costs by eliminating the waste in processes.

Correlation: A statistical relationship between two sets of data such that when one brings about some change in the other it is explained and is statistically significant.

Cp process capability: Process capability is the measured, inherent reproducibility of the product turned out by a process. The most widely adopted formula for process capability (Cp) is

$$\text{Process capability} \left(\text{Cp}\right) = 6\sigma = \text{total tolerance} \div 6$$

where σ is the standard deviation of the process under a state of statistical control. The most commonly used measure for process capability within ASA is a process capability index (Cpk), which is

$$\text{Cpk} = \text{lesser of Cpu or Cpl}$$

where

$$\text{Cpu} = \left(\text{upper specification} - \text{process mean}\right) \div 3$$

and

$$\text{Cpl} = \left(\text{process mean} - \text{lower specification}\right) \div 3$$

Interpretation of the index is generally as follows:

Cpk > 1.33	More than adequate
Cpk ≤ 1.33 but > 1.00	Adequate, but must be monitored as it approaches 1.00
Cpk ≤ 1.00 but > 0.67	Not adequate for the job
Cpk ≤ 0.67	Totally inadequate

CPIM: APICS—acronym for certified purchasing and inventory manager. Rigorous course material required with five modules of testing to be certified.

CPM: Acronym stands for certified purchasing manager—this is a NAPM (national association of purchasing managers) certification for purchasing professionals. Requires passing rigorous testing and experience criteria.

Cross-functional management: Cross-functional management is the overseeing of horizontal interdivisional activities. It is used so that all aspects of the organization are well managed and have consistent, integrated quality efforts pertaining to scheduling, delivery, plans, etc.

Cross-training: Training an employee in many different jobs within or across cells.

Customer relations: A realization of the role the customer plays in the continuation of your business. A conscious decision to listen to and provide products and services for those who make your business an ongoing concern.

Customer service: Any specifications required to meet the customer demands, needs, or requests for information and service. Everyone in the company should be a customer service representative.

Cycle: Completion of one whole series of processes by a part or person.

Cycle time: Available time divided by the factory capacity demand, the time each unit is coming off the end of the assembly line or the time each operator must hit, or the total labor time divided by the number of operators.

Cumulative: The progressive total of all the pieces.

Cumulative time: Is equivalent to adding up the total times as you progress. For instance, if step 1 is 5 seconds and step 2 is 10 seconds, the cumulative time is 15 seconds.

Daily control: The systems by which workers identify simply and clearly understand what they must do to fulfill their job function in a way that will enable the organization to run smoothly. These items are usually concerned with the normal operation of a business. Also a system in which these required actions are monitored by the employees themselves.

Data: Any portrayal of alphabetic or numerical information to which some meaning can be ascribed. Data can be found in a series of numbers or in an answer to a question asked of a person.

Data box: Term apportioned to a box in a value stream map that underlies a process box and contains elements such as process cycle time, number of persons, change over time, lot size, etc.

Demand flow: Material only moves to a work center when that work center is out of work. Subject of the book *Quantum Leap* by the World Wide Flow College of Denver. Layouts are typically a conveyor down the middle of the line with subassembly lines feeding in both sides.

Deming cycle: A continuously rotating wheel of plan, do, check, act.

Demonstrated capacity: Term to depict capacity arrived at by nonscientific means. Generally, it is arrived at by feel or observing actual output without determining what the process could generate if all the waste was removed.

Deviation: The absolute difference between a number and the mean of a data set.

Direct labor: Labor attributable specifically to the product.

Direct material: Raw material or supplied materials that when combined become part of the final product.

Distribution: Term generally refers to a supply chain of intermediaries.

Distributor: A company that generally does not manufacture material but is a middle man. They normally hold some finished goods but not always. Sometimes they may make some modifications to the finished goods.

Dock to stock: Process where suppliers are certified by the company's supplier quality engineers or purchasing and quality professionals that result in the supplier's products bypassing inspection or sometimes receiving to go directly to the stock room or shop floor where it is used.

Download: Transfer of information from a central computer (cloud) to a tablet, PC, phone, or other type of device.

Downstream operation: Task that is subsequent to the operation currently being executed or planned.

Downtime: Time when a scheduled resource is not operating.

Earned hours: Standard hours credited for actual production during the period determined by some agreed upon rate.

Economic order quantity: Model used to determine the optimum batch size for product running through an operation or a line. It is equal to the square root of two times the annual demand times average cost of order preparation divided by the annual inventory carrying cost percentage times unit cost.

Economy of scale: Larger volumes of products realize lower cost of production due to allocating fixed costs against a larger output size.

EDI: Acronym stands for electronic data interchange which is the ability for computer systems between supplier and customer to talk to each other without human involvement. In some cases, this requires programing of an interface between computers so they can talk to each other.

Effectiveness: Is the ability to achieve stated goals or objectives, judged in terms of metrics that are based on both output and impact. It is (a) the degree to which an activity or initiative is successful in achieving a specified goal and (b) the degree to which activities of a unit achieve the unit's mission or goal.

Efficiency: Production without waste. Efficiency is based on the *energy* one spends to complete the product or service as well as timing. For example, we all know of the *learning curve*. The more one performs a new task, the better they become each time the task is practiced. As one becomes more efficient, they definitely reduce stress and gain accuracy, capability, and consistency of action. A person has achieved efficiency when they are getting more done with the same or better accuracy in a shorter period of time, with less energy and better results.

Eight dimensions on quality: Critical dimensions or categories of quality identified by David Garvin of the Harvard Business School that can serve as a framework for strategic analysis. They are performance, features, reliability, conformance, durability, serviceability, esthetics, and perceived quality.

Elimination of waste: A philosophy that states that all activities undertaken need to be evaluated to determine if they are necessary, enhancing the value of the goods and services being provided and what the customer wants. Determining if the systems that have been established are serving their users or are the users serving the system.

Ending inventory: Inventory present at the end of a period. Sometimes validated by taking a physical inventory.

EPE: Acronym stands for every part every—this denotes batch size of lots running through the process.

Ergonomics: The study of humans interacting with the environment or workplace.

ERP: Acronym for enterprise resource planning system. It is a business management software to integrate all business phases to include marketing/sales, planning, engineering, operations and customer support the third generation of MRP systems usually used to link company plants locally, nationally, or globally. SAP, ORACLE, and BPCS are examples of these types of systems.

Excess inventory: More inventory than required to do any task.

Expedite: To push, rush, or walk a product (or information, signatures, etc.) through the process or system.

Expeditor: One who expedites.

External setup time: Time utilized and steps that can be done preparing for changeovers while the machine is still running. Example—prepping for a racing car pit stop like getting tires in place, having fuel ready, etc. Focus of changeovers or setups moving internal elements to external elements.

Fabrication: The process of transforming metals into a final product or subassembly usually by machine. Generally, a term to distinguish activities done in a machine shop versus manually assembling components into a final product.

Facility: The physical plant or office (transactional areas).

Failure analysis: The process of determining the root cause of a failure usually generating a report of some type.

Family: A group of products (or information) that shares similar processes.

FIFO: First in, first out inventory management system.

Flex fence: Purchasing term used in contracts to mitigate demand risk by having the supply chain capable of flexing production plus or minus 10%, 20%, or 30%. This is accomplished by identifying long lead items and developing plans to stock some of those parts at the buyer's expense.

Flexible workforce: A workforce totally cross-trained, capable, and allowed to work in all positions.

Floater: Cross-trained workers moved around throughout the day to different positions depending on the takt time or cycle time and the staffing requirements for the day.

Floor stock: Generally less expensive C-type parts stored centrally on the floor and owned by the company.

Flow: Smooth, uninterrupted movement of material or information.

Flow chart: A problem-solving tool that illustrates a process. It shows the way things actually go through a process, the way they should go, and the difference.

Flow production: Describes how goods, services, or information are processed. It is, at its best, one piece at a time. This can be a part, a document, invoice, or customer order. It rejects the concept of batch, lot, or mass producing. It vertically integrates all operations or functions as operationally or sequentially performed. It also encompasses pull or demand processing. Goods are not pushed through the process but pulled or demanded by succeeding operations from preceding operations. Often referred to as *one-piece-flow*.

FMEA: Failure mode and effects analysis. A structured approach to assess the magnitude of potential failures and identify the sources of each potential failure. Each potential failure is studied to identify the most effective corrective action. FMEA is the process of mitigating risk by looking at a process to determine what is likely to go wrong, the probability of it going wrong, the severity if it does go wrong, and the countermeasures to be taken in the event it does go wrong.

FOB: Free on board—logistics term used to designate where title passes to the buyer.

Focused factory: A plant or department focused on a single or family of products. Where everything can be done within the four walls. Does not necessarily mean cellular or one-piece flow.

Forecast: An attempt to look into the future in order to predict demand. Companies use techniques that range from historical statistical techniques to systematic wild ass guesses (SWAGs). The longer the forecast horizon, the less accurate the forecast.

FTE: Acronym standing for full-time equivalent. The formula is to take the total number of hours being worked by one or multiple people and divide by 2,080 hours (per year) and come up with the equivalent of one person's worth of labor per year.

Functional: Organized by department.

Functional layout: Layouts where the same or similar equipment is grouped together. These layouts support batch production.

GAAP: Acronym for generally accepted accounting principles.

Gain sharing: Method of compensating employees based on the overall productivity of the company. The goal is to give the employee a stake in the company and share based on productivity. Measures and participatory schemes vary by company and philosophy. There are many different methods of gain sharing. Normally differentiated from profit sharing, which is based on formulas relating only to company profits.

Grievance: Term refers to complaint (contract violation) filed by an employee (normally union based) against someone who is union or nonunion in the company.

Hanedashi: Device or means for automatic removal of a workpiece from one operation or process, which provides proper state and orientation for the next operation or process. In manufacturing, a means for automatic unloading and orientation for the next operation or process. In manufacturing, a means for automatic unloading and orientation for the next operation, generally a very simple device. Crucial for a *Chaku-Chaku* line.

Heijunka: Japanese term for level loading production. Necessary to support Kanban-based systems.

Histogram: A chart that takes measurement data and displays its distribution, generally in a bar graph format. For example, a histogram can be used to reveal the amount of variation that any process has within it based upon the data available.

Hoshin: Type of corporate planning, strategy, and execution in a setting where everyone participates in coming up with goals through a process called catchball and everyone down to the shop floor knows what they are doing is directly supporting the top three to five company goals.

Housekeeping: Keeping an orderly and clean environment.

Idle time: When a person is standing around with nothing to do, visible by arms crossed. Also known as pure waste.

Indirect costs: Traditional accounting costs that are not directly related or accounted to the product. Also known as overhead costs.

Indirect labor: Traditional accounting of labor required to support production without directly working on the product.

Indirect materials: Traditional accounting of materials used to support production but not directly used on the product.

Information: Data presented to an individual or machine.

Information systems: Term used to designate manual or computer-based systems, which convey information throughout the department or organization as a whole. Term used in value stream mapping for boxes located at the top of the map with lines to the process (information) boxes with which they interact.

Input: Work or information fed to the beginning of a system or process.

Inspection: The act of multiple (two or more) checks on material or information to see if it is correct. Can also refer to a department of humans that checks incoming materials (receiving inspection), WIP (in-process inspection), or final inspection before the product leaves the plant.

Internal setup time: Term used to designate time when machine or process is down (not running). Example is time when the racing car is in the pit stop having tires replaced and fuel added, etc.

Interrelationship diagram: A tool that assists in general planning. This tool takes a central idea, issue, or problem and maps out the logical or sequential links among related items.

It is a creative process that shows every idea can be logically linked with more than one idea at a time. It allows for *multidirectional* rather than *linear* thinking to be used.

Inventory: Purchased materials used to assemble any level of the product or to support production. Inventory can be in various stages from raw materials to finished goods.

Inventory turnover or turns: The number of times inventory cycles or turns over during the year. Generally calculated by dividing average cost of sales divided by the average inventory (normally three months). This can be a historical or forward-looking methodology. Can also be calculated by dividing days of supply into the number of working or calendar days.

Ishikawa diagram: Referred to as a fishbone used to graphically display cause and effect and to get to the root cause.

Item number: Normally a part number or stock number for a part.

Jidoka: Automation with a human touch or mind, autonomation. Automatic machinery that will operate itself but always incorporates the following devices: a mechanism to detect abnormalities or defects and a mechanism to stop the machine or line when defects or abnormalities occur.

Job costing: Where costs are collected and allocated to a certain job or charge number. Can be based on actual or standard costs.

Job description: List of roles and responsibilities for a particular job.

Job rotation: Schedule of movement from machine to machine or process to process. Used to support and encourage cross-training.

Job shop: Term used for factories that have high mix and low volume typically nonrepeatable or customized products.

Just-in-time manufacturing: A strategy that exposes the waste in an operation, makes continuous improvement a reality, and provides the opportunity to promote total employee involvement. Concentrates on making what is needed, when it is needed, no sooner, no later.

Kaizen (Kai = change; zen = good): The process improvement that involves a series of continual improvements over time. These improvements may take the form of a process innovation (event) or small incremental improvements.

Kanban: Japanese for a sign board. Designates a pull production means of communicating need for product or service. Originally developed as a means to communicate between operations in different locations. It was intended to communicate a change in demand or supply. In application, it is generally used to trigger the movement of material to or through a process.

Kit: Collection of components used to support a sub- or final assembly of a product.

Kitting: Process of collecting the components used to support a sub- or final assembly of a product.

Knowledge worker: A worker, who acquires information from every task, analyzes and validates the information, and stores it for future use.

Labor cost: Cost of labor, can be direct or indirect. In Lean, we look at total labor cost versus indirect or direct associated with traditional cost accounting systems.

Layout: Physical arrangement of machines and materials or offices.

LCL: Lower control limit, used on control charts.

Lead time: The time to manufacture and deliver a product or service. This term is used in many (often contradictory) contexts. To avoid confusion, lead time is defined as the average total lapse time for execution of the product delivery process from order receipt to delivery to the customer under normal operating conditions. In industries that operate in a build-to-order environment, lead times flex based on the influences of seasonal demand loads. In environments where production is scheduled in repeating, fixed-time segments or cycles, the lead time is usually determined by the length of the production cycle (i.e., days, weeks, months, etc.).

Lead time or throughput time: Time it takes to get through the entire process or time quoted to customers to receive their orders (from order to cash).

Lean production: The activity of creating processes that are highly responsive and flexible to customer demand requirements. Successful Lean production is evident when processes are capable of consistently delivering the highest quality (defect-free) products and services, at the right location and at the right time, in response to customer demand and doing this in the most cost-effective manner possible.

Learning curve: A planning technique used to predict improvement based on experience. Uses log charts to trend the data.

Level load: Process of leveling or equally distributing demand or products across a cell or plant. Also known as heijunka.

LIFO: Last in, first out inventory management.

Limit switch: Various electronic devices used to trigger an action when a particular limit is reached. Used to control machines or count parts, used to turn on or off machines, used often for poka yoke, etc.

Little's Law: Throughput time divided by cycle time = amount of inventory in the system.

Logistics: The art and science of shipping materials, distribution, warehousing, and supply chain management.

Lot: Refers to a group of parts or information generally batched together through the process.

Lot size: Number of parts in a batch to be produced.

LTA: Acronym for long-term agreement. An agreement negotiated with a supplier for a longer term and more complex than a simple blanket (pricing) agreement, normally three to five years with other conditions centering on the supplier's improvement, quality and delivery certification, and price reduction goals.

Machine hours: Total hours a machine is running. Can be value-added or non-value-added time normally used for capacity planning. May or may not include setup time or unplanned downtime.

Machine utilization: The amount of time a machine is available versus the amount of time the machine is being used. Includes setup and run time compared to available time. It used to be the *be all and end all* for traditional cost accounting measures. With Lean, it is not as important unless it is a true bottleneck machine.

Make or buy: Study of costs of purchasing a part versus purchasing the raw materials and making it in house.

Make to order: A product that is not started until after the customer orders it. In some cases, a Kanban or inventory of parts produced to a certain level may then be modified to fit the customer requirements.

Manufacturing resources planning (MRP II): A second-generation MRP system that provides additional control linkages such as automatic purchase order generation, capacity planning, and accounts payable transactions.

Master schedule: Schedule with customer orders loaded by due date or promised date.

Master scheduler: Person who enters sales orders into the master schedule.

Material requirements planning (MRP): A computerized information system that calculates material requirements based on a master production schedule. This system may be used only for material procurement or to also execute the material plan through shop floor control.

MBO: Management by objectives—a system where goals are handed down from manager to employee where the employee participates in the process.

Means (measure): A way to accomplish a target.

Min max: Refers to a type of inventory system where once the minimum level is reached or a reorder point is reached, a quantity is reordered, which brings the quantity back up to the maximum level. Some computer MRP systems (Oracle) have this as an option to manage inventory.

Milk run: Term used to identify the path water spider uses to replenish materials for a line.

Mistake proofing: Also known as poka yoke or foolproofing. A system starting with successive checks by humans to inspection devices built into or added to machines to detect and or prevent defects.

Mixed model production: The ability to produce various models with different levels of customization one by one down the production line.

Monthly audit: The self-evaluation of performance against targets. An examination of things that helped or hindered performance in meeting the targets and the corrective actions that will be taken.

MPS: Master production schedule.

MRO: Term used to designate maintenance repair and operating supplies.

MRP: Material requirements planning; a computerized system developed by Olie Wright using lead time offsets, bill of material, and various planning parameters used to predict when to release requisitions or work orders in order to schedule the production floor.

MRPII: Material resource planning; a more advanced MRP system, which ties various systems together within a single company, that is, manufacturing and finance.

MTM: Methods time measurement; system that has studied and determined times for various operations or movements by operators. Generally used with motion study.

Muda: Japanese term for waste.

Multiskilled or process workers: Description for individuals at any level of the organization who are diverse in skill and training. Capable of performing a number of different tasks providing the organization with additional flexibility.

Mura: Japanese term for uneven.

Muri: Japanese term for overburden.

Nemawashi: Refers to the process of gaining consensus and support prior to implementing a strategy.

Net sales: Total sales less returns and allowances.

Noise: Randomness within a process.

Nominal group technique: Process of soliciting information from everyone in the group.

Non-value added: Designation for a step that does not meet one of the three value-added criteria.

Non-value added but necessary (sometimes called business value added): Any step that is necessary but the customer is not willing to pay for it but it is done right the first time.

Normal distribution: Statistical term where most data falls close to the mean (±1 sigma), less fall away from the mean (±2 sigma), and even less fall even further away (±3 sigma), where the distribution when graphed looks like a bell-shaped curve.

NTED: No-touch exchange of dies.

Objective: What you are trying to achieve with a given plan. The desired end result. The reason for employing a strategy and developing targets.

Obsolete: Loss of product value due to engineering, product life decisions, or technological changes.

Offset: Time entered into MRP systems to designate how long it takes to get through a part of the system, that is, purchasing time entered as two days. MRP uses this information to develop a timeline to predict when to release the order or purchase requirement. When added up, it equals the total lead time of the product in the system.

OJT: Acronym for on-the-job training.

One-year plan: A statement of objective of an organizational event for a year.

Operating system: Refers to the type of system computer is using, that is, DOS, windows, etc.

Operation: A series of tasks grouped together such that the sum of the individual task times is equal to the takt time (cycle time to meet product demand requirements). It is important to distinguish between operations and activities. Operations are used to balance work content in a flow manufacturing process to achieve a particular daily output rate equal to customer demand. An operation defines the amount of work content performed by each operator to achieve a balanced flow and linear output rate.

Opportunity cost: Return on capital, which could have been achieved had it been used for something else more productive.

Order policy: Term used in MRP to decide lot sizing requirements.

Organization structure: The fashion in which resources are assigned to tasks. Includes cross-functional management and vertical work teams. Also includes the development of multiskilled workers through the assignment of technical and administrative personnel to nontraditional roles.

Organizational development: Process that looks at improving the interactions within and between departments across the overall organization. Generally led by a consultant or company change agent.

Organizational tools: These provide a team approach in which people get together to work on problems and also get better at what they are doing. Organizational tools include work groups and quality circles.

OTED: One-touch exchange of dies. Uses a human touch to changeover one or more machines at the same time.

Overhead: Costs not directly tied to the product. Normally refers to all personnel who support the production process whether it is physical or transactional.

Overtime: Work beyond the traditional 40 hours usually results in a premium paid per hour.

Pareto chart: A vertical bar graph showing the bars in order to size from left to right. Helps focus on the vital few problems rather than the trivial many. An extension of the Pareto principle that suggests the significant items in a given group normally constitute a relatively small portion of the items in the total group. Conversely, a majority of the items in the total will, even in aggregate, be relatively minor in significance (i.e., the 80/20 rule).

Participative management: Employees collaborate with managers to work on improvements to the process. Basis for QC circles.

Pay for performance: Pay is tied to overall output by a team.

Perpetual inventory system: System designed to always have the correct amount of inventory in the system.

PFA: Process flow analysis, looks at the flow of just the product through the process using TIPS.

Phantom: A bill of material (BOM) or non-production work order used to determine if there are any parts shortages. How to create the phantom varies depending on the type of MRP or

ERP system. In general, a work order is created and then backed out of the system prior to MRP running again.

Physical layout: A means of impacting workflow and productivity through the physical placement of machinery or furniture. Production machinery should be grouped in a cellular arrangement based upon product requirements, not process type. In addition to this, in most instances, there is an advantage in having the workflow in counterclockwise fashion. Similarly, in an office environment, furniture should be arranged such that there is an efficient flow of information or services rather than strictly defined departments.

PDCA cycle: Plan-Do-Check-Act. The PDCA system, sometimes referred to as the Deming cycle, is the most important item for control in policy deployment. In this cycle, you make a plan that is based on policy (plan); you take action accordingly (do); you check the result (check); and if the plan is not fulfilled, you analyze the cause and take further action by going back to the plan (action).

Piece rate: Form of worker compensation based on individual output targets that vary by employee and process.

Pilot: Trying something out for one or several pieces in a controlled environment to test a hypothesis.

Plan: The means to achieve a target.

Planned downtime: Downtime that is scheduled for a machine or line.

Planner/buyer: Combines planning and buyer jobs.

Planner/buyer/scheduler: Combines planning, buying, and scheduling jobs.

Poka yoke: Japanese expression meaning *common or simple, mistake proof.* A method of designing processes, either production or administrative, which will by their nature prevent errors. This may involve designing fixtures that will not accept a defective part or something as simple as having a credit memo be a different color than a debit memo. It requires that thought be put into the design of any system to anticipate *what* can go wrong and build in measures to prevent them.

Policy: The company objectives are to be achieved through the cooperation of all levels of managers and employees. A policy consists of targets, plans, and target values.

Policy deployment: Hoshin Kanri—policy deployment orchestrates continuous improvement in a way that fosters individual initiative and alignment. It is a process of implementing the policies of an organization directly through line managers and indirectly through cross-functional organization. It is a means of internalizing company policies throughout the organization, from highest to lowest level. Top managers will articulate its annual goals that are then deployed down through lower levels of management. The abstract goals of top management become more concrete and specific as they are deployed down through the organization. Policy deployment is process oriented. It is concerned with developing a process by which results become predictable. If the goal is not realized, it is necessary to review and see if the implementation was faulty. It is most important to determine what went wrong in the process that prevented the goal from being realized. The Japanese name for policy deployment is Hoshin Kanri. In Japanese, Hoshin means *shining metal, compass,* or *pointing in the direction.* Kanri means *control.* Hoshin Kanri is a method devised to capture and concretize strategic goals as well as flashes of insight about the future and to develop the means to bring these into reality. It is one of the major systems that make world-class quality management possible. It helps control the direction of the company by orchestrating change within a company. The system includes tools for continuous improvement, breakthroughs, and implementation. The key to Hoshin planning is it brings the total organization into the strategic planning process, both top down and bottom up. It ensures the direction, goals, and objectives of the company are rationally developed, well defined, clearly communicated, monitored, and adapted based on system feedback. It provides focus for the organization.

POU: Point of use, designates location where product or tooling or information is used.

Preventative maintenance: Term given to duties carried out on machines in order to prevent a breakdown or unplanned stoppage.

Prioritization matrices: This tool prioritizes tasks, issues, product/service characteristics, etc., based on known weighted criteria using a combination of tree and matrix diagram techniques. Above all, they are tools for decision-making.

Problem-solving tools: These tools find the root cause of problems. They are tools for thinking about problems, managing by fact, and documenting hunches. The tools include check sheet, line chart, Pareto chart, flow chart, histogram, control chart, and scatter diagram. In Japan, these are referred to as the seven QC tools.

Process: A series of activities that collectively accomplish a distinct objective. Processes are cross-functional and cut across departmental responsibility boundaries. Processes can be value added or non-value added.

Process capability: See CPK.

Process control chart: Chart that represents tracking the sequence of data points over a number of or 100% samplings. It serves as a basis to define common cause versus special cause variation and to predict when a part or machine is likely to fail.

Process decision program chart: The process decision program chart (PDPC) is a method that maps out conceivable events and contingencies that can occur in any implementation plan. It, in time, identifies possible countermeasures in response to these problems. This tool is used to plan each possible chain of events that need to occur when the problem or goal is an unfamiliar one.

Process hierarchy: A hierarchical decomposition from core business processes to the task level. The number of levels in a hierarchy is determined by the breadth and size of the organization. A large enterprise process hierarchy may include core business processes, processes, subprocesses, process segments, activities, and tasks.

Process management: This involves focusing on the process rather than the results. A variety of tools may be used for process management, including the seven QC tools.

Process segment: A series of activities that define a subset of a process.

Product delivery process: The stream of activities required to produce a product or service. This activity stream encompasses both planning and execution activities to include demand planning, order management, materials procurement, production, and distribution.

Production control: Employee that tracks status of daily production; normally used in batch environments but sometimes in Lean environments.

Production schedule: Orders lined up in order of priority based on due date, promised date, or some other planning parameters.

Productivity: Productivity is the *amount* of products produced in a certain amount of time with a certain amount of labor. The products could be physical products or transactional such as processing an invoice or Internet blogs. Productive means getting things done, outcomes reached, or goals achieved and are measured as output per unit of input (i.e., labor, equipment, and capital).

Prototype: First piece on which new process is tried.

Pull production: In a pull process, materials are staged at the point of consumption. As these materials are consumed, signals are sent back to previous steps in the production process to pull forward sufficient materials to replenish only those materials that have been consumed.

Push production: In a push process, production is initiated by the issuance of production orders that are offset in time from the actual demand to allow time for production and delivery. The idea is to maintain zero inventory and have materials complete each step of the production process just as they are needed at subsequent (downstream) activities.

+QDIP: Acronym stands for safety, quality, delivery, inventory, and production. Ideally, parameters are set by the employees on the shop floor or in the workshop.

Quality: Refers to the ability of the final product to meet both the customers required specification and unspecified specifications.

Quality circles: Quality circles are an organizational tool that provides a team approach in which people get together to work on problems and to improve productivity. Their primary objective is to foster teamwork and encourage employee by involvement employing the problem-solving approach.

Quality function deployment: A product development system that identifies the wants of a customer and gets that information to all the right people so the organization can effectively exceed competition in meeting the customer's most important wants. It translates customer wants into appropriate technical requirements for each stage of product development and production.

Quality management: The systems, organizations, and tools that make it possible to plan, manufacture, and deliver a quality product or service. This does not imply inspection or even traditional quality control. Rather, it involves the entire process involved in bringing goods and services to the customer.

Queuing theory: Applies to manufacturing orders, people, or information that is waiting in line for the next process. Based on Little's law.

Queue time: Amount of time an order, people, or information is waiting for the next process.

Quick changeover: Method of increasing the amount of productive time available for a piece of machinery by minimizing the time needed to change from one model to another. This greatly increases the flexibility of the operation and allows it to respond more quickly to changes in demand. It also has the benefit of allowing an organization to greatly reduce the amount of inventory that it must carry because of improved response time.

Rate-based order management: This order management system employs a finite capacity loading scheme to promise orders based upon the agreed demand bound limits. These minimum and maximum demand bounds reflect potential response capacity limits for production and materials procurement.

Rate-based planning: A procedure that establishes a controlled level of flexibility in the product delivery process in order to be robust to anticipated variations in demand. This flexibility is achieved by establishing minimum and maximum bounds around future demand forecasts. The idea is that both the production facility and the material supply channels will echelon sufficient capacity to accommodate demand swings that do not exceed the established demand bounds. As future demand forecasts move closer to the production window, updated demand bounds are periodically broadcasted to the material suppliers. At the point of order receipt and delivery promising (within sales or customer service), demand bounding limits are enforced to insure that the rate-based production plan remains feasible.

Regression analysis: Statistical technique that determines or estimates the amount of correlation explained between two or more variable sets of data.

ROI: Return on investment, generally compares investment versus the return to determine the payback that is often stated in years and expressed as a percentage of earnings.

RONA: Return on net assets.

Root cause: The ultimate reason for an event or condition.

Run chart: A statistical problem-solving tool that shows whether key indicators are going up or down and if the indicators are good or bad.

Safety: Ensuring that the work environment is free of hazards and obstacles of which could cause harm.

Scanlon plan: A system of group incentives that measures the plant-wide results of all efforts using the ratio of labor costs to sales value added by production. If there is an increase in production sales value with no change in pricing, mix, or labor costs, productivity has increased and unit costs have decreased.

Scatter diagram: One of the seven QC tools. The scatter diagram shows the relationship between two variables.

Scheduled (planned) downtime: Planned shutdown of equipment to perform maintenance or other tasks or lack of customer demand.

Self-diagnosis: As a basis for continuous improvement, each manager uses problem-solving activity to see why he or she is succeeding or failing to meet targets. This diagnosis should focus on identifying personal and organizational obstacles to the planned performance and on the development of alternate approaches based on this new information.

Self-directed work team: Normally, a small group of employees that can plan, organize, and manage their daily responsibilities with no direct supervision. They can normally hire, fire, or demote team members.

Setup: The changing over of a machine or also the loading and unloading of parts on a machine.

Setup time: The amount of time it takes to changeover a machine from the last good part to and including the first good part.

Setup parts: Preparation, mounting and removing, calibration, trial runs, and adjustments.

Seven new tools: Sometimes called the seven management tools. These are affinity and relationship diagrams for general planning; tree systems, matrix, and prioritization matrices for intermediate planning; and activity network diagrams and process decision program charts for detailed planning.

Seven QC tools: Problem-solving statistical tools needed for customer-driven master plan. They are cause and effect diagram, flow chart, Pareto chart, run chart, histogram, control chart, and scatter diagram.

Seven wastes: Seven types of waste have been identified for business. They are as follows:

1. Waste from overproduction of goods or services
2. Waste from waiting or idle time
3. Waste from transportation (unnecessary)
4. Waste from the process itself (inefficiency)
5. Waste of unnecessary stock on hand

6. Waste of motion and effort
7. Waste from producing defective goods

The eighth waste: Waste of talent and knowledge

Shojinka: Means labor flexibility. The term means employees staffing the line can flex up or down based on the incoming demand, which requires employees to be cross-trained and multi-process/machine capable. It also means continually optimizing the number of workers based on demand. This principle is central to baton zone line balancing (bumping).

Shoninka: Means *manpower savings*. This corresponds to the improvement of work procedures, machines, or equipment to free whole units of labor (i.e., one person) from a production line consisting of one or more workers.

Shoryokuka[1]: Shoryokuka means *labor savings* and indicates partial improvement of manual labor by adding small machines or devices to aid the job. This results in some small amount of labor savings but not an entire person as in shoninka. Again this becomes a goal of all follow-up point kaizen events.

Simultaneous/concurrent engineering: The practice of designing a product (or service), its production process, and its delivery mechanism all at the same time. The process requires considerable up-front planning as well as the dedication of resources early in the development cycle. The payoff is in the form of shorter development time from concept to market, lower overall development cost, and lower product or service cost based upon higher accuracy at introduction and less potential for redesign. Examples of this include the Toyota Lexus 200 and the Ford Taurus.

SMED: Single-minute exchange of dies, 9 minutes 59 seconds or less setup time.

Smoothing/production smoothing: The statistical method of converting weekly or monthly schedules to level-loaded daily schedules.

SPC: Acronym for statistical process control.

Standard deviation: Statistical measurement of process variation (σ) which measures the dispersion of sample observations around a process mean.

Standard work: Standard work is a tool that defines the interaction of man and his environment when processing something. In producing a part, it is the interaction of man and machine, whereas in processing an invoice, it is the interaction of man and the supplier and the accounting system. It details the motion of the operator and the sequence of action. It provides a routine for consistency of an operation and a basis for improvement. Furthermore, the concept of standard work is it is a verb, not a noun. It details the best process we currently know and understand. Tomorrow it should be better (continuous improvement), and the standard work should be revised to incorporate the improvement. There can be no improvement without a basis (standard work).

Standard work has three central elements:

1. Cycle time (not takt time)
2. Standard operations
3. SWIP

Standard work (as a tool): Establishes a routine/habit/pattern for repetitive tasks, makes managing such as scheduling and resource allocation easier, establishes the relationship between man and environment, provides a basis for improvement by defining the normal and highlighting the abnormal, and prohibits backsliding.

Standard work in process: The amount of material or a given product that must be in process at any time to insure maximum efficiency of the operation.

Standardization: The system of documenting and updating procedures to make sure everyone knows clearly and simply what is expected of them (measured by daily control). Essential for application of PDCA cycle.

Statistical methods/tools: Statistical methods allow employees to manage by facts and analyze problems through understanding variability and data. The seven QC tools are examples of statistical tools.

Store, storage: Any time a product (part, information, or person) is waiting in the process.

Strategy: The business process that involves goals setting, defining specific actions to achieve the business goals, and allocating the resources to execute the actions.

Subprocess: A series of interrelated process segments that forms a subset of a total process.

Supplier partnerships: An acknowledgment that suppliers are an integral part of any business. A partnership implies a long-term relationship that involves the supplier in both product development and process development. It also requires a commitment on the part of the supplier to pursue continuous improvement and world-class quality.

System: A system is the infrastructure that enables the processes to provide customer value. Business systems comprise market, customer, competition, organizational culture, environmental and technological influences, regulatory issues, physical resources, procedures, information flows, and knowledge sets. It is through physical processes that business systems transform inputs to outputs and, thereby, deliver products and services of value in the marketplace.

Takt time: The frequency with which the customer wants a product or how frequently a sold unit must be produced. The number is derived by taking the amount of time available in a day and dividing it by the number of sold units that need to be produced. Takt time is usually expressed in seconds.

Target: The desired goal that serves as a yardstick for evaluating the degree to which a *policy* is achieved. It is controlled by a *control point, control item,* or *target item*.

Target costing: Method for establishing cost objective for a product or service during the design phase. The target cost is determined by the following formula:

$$\text{Sales price} - \text{target profit} = \text{target cost}$$

Target/means matrix: Shows the relationship between targets and means and to identify control items and control methods.

Target value: Normally a numeric definition of successful target attainment. It is not always possible to have a numeric target, and you must never separate the target from the plan.

Theory of constraints: A management philosophy first put forth in the book *The Goal* by Eliyahu Goldratt to identify bottlenecks in the process. In the book, he follows a young boy scout named Herbie. We call bottlenecks *Herbies* today in some cases. His approach was to identify the constraint, exploit the constraint, subordinate all non-constraints, elevate the constraint, and if the constraint is broken in step 4, then go back to step 1.

Throughput time: A measure of the actual throughput time for a product to move through a flow process once the work begins. Many people incorrectly label this measure as manufacturing lead time but it is actually a small subset and often has little to do with the total time from order inception to fulfillment.

TIPS: Acronym for parts of process flow analysis—transport inspect process store.

Total density: One of the eight Lean wastes is the *waste of motion*. One of the first things we advise when trying to identify wasted motions is do not confuse motion with work. In offices, this concept is revised slightly to the following: *do not confuse effort with results*.[2] Total density = work divided by motion.[3] Not all motion is work. It is important to separate needed motions versus wasted motions.

Total employee involvement (TEI): A philosophy that advocates the harnessing of the collective knowledge of an organization through the involvement of its people. When supported by the management, it is a means of improving quality, delivery, profitability, and morale in an organization. It provides all employees with a greater sense of ownership in the success of the company and provides them with more control in addressing issues that face the organization. TEI does not allow top management to abdicate its obligation to properly plan and set objectives. It does, however, provide more resources and flexibility in meeting those objectives.

Total labor time: The sum of labor value-added and labor non-value-added times.

Total productive maintenance: TPM is productive maintenance conducted by all employees. It is equipment maintenance performed on a companywide basis. It has five goals:

1. Maximize equipment effectiveness (improve overall efficiency).
2. Develop a system of productive maintenance for the life of the equipment.
3. Involve all departments that plan, design, use, or maintain equipment in implementing TPM (engineering and design, production, and maintenance).
4. Actively involve all employees—from top management to shop-floor workers.
5. Promote TPM through motivational management (autonomous small group activities).

The word total in *total productive maintenance* has three meanings related to three important features of TPM: total effectiveness (pursuit of economic efficiency or profitability), total PM (maintenance prevention and activity to improve maintainability as well as preventative maintenance), and total participation (autonomous maintenance by operators and small group activities in every department and at every level).

Transport: Any travel a part or information does throughout the process.

Tree diagram: The tree diagram systematically breaks down plans into component parts and systematically maps out the full range of tasks/methods needed to achieve a goal. It can either be used as a cause-finding problem-solver or a task-generating planning tool.

Value added: Must meet three criteria from the AMA video *Time The Next Dimension of Quality*: customer cares, physically changes the thing going through the process, and done right the first time. Value added was expanded for hospitals to physically or emotionally change the patient for the better in addition to the other two criteria.

Value-added work content ratio: The steps that actually transform and increase the value of the product or test requirements legislated by industrial licensing agencies. The value-added work content ratio is formed by simply dividing the sum of all value-added work steps by the product lead time for the total process. This ratio can also be used to evaluate waste only in the manufacturing process segment by dividing the numerator by the manufacturing flow time.

Vertical teams: Vertical teams are groups of people who come together to meet and address problems or challenges. These teams are made up of the most appropriate people for the issue, regardless of their levels or jobs within the organization.

Vision: A long-term plan or direction that is based on a careful assessment of the most important directions for the organization.

Visual management: The use of visual media in the organization and general administration of a business. This would include the use of color, signs, and a clear span of sight in a work area. These visuals should clearly designate what things are and where they belong. They should provide immediate feedback as to the work being done and its pace. Visual management should provide access to information needed in the operation of a business. This would include charts and graphs that allow the business status to be determined through their review. This review should be capable of being performed at a glance. To facilitate this, it is necessary to be able to manage by fact and let the data speak for it.

Water spider: New role for material handler. Water spiders can be a low-skill or high-skill job. The water spider job is to replenish empty bins on the line daily, plays a vital role in mixed model parts sequencing, should stay 15 minutes or more ahead of the line, can be utilized as a floater, can be utilized to release parts orders from suppliers, and should have standard work and walk patterns/milk runs.

Work groups: Work groups are an organizational tool providing a team approach in which people work together on problems to improve productivity.

World-class quality management: The commitment by all employees. It is a philosophy/operating methodology totally committed to quality and customer satisfaction. It focuses on continuous process improvement in all processes. It advocates the use of analytical tools and scientific methods and data. It establishes priorities and manages by fact. World-class quality management has perfection (world class) as its goal. We should benchmark to be better than the competition by a large margin, the best. To obtain this status, all employees must be involved, everyone, everywhere, at all times. The result will be products and services that consistently meet or exceed the customers' expectations both internal and external. This group is always passionate with respect to improving the customer experience.

Yo-i-don[4]: It means ready set go. It is used to balance multiple processes and operators to a required cycle time using andon. This means each station or line is station balanced to one cycle time. When each operator completes their work, they press the andon button. Once the count-down or count-up clock reaches the prescribed cycle time, any station not completed, immediately turns the andon light to red. At this point, the supervisor and other team members will come to help that station.

Yokoten[5]: It is a process critical for creating a true learning organization. Sharing best practices (successes) is critical across the entire organization. In kanji, yoko means beside, side, or width and ten has several meanings but here it would mean to cultivate or comment. Yokoten is a means of *horizontal or sideways transfer of knowledge*, that is, peer-to-peer across the company. People are encouraged to Gemba, to see the kaizen improvement made for them, and see if they can apply the idea or an improved idea in their area. At Honeywell, this is referred to as horizontal linking mechanisms (HLMs).

Notes

1. *Lean Lexicon*, John Shook, LEI, 2004.
2. Source unknown.
3. Kanban JIT at Toyota—Ohno, Japan Management Association.
4. Monden Yasuhiro, *Toyota Production System*, 3rd edition.
5. http://eudict.com/?lang=japeng&word=ten.

Index

Note: Locators in *italics* represent figures and **bold** indicate tables in the text

Printed in the United States
by Baker & Taylor Publisher Services